THE EVOLUTION OF AMERICAN DEMOCRACY

TWO CENTURIES OF AMERICAN LIFE:
A Bicentennial History
Harold M. Hyman and Leonard W. Levy, Editors

WILLIAM R. BROCK

THE
EVOLUTION
OF AMERICAN
DEMOCRACY

The Dial Press, New York, 1970

Library of Congress Catalog Card Number: 79–111451

Printed in the United States of America

First printing, 1970

Book design by Larry Alexander

CONTENTS

INTRODUCTION

This book is not a political history of the United States, or a constitutional history, or a history of political ideas. It is a study of the way in which American democracy has evolved over two centuries of national existence. It shows how the processes and aims of democracy have responded to events, changing in some respects, and preserving continuity in others. The United States is the oldest democratic country in the world, but it would be wrong to assume that democracy in the late twentieth century is the same as Jeffersonian democracy, or Jacksonian democracy, or democracy as Lincoln knew it, or even democracy as it was fifty years ago.

It is true that certain characteristics persist. Americans today can vote frequently for a large number of officials and legislators; they did so in 1776. With a few exceptions they have always chosen representatives in single member constituencies. Democratic processes have always taken place within the framework of constitutions which limit and define authority, including that of majorities. Set beside these great elements of continuity, the changes may seem elusive and of secondary importance. Yet one would also expect men living in a huge, industrialized society, with enormous cities and rapid means of communication, to have a different view of the world from that of men living in small, isolated and rural societies, and to reflect these differences in their political attitudes. If changes have been slow, and sometimes imperceptible, they have, nevertheless, been profound.

For this reason the word "evolution" is used. Evolution is adaptation; it is change as the result of an incredible number of tiny modifications; it is the elimination of unsuccessful variants and the survival of the forms best fitted to the environment. There have been periods of crisis in the history of American democracy which can be compared to the effects of sudden changes in environment upon biological evolution. Of necessity one dwells upon these crises and neglects the flat periods when nothing much seems to happen; but quiet times may be as important in fixing and confirming ways of life as are the cataclysmic events which alter them. Though this book necessarily dwells upon familiar and significant episodes, it also deals with the longer and slower movements which gradually transform life.

The theme, therefore, is American democracy as a living, growing, and changing institution. It does not attempt to rival political science in detailed analysis of political mechanism, but it seeks to place American political processes in their social and historical context. There is a task for the political analyst, but there is also a need to see politics in history as an aspect of a growing society. The approach is modest but the aim is ambitious.

THE EVOLUTION OF AMERICAN DEMOCRACY

CHAPTER I

DEMOCRACY AND AMERICAN IDEOLOGY

Few words suffer from such a variety of usages as "democracy"; it describes states which prize individual freedom and states which are rigidly totalitarian; it comprises two-party systems, one-party systems, and multi-party systems; it is applied to societies in which citizens can vote to choose a multitude of elected officials and to others where the right is limited to the approval of a single list of candidates; it is used of countries in which there is virtually no check upon the legislative authority of elected majorities, and to countries in which their power is limited by strict constitutional restraints. Even in democracies which share so many common traditions, such as those of America, Britain, Canada, Australia, and New Zealand, there are marked differences in practice and purpose; democracy in new African states superficially resembles one or other of the older democracies while fundamentally different in political attitudes.

It is therefore necessary to qualify the word "democracy" by a national adjective. This book is about American democracy, and its characteristics can be briefly enumerated. It is a democracy in which all adults have the legal right to vote, ballots are cast in secret, a very large number of officials and legislators are chosen, and elections at all levels are frequent. Not every voter participates on every occasion, but, in general, more Americans vote, more often, for more candidates and on more issues, than the citizens of any other country. In addition there are frequent primary elections in which the voters of a party choose its nominees for office. It is a safe guess that there is also more talk about politics, more literature about politics, and more political rhetoric than in any other country.

The proliferation of political activity is therefore a distinguishing characteristic of American democracy. It is also a constitutional democracy, living under a written law, with the intense and restless activity of the people balanced by the statuesque quality of a Supreme Court which is, in the last resort, the only authority able to decide what law is. It is also a Federal democracy in which state governments still retain important powers and responsibilities despite the vast increase in national authority during the present century. Finally it is a democracy which inherited and modified the Common Law of England together with a bundle of ideas and arguments about political life derived from the Bible, the Ancient World, medieval England, the Reformation, the constitutional conflicts of the seventeenth century, John Locke, Montesquieu, and Thomas Jefferson. In about equal measure it combines a faith in the ability of men to make good laws with a respect for fundamental or natural laws which ought to be beyond the range of human interference.

It is a complex system, and many political scientists have found the occupation of a lifetime in describing and analyzing its operation.

It has the fascination of a countryside with easily traced contours, but with hundreds of byways amid the trees and valleys where strange creatures of every kind can be sought out by the diligent hunter. It is the oldest democracy in the world, and its peculiarities are not the product of ignorance or inexperience, but of two centuries of adaptation and selection. If the observer sometimes pays most attention to the oddities and errors, he should also consider the rocks which have endured.

Americans sometimes speak as though their democracy has been handed down from Heaven; that it existed from the beginning of national life and that the task has been to defend the pure stream from pollution. Stated thus, this belief is absurd; but it is true that Americans constantly trace their political ideas back to the Revolutionary mainspring. In this they resemble the eighteenth-century English who proclaimed their adherence to the principles of 1688 (or, for that matter, the twentieth-century Russians who look back to 1917) rather than the modern British whose democracy seems to have dragged all the anchors which held them to past principles. This backward-looking mode does not, however, prevent American democracy in the twentieth century from being unlike that of the nineteenth century, and very unlike the political world envisaged by eighteenth-century Americans. It has become what it now is because it has responded to various needs and pressures through two centuries of history.

The story is one of evolution however, not sudden change or violent alterations in course. The cataclysm of the Civil War affected American democracy in many ways, but it did not cause rejection of any fundamental principles. Indeed, the Confederate States made a virtue of taking over the Constitution and political machinery of the Union which they had disrupted (though alterations, to fit their circumstances as slave-owning societies, may have affected the fundamental principles more than they realized). American history has its drama, but since 1776 it has not been the drama of political revolution. An evolutionary process offers few striking incidents to exploit; one deals instead with influences, slow changes in attitude, and only occasionally with innovation. Moreover, political practices exist within the framework of a national ideology which has grown even more slowly, and in which consciousness of the past plays an extraordinarily powerful part among a people who are sometimes accused of living too much in the present.

Two centuries ago the enlightened men of western Europe and North America congratulated themselves upon the achievement of religious toleration and the prospect of a rational world; many battles had still to be fought against bigotry and obscurantism, but the promise of the future was a world in which the mind of man would be free. The dark history of persecution justified by the need to ensure salvation lay behind, and judicial murder in the name of religion was obsolete. They could not foresee that they stood on the threshold of an age in which many more men would die for political heresy than had ever been executed by the Inquisition. Moreover, the terrible paradox of the future would be justification of political persecution by the promise of a better life on earth. A powerful instrument in the destruction of traditional authority was the claim that man had a right to be happy, but political ideologies of the future would insist that men could be happy only in a prescribed way and that they must be ready to sacrifice lives and minds in the struggle against rival concepts.

It may seem unjust to place the history of the United States in this somber perspective, and many modern Americans, associating the word "ideology" with doctrinaire totalitarianism, would deny its relevance for their experience. "Ideology" can, however, be interpreted in a broad sense as a system of ideas grouped around a nucleus of concepts concerning man's place in society. In this sense America was the first modern nation to make ideology the central fact of national existence. Here was the first decisive break with traditional authority, here was the first assertion that the pursuit of happiness was an inalienable right of man, and here was the first attempt to build a nation around a liberal political philosophy. Within a short period the principles of the Revolution crystallized into a total view which embraced not only political mechanism but the whole way of life. It is true that this political creed contained many negative commandments about the scope and authority of government, and that the early citizens of the United States feared excess of power more than they respected the ability of government to perform positive tasks. The idea that the best government is the one that governs least was one of the most familiar and most widely accepted maxims of the American political creed, though always applied more strictly against the federal than against state governments. Subsequent enlargements of federal responsibility were made apologetically and only upon the plea of urgent national need; but "thou shalt not" can be as powerful a precept as "thou shalt" and these negative precepts helped to give the United States the first of the great political ideologies which have struggled for supremacy in the modern world.

The American ideology is distinct, but it should not be considered in isolation. The American nation has developed during two centuries of profound changes which have helped to fulfill the hopes of the eighteenth century as much as wars and conflicts have worked to frustrate them. The vast achievements of science and technology have led to standards of life never before envisaged, to education and to the diffusion of knowledge on an unprecedented scale. Throughout the greater part of human history the large majority of the human race lived in ignorance, poverty, and disease, and social systems held out to them no hope on earth save that of unremitting toil; it is only the modern age that has given leisure, comfort, and health to the masses. Against the sad record of war and destruction can be set an ever-growing concern with human suffering. Former centuries regarded misery as a part of the natural order which could not be altered by human agencies; Christianity might teach compassion for individuals, but attempts to alleviate distress ended with private action, and even the charitable might display attitudes which seem callous to modern eyes. By contrast modern societies have accepted the proposition that the causes of suffering can be identified, and that once identified there is a public responsibility to provide a cure. Science, medicine, and economic management have placed tools for social amelioration in the hands of governments, and to an increasing extent democratic societies have demanded that these tools should be used. It is a major claim of the Americans that their system of government has met these demands without the sacrifice of individual achievement and without the use of authoritarian government.

Many Americans of the present age question their own success in fulfilling the promise of a better life. It is asked whether material success has not deadened the spirit without eradicating poverty or relieving the large Negro minority from neglect, discrimination, and injustice. Communist critics put the case more forcibly: for them the pursuit of material betterment has enthroned the capitalists as the real rulers of America, while the condition of the Negro minority proves that Americans share the characteristic vices of white imperialism. With many variations these criticisms are echoed by militant radicals of the twentieth century. Yet American critics—and, to a large extent, foreign critics—make their points by contrasting what has been achieved with what should have been achieved if the American ideological commitments had been honored. The promise is the standard by which results are judged, and the appeal is made to the principles of the American ideology, not against them.

All modern societies experience a tension between the enormous powers of government and the desire of men to live their own lives; between the objectives set by men who control government and the desire of humbler men to satisfy their own needs. This tension is not more acute in the United States than in other nations, but it is more frequently exposed in the forum of public debate. Criticism is nourished by the hope that people will be convinced and overstatement is fostered by controversy. The frequent accusations that one group or another is betraying American traditions is evidence of strength, not weakness. On the basic elements of political and social life the Americans exhibit a solidarity which might well be the envy of more authoritarian systems.

American controversies have been concerned with the meaning of principles which most Americans accept; but, like other nations based upon a revolution the United States has experienced a tension between people's attachment to ideas that provide the core of their national experience and a utopian conviction that society could and should be made more perfect. The idea of amelioration was built into the revolutionary foundations, and in theory conservatism should embrace the impulse to improvement; on these lines some recent historians have constructed an interpretation of American history which takes consensus, not conflict, as its guiding theme. In practice conservative and reforming principles have found it difficult to live together. A classic example is provided by the history of the antislavery movement which displayed the clearest clash between constitutional right and the hope of reform. In the twentieth century the crowding problem of an urban and industrial society have made the tension greater than ever before; the men of the "right" and the men of the "left" stand further apart and find it increasingly difficult to communicate with each other.

The contemporary conflicts are made more severe by the traditional suspicion between the political establishment and the intelligentsia. Modern government cannot dispense with the services of economists, political analysts, scientific aides, and speech writers; but the great body of the intellectual community stands outside as critics (and often as unfriendly critics) of the political establishment. Inasmuch as intellectuals are the most articulate interpreters of the American tradition —and tend to identify themselves with the impulse to reform—the impression of a divided society is heightened. The recurrent campaign against "un-American" activities is one example of the way in which the political establishment counterattacks intellectual criticism; but in the long run it is the intellectuals who win the battle of the books and perpetuate the impression of ignorance, prejudice, and selfish interest in high places. It may not be necessary to go all the way with the prophets of consensus to agree that there has been too much black and white in the writing of American history.

The words and slogans used in these controversies are abstractions or symbols rather than descriptions of what actually occurs: "democracy," "communist," "free enterprise," or "the free world" may convey ideas which stir the emotions, but they are tools for political rhetoricians, not for political analysts. "Democracy" is a symbolic word to denote a number of associated characteristics including popular participation in government, free elections, majority decisions, free speech, and free association. But what do these things mean in practice, and how are they combined together? Some recent examples may help to illustrate the difficulties. An American political party—the Communist party—is subjected to restraints that virtually deprive its members of the right of free speech, free association, and several common law safeguards which apply to other citizens. These restraints are justified by the highest legal authority on the ground that Communists endanger national security and that the blessings of "democracy" cannot be extended to men who endanger its survival. The Congress of the United States can delegate such wide powers to the President—especially in foreign affairs and defense—that his authority may be as unfettered as that of any dictator. There are important differences between this course of action and that by which the rulers of a communist state can commit their country to military action; but there are also similarities. An American citizen has more opportunity for participation in voting processes than the citizens of any other nation; but it was riot and violence, not voter participation, which persuaded the government to tackle the problems of poverty and Negro unrest in the hearts of the nation's largest and most affluent cities. American enterprise is "free" but the success of that enterprise depends very much upon economic policies adopted by the national government; the economic life or death of whole regions is determined by the allocation of defense contracts, while the small businessman may sometimes wonder which "freedom" can prevent him from being overwhelmed by giant competitors. The "free world" may be a valuable concept, but outsiders may well be puzzled when it embraces dictatorial regimes, and when a conservative posture seems to deny America's own origin as a revolutionary nation.

Words may not always describe things as they are. As systems change language continues to explain them in inherited terms, and national ideologies may be rooted in the past or even in the aspirations of the past rather than in the world as it was. The basic ideas of Marxism were forged in the middle of the nineteenth century, crystallizing the hopes of an alternative to capitalism as it then was; so that today the lives of millions are directed by past ideas about a society that never came into being. An American might well recognize this argument when applied to others without admitting that it might also apply to his own society; yet the formative ideas of American democracy are older than Marxism and were launched in a rural society containing fewer people, spread along a thousand miles of the Atlantic coast, than now occupy Los Angeles County. To say that ideas are old, or that they were formulated in a different environment, does not deny that they may be valid for all time, but it does convey a warning against a dogmatic attachment to concepts which no longer correspond with realities. Freedom, justice, tolerance, equal rights, and government by consent have permanent value; but changing circumstances require their application in different ways.

An ideology should not be a static thing; it should be a growing body of ideas about society, constantly discarding what no longer applies and assimilating the new. The experience of the past demonstrates the constructiveness of visionaries whom contemporaries regarded as dangerous or impractical; and in a later generation the dreams and aspirations may be as difficult to shed as they once were to assimilate. Facts which are enshrined in national histories, the commanding rhetoric of the past, and literary expressions of national character, have a life of their own, and these ghosts cannot be exorcised by sophisticated criticism. The contemptuous use of the word "mythology" can reveal a deep misunderstanding of the historical process; national existence is real, the political institutions are real and the ideas which sustain them are real even when fallacious. This is particularly true in the United States where it is impossible to explain national existence without giving an historical account of national development (and especially of development in those early and formative years of the eighteenth century). The historian is compelled to stand midway between the exponents of everyday popular patriotism and the social analysts; he must be aware that slogans are not descriptions, but he must also accept the fact that what people think may be more potent than a realistic appraisal of their actual condition.

The United States belongs to a large family of nations with intellectual roots in Israel, Greece, and Rome. The ancestors of all white Americans belonged to what was once known as Christendom, but the dominant portion of the early American population came from northern Europe and especially from the British Isles. Here the heritage of ancient Mediterranean civilization had been assimilated with a Teutonic tradition, and the memory of a supposedly "free" Anglo-Saxon constitution was to have a marked effect upon American development. This blend of ideas about human destiny, man's reasoning capacity, and the institutions of civilized society gave a characteristic and ineradicable texture to the American political mind.

Like the ancient Jews, the first Puritan settlers were the people of a book and the product of a religious revolution. The Bible was their authority and the persecution of the Godly in the Old World was their justification; they compared their transatlantic migration with the Exodus from Egypt, and the purpose of escape was the creation of a new society in a promised land. Their mission was to carry with them the hopes of mankind; they were a chosen people, but they worked under Providence to carry out God's purpose in the world. The inspiration of a mission, both exclusive and universal, was a basic element in the American heritage. So, too, was the Puritan emphasis upon individual salvation combined with the Divine command to build an ordered society where the Godly could live uncontaminated by the evils of European civilization. New Englanders were not all Puritans, and commercial motives mingled with the religious impulse, but the Puritan mind set the pattern of thought and sketched out the lines of development. The new society was to be a haven for the Godly, but to accomplish this it had to be successful. It had to find ways of supporting a vigorous and ambitious people who believed that it was their destiny to inherit the earth. Piety and strict moral standards came first, but material success was a social necessity and earned its own rewards. The Puritans rejected the aristocratic disdain for trade; but they also rejected the paganism and indulgence which accompanied the accumulation of wealth in sixteenth-century Europe. Material success was a means; moral society was the goal.

The Southern plantation colonies were settled by man under very different influences. Here the commercial motive was uppermost, but successful agriculture could support a way of life that was more important than its profits. If New England perpetuated the spirit of Puritan revolt against authority in Church and State, Virginia carried across the Atlantic the sturdy independence of the English country gentry who respected authority only so long as it contributed to their own local power and influence. Their difficulty was to find a laboring force to replace the peasantry of the home country, but this problem was solved by African slavery. Meanwhile the earlier poor settlers spread out over the country as an independent yeomanry, and, if the Puritan settlements offered a well-ordered society where religion and virtue could flourish, the Southern colonies fulfilled other aspirations of the submerged classes in England. Here a man could own land; and, despite the fact that planter gentry monopolized political authority, poor men owed them no economic services and could live more freely than any other people in the world.

Both types of colonies shared the heritage of English law. In England a customary law of Teutonic origin had persisted in spite of the challenge from the more orderly concepts. Roman law consisted of a large body of precepts which were adapted to the needs of a particular society by command of the sovereign; common law was a body of rules built up through the centuries and derived its authority from use rather than command. The law was discovered by reason working upon precedent, and it existed independently of the sovereign.

In practice Englishmen might appeal to the law against their King at their peril, but the principle that authority was bound by law was always present and became decisive during the constitutional conflicts of the seventeenth century. The King, said Bracton, the English medieval jurist, was under no man but under God and the Law, and Sir Edward Coke, the cantankerous Chief Justice under James I, made the law a mystic embodiment of justice which could protect the subject against all actions which were not authorized by it. Generations of American colonial lawyers would learn their jurisprudence from Coke, and this concept of law as a majestic principle brooding over all human affairs was easily assimilated with the Puritan idea of Divine Providence. The Bible showed how kings and people had been punished when they strayed from the law and the prophets; it counseled obedience but showed how rulers had been judged and found wanting. It was but a short step to see the English common law as the expression of God's wish to see justice among men.

Other aspects of the American heritage may be more difficult to define. Every educated American was bred on the Roman classics: Ciceronian orations were the model of oratory and the expression of a social philosophy in which justice and right dealing were the major concerns, and the history of the Roman republic was more familiar to Americans than that of any other epoch except seventeenth-century England. To many Americans Latin was, perhaps, no more than a disagreeable linguistic exercise, endured in youth and forgotten in later life; yet certain lessons and impressions remained. The Roman Republic proved that nations could be great without hereditary kings, while the history of the Empire proved that greatness could be won at the expense of virtue. It was corruption, a decay of public spirit, and a relaxation of vigilance which had brought about the downfall of the ancient republic, and eighteenth-century Americans were to apply the same standards to imperial Britain. The Revolution would reverse the process of decline and decay; new institutions would create "republican virtue," and an imperial destiny would open before the men of the new world. Certainly the Roman example had a deep and pervasive influence upon the Americans of the Revolutionary generation as they envisaged their work under the judgment of history.

The ancient world also provided a laboratory for politics. When James Madison prepared himself for the Federal Constitution of 1787 he did so by immersing himself for six months in the study of ancient states, and particularly of federal and republican constitutions. Plato was little read, and not appreciated when read, but the history of Athenian democracy was well known to well-educated Americans. They learned that democratic government was possible but also learned that democracies were vulnerable when they succumbed to the unrestrained passions of the multitude. Aristotle's *Politics* was probably known directly to very few, but Aristotle's doctrine of a government of laws, not men, of constitutions, and of social balance had flowed down to them through many channels.

Of more immediate influence was the Americans' concept of the British constitution, and their own experience of representative government in the colonies. The constitution, though unwritten, was the formal expression of the authority of law. Its essential idea was that a body of legal principles, augmented by charters and statutes, protected individuals against arbitrary authority. Legally established institutions provided a part of this barrier between men and government: parliament, colonial assemblies, churches, incorporated towns, and chartered commercial companies had duties and rights; they could neither be deprived of their rights (save by process of law) nor divest themselves of their duties. Wherever a right was infringed there was a legal remedy to be found, and the whole of society was, in this way, bound together by laws which could not be abrogated and rights which could not be diminished. In some passages Coke had even seemed to suggest that the legislative authority itself was limited in the laws which it could enact by the principles of natural law embodied in the unwritten constitution. Blackstone, the British legal philosopher, was to demonstrate that logically nothing could restrain the legislative power of Parliament, but constitutional limitations would have momentous consequences in America.

Superimposed upon the idea of constitutionalism was the eighteenth-century idea of a "mixed government." This rationalized what actually existed in England—a hereditary monarchy, a hereditary upper house, an elected lower house, and an independent judiciary—and deduced that this separation of powers balanced the principle of authority, the permanent interests of property, the wishes of the people, and the supremacy of the law. Order was maintained and liberty was preserved when no part of society had the power to act alone, and when each power to act was balanced by a power to check. This formal expression of a system of "checks and balances" coincided with the experience of colonial government. Governors, councils, elected assemblies, and judges appointed for life set up a balance which worked harmoniously most of the time; when controversies arose they had been resolved and usually by compromises in which the elected assemblies gained more than the appointed governors and councils. Colonial experience had also made Americans familiar with the notion that there were different kinds of law, a hierarchy of laws each with their respective spheres. The common law, parliamentary statutes, colonial charters, and the enactment of colonial assemblies were all operative, and American colonists were being trained in a system of plural law at the very time that Englishmen were resolving the unanswered questions of the seventeenth century by agreeing that Parliament was the supreme legislative authority. In legalistic terms, this is what the American Revolution was about.

This blend of ancient ideas and recent experience might have occurred in a very different way if the American Revolution had not taken place in an age of rationalist thought. Medieval Europe had not been an irrational society, but human reason operated within well-defined channels and implicitly accepted the existence of an unknown world which men could not know and only God could reveal. The frontiers of knowledge were fixed by divine wisdom, and beyond them men must look to such information as God had chosen to reveal in Holy Scriptures. The civilization which built Gothic cathedrals and laid the foundations of the modern world, kept knowledge under the discipline of the unknowable, but by the eighteenth century the most active intellects of Europe had broken out of these traditional bonds. A new spirit claimed that man was master of his world and could solve any problem through reason.

This intellectual revolution is the root of all those changes which separate the modern world from the past. The conviction that men need not be limited by the past but can make the world as they want it—provided they discover the rational principles for action— has been the inspiration, and has provided the intellectual tools, for all the vast changes in science, technology, medicine, and social engineering that have transformed civilization. Eighteenth-century Americans were conservative in many ways, and Puritan theology continued to subject knowledge to divine inspiration; but in one very significant way the Americans were to lead the world in the great revolution of modern times. Since the earliest days of settlement the colonists had experimented with the building of communities, and the Revolution provided them with an opportunity for making governments as they wished. If they took over much from the past, there was a principle of selection at work. They did not passively accept, but consciously created, the institutions under which they wished to live. In 1787, for the first time, a group of men sat down to *make* a system of government, and to decide what they wanted through a process of rational enquiry and debate. Since that time most countries of the world have followed this example, though often with less conspicuous success.

Among the discoveries of this period was the idea that the institutions and powers of government must be written down and perpetuated in a constitution. The bonds of the unwritten constitution had been insufficient, and it was now necessary to record for all time the fundamental law in a document which would be the supreme law of the land. Hitherto constitutions, so far as they existed, had been principles of natural law recognized in concessions wrung from princes. Even later, in some European countries, men would speak of rulers *giving* constitutions to their people. American constitution-making was guided by a different principle: here the people themselves would decide what institutions and laws they would have. For the first time in the modern world the Aristotelian ideal—of a government of laws, not men—became a reality. In this revolutionary event one paradox was concealed: the Constitution did not restrain princes but the people who made it. The rational and free men of the eighteenth century had set up a constitutional god which would set the limits of experimentation in the political and social sphere, and in this paradox is comprised the future constitutional history of the United States.

These are the basic elements of the American political ideology; but an ideology is a living thing, and it is impossible to separate the roots from the organism, or to weigh exactly the importance of fundamental ideas against that of subsequent experience. Physical environment, the vast areas of unoccupied land, the population explosion in Europe which sent millions of migrants across the Atlantic, economic growth in an age of technicological innovation, sectional controversy, slavery and its heritage of racial tension—all these influences and many more have played their part. It is profitless to seek explanations which extract one of these influences and give it a primacy which is denied to others; we deal with total history and not with partial history; and with a nation that spreads over a continent and now includes more than two hundred million people, not with a city state in which it might be possible to enumerate and evaluate a precise list of formative influences.

Democracy as it is understood today was not a part of the original American heritage. The essence of republicanism, as understood by the revolutionary generation, was representation of the people but not automatic entitlement to participation in politics. Women, minors, and slaves were excluded without question; most men without property were denied the vote, and so were large numbers of men with very small property. In spite of these restrictions the colonies were wide suffrage societies—at a time when only a tiny fraction of the English population could vote—because property was so widely diffused. There was also a tendency to open the doors wider by accepting qualifications other than property—such as payment of taxes or service in the militia—and it is probable that in many cases votes were accepted from men who were known and respected in their districts, even if their property was technically insufficient for the suffrage. The Revolution accelerated this process, but it was not until 1830 that all resident males in most states were allowed to vote, and even then there were exceptions. Thus the idea of universal white male suffrage was slow to emerge, and even today the idea survives that certain kinds of citizens should carry more weight than others. Until recently, the apportionment of seats in the legislatures of many states insured that rural counties would carry more weight than densely populated urban areas, and even a Supreme Court ruling that representation must be in proportion to numbers has not entirely eradicated the practice of unequal apportionment. Another idea, generally accepted at the time of the Revolution, was that large property must have special representation in the legislature (usually by provisions that members of the Senate should have higher property qualifications or be elected on a more restricted franchise than the lower house), and these safeguards against the power of numbers were slow to die. Thus ideas which are today accepted as axiomatic grew into the American system and were not born with it. One citizen, one vote, each vote carrying equal weight; no special representation for classes or interests—these are principles which command themselves today without much argument, yet earlier principles have left their legacy.

More important than the mechanics of voting and qualifications for suffrage is the purpose which voting is intended to serve. Eighteenth-century ideas about voting were formulated in a society which possessed a well-defined social hierarchy. The tasks of government were carried out by members of the social elite, and no eighteenth-century theorists contemplated a system that would turn society upside down or give the poor authority over the rich. Voters could select between rival members of the elite and rebuke men or policies at the ballot box; they had the right to choose, the right to reject, and the right to consent. By voting humble men could make their wishes known to men in authority and effectively prevent the abuse of power, but the people did not force their will upon government or project their own kind into office. Voting was a defense mechanism, and the way the people at large played their part in a system of checks and balances. Two centuries of experience have brought about substantial modifications in this view, and most modern Americans would assume that the purpose of voting is to translate political views into political policies. Even so, there remains a significant difference between the climate of American democracy—with its rural origins—and European democracy, which came later in time and at a period when the urban masses demanded political participation to achieve political objectives.

In European democracy it is assumed that the will of majorities should be the mainspring of policy, but Americans assume that the will of one area or of one class (even of the majority) must seek reconciliation with conflicting views expressed in other regions and by other classes. The result must be a compromise in which the national majority is bound to make concessions to local majorities, and the roots of this respect for local autonomy lie deep in the colonial experience. The colonies existed as separate political units, under the Crown, but owing no obligation to each other. In Europe the course of history had set against local autonomy; even liberal historians have commended the centralizing process by which the rulers of national states stamped out regional particularism, and the scales of judgment have been heavily weighted against men who set the interest of an area against the interest of the nation. In America this kind of nationalism was unacceptable. Even though much argument and blood was to end in a drastic curtailment of local autonomy, the states continued to exist as independent authorities. The Revolution sprang from the need to defend the rights and powers of colonial legislatures against imperial centralization and this freedom, once gained, could not be lightly sacrificed. This independence of the states from external control was reinforced by a favorite eighteenth-century axiom that free institutions were possible only in small societies: the greater the size, the greater the need for despotic control, and the more remote a government, the more impractical popular control.

Yet the independence of states became possible only because there was union between them. If the states separately could put the case for autonomy, only the states united could succeed in war and act on a par with older nations. If the Revolution pulled men in the direction of local separatism, it also provided the strongest practical and emotional arguments for union. Union was a by-product of the struggle, not its first objective; but once achieved, the idea of union acquired a life of its own, with a powerful attraction for American minds. The synthesis was to be found in American federalism, which was to be a major contribution of American experience to modern political development. The idea of the unitary national state prevailed in some older European nations, but as new nations came into the field during the nineteenth and twentieth centuries, most of them adopted some version of American federalism. Americans would often divide sharply between the adherents of the states and those of the national Government, but this conflict does not represent the true and permanent condition of American opinion, which goes all the way neither to a unitary system nor to provincial separatism. Even in 1861 the seceding states immediately formed a new national union.

The new men of America presented distinctive ideas about political organization; the vitality of these ideas was to be tested and reinforced by the experience of immigration. Millions crossing the Atlantic repeated the drama of rejecting the old world and accepting the new, and though immigration changed the social complexion of America, the basic tenets of the American system survived; they were accepted, and acceptance gave them new strength in every generation. Economic opportunity played a large part in making America attractive to immigrants; but over the years the democratic system exercised an even greater attraction. For the immigrant America offered not only a chance to better himself but to do so without interference from squire or parson, landowner or royal official. Until late in the nineteenth century most immigrants from the British Isles had been denied the vote in their own countries, and later immigrants from eastern Europe came from countries still under authoritarian rule; for all these people the experience of political participation, after a comparatively short naturalization period, was novel and exhilarating. Thus each generation of immigrants provided new waves of willing and enthusiastic converts to the American political ideology and passed on their faith to their children.

For one group of Americans, however, the world looked very different. Africans came to America because they were forced to come, and under circumstances which completely disrupted their traditional culture. As slaves they were stripped of most of their attributes of personality and became chattels without wills of their own. Even when free they were treated as inferior men, and only occasionally could they participate in politics. Yet the pervasive appeal of the American ideology sank into the Negro mind, and when free his highest ambition was to become a citizen on the American model. Negroes appealed to the American tradition in order to win status for themselves, and in spite of the wrongs they endured asked for assimilation with American civilization. Not all Negroes accepted this attitude, but their most prominent spokesmen did, until the terrible urban riots of the 1960s— carried out by men who had all the civil and political rights for which earlier generations had asked—sowed doubt among Negro leaders and their white friends. Black nationalism may or may not have a future, but weak or powerful, it carries a warning. For the first time a substantial group of Americans have rejected the American ideology though the emotions of the white "backlash" may constitute an equal denial of basic principles.

An expanding nation in the nineteenth century experienced one problem which had hardly been contemplated in the hopeful era of the Revolution. Early Americans knew of the rights of individuals and of the rights of states; they realized the broad difference between the "planting" states and the "commercial" states, but they hardly contemplated the situation in which a group of states would claim a destiny different from that of the others. Sectionalism was perhaps inevitable; specialization of economic function bred social differentiation and generated political separatism. The American system was called upon to hold the balance between different regions, and to adjust conflicting interests among different social systems. Its failure to perform this task in the case of the South produced a tragic war, but its success in other respects deserves more notice than it sometimes receives. Throughout the nineteenth century the American heartland was throwing off colonies of settlement in much the same way as the older European nations. A Western Territory could be compared to a colony, and for the early part of its existence it was governed as a dependency. One of the greatest achievements of the American political system was to bridge the gap between colonial status and equality in the Union, without any of the recurrent disputes which vexed the relationship between European countries and their colonial offshoots. As colonists the Americans had protested vigorously against the notion that their forefathers had forfeited some of their rights as British subjects by removing themselves to America. In the old British Empire the idea survived for long that colonists were in some indefinable way inferior to the native population of the British Isles, and that they should be kept in political tutelage. In the United States an early decision meant that men going to new areas out of the existing states lost none of their rights as American citizens, and their settlements were promised equality in the Union as states as soon as population had reached a required level. In this way the "colonies" were assured of early participation in national affairs, and once represented in the government at Washington they could employ normal political tactics to satisfy the needs of their regions. The process worked in spite of frequent and inevitable tension between the newly developing regions and the older colonies where economic power was concentrated.

The political representation of economically weaker regions was not enough to satisfy the South. The profound differences over slavery made it increasingly difficult to reconcile more superficial differences, and four years of war saved the Union without erasing sectionalism. It is wrong to say that the South rejected the American ideology because the Southern version was a reasonable deduction from the original premises. What it did mean was that after the war the South would continue to use the ideas and slogans of American political thought, but for different purposes. "States' Rights" meant the right to evade the Constitution, "democracy" meant white supremacy, "minority rights" meant the right to obstruct by filibuster or by other means. The resources of the law were used to prevent the law from operating, and rational argument was used to explain why reason should not prevail. There is no need to heap hysterical abuse upon the Southerners for behaving in this way; they were using the right of political participation in the Union—which the other states insisted they must have—in order to win the autonomy which had been denied by war. They were resisting tendencies which they thought would undermine their society, and recent experience in the North may suggest that they were not so oddly obscurantist as is sometimes suggested. Still, there was something very significant in all this; the American ideology was being used against itself, and the result left no one happy.

It has been suggested that the American experience played a primary role in the political revolutions which have inaugurated modern times; it is also true that in the two subsequent centuries American experience was intertwined with the whole course of events in Euro-American civilization. Nineteenth-century Europe saw a continuing dialogue between traditional society, commercial society, the intelligentsia, and the rising class of what would later be called "white collar" workers. The traditional society was one in which custom was accepted as a guide for action, and the existence of an elite was taken for granted. Commercial society was ready at times to ally with traditional society but its guiding principle was the maximization of profit; economic success was treated as a qualification for authority, but free enterprise would also continually improve general welfare. The employed and self-employed middle class grew as ancillary to commercial society; it provided the bureaucracies for public and private enterprise but also promoted political demands for a relaxation of privilege, for education, for wider political participation, and for a host of social reforms. Where the traditional authority was too inflexible, or where commercial society failed to provide sufficient economic opportunities, the middle class also provided the leadership for revolutionary movements. Often allied with one or more of these groups, but usually separate from them, was the intelligentsia which claimed to pursue the truth without allegiance to Church or State. The intellectuals could be called "irresponsible" because they often advanced theories without regard to the consequences, but the intellectuals could claim that the advancement of knowledge was a transcendent responsibility. It is a curious fact that these claims were advanced most emphatically, and with greatest influence, in nineteenth-century England where the intelligentsia was most closely allied with the political establishment.

In this four-cornered dialogue between traditional authority, commercial society, the employed and self-employed middle class, and the autonomous intelligentsia the United States has played a vital role. First among modern nations it rejected traditional authority and constructed a new system on principles expressed by the intelligentsia; the lawyers, merchants, and planters who led the Revolution were not cloistered intellectuals but assumed that reason could uncover and apply correct ideas of government. If they began by claiming that the correct principles were already found in the British constitution, they ended by asserting that these truths were "self-evident." They were not "doctrinaires," in the rigid sense in which the word is now used, but they were men of books and reflective thought, who based a new system on rational argument, not upon custom, theology, or hereditary right. It is these prophets—albeit the unconscious and often unwilling prophets—of American democracy, who provide the theme for the next chapter.

CHAPTER II

REVOLUTION

In 1777 Benjamin Franklin rebuked a lady correspondent, saying, "You are too early, *Hussy*, as well as too saucy, in calling me Rebel; you should wait for the event, which will determine whether it is a *rebellion* or only a *revolution.*"* "Rebellion" (perhaps with the events of 1745 in mind) was an unjustifiable attack upon legitimate authority; a "revolution" (certainly with 1688 in mind) was justifiable action against authority which had forfeited its claim to legitimacy. Rebellion repudiated rightful allegiance; revolution derived its authority from allegiance to a higher law. If cynics might say that a revolution was, then, nothing but a successful rebellion, the jibe misfired among men brought up to believe in God's Providence; defeat was evidence of divine displeasure, success bore witness to God's blessing.

This view of revolution explains the way in which Americans regard the revolutionary origin of their nation. This revolution (unlike the French Revolution) is not the fountainhead of a radical tradition which renews itself in each generation; nor is it (like the Russian Revolution) the work of an intelligent minority interpreting history in the interest of the masses. Rather the American Revolution was the deposition of bad government, and the assertion of good principles which have remained in force to this day. The Revolution was concerned with the legal relationship between Great Britain and the American colonies; it did not begin with an ambitious attempt to make a new society, but with the hope that a few concessions and reforms would resolve the tension which had been created. Yet this limited objective came to involve major statements about the rights of men and their relationship to government. As Bernard Bailyn has said,

> These closely related changes—in the view of what a constitution was and of the proper emphasis in the understanding of rights—were momentous; they would shape the entire future development of American constitutional thought and practice. Yet they did not seem momentous at the time.†

This blend—of expedients with principles of universal significance—marks out the special character of the American revolutionary heritage.

To contemporaries the dominant fact was that British policy, ordained by a supreme Parliament, threatened to alter the fabric of colonial life. There was no deep-seated drive toward independence and no utopian substitutes for things as they were; the leaders of the

---

* Franklin to Mrs. Thompson, 8 February 1777.
† Bernard Bailyn, *The Ideological Origins of the American Revolution* (Cambridge, Mass., 1967), p. 189.

Revolution risked the penalties for treason, organized for war, and became the architects of a new nation because unexpected circumstances dictated their actions. But, if the direction of the Revolution was unsought, it was not taken blindly but guided by a long tradition, forged in the mother country, of constitutional liberty and resistance to arbitrary power. Theoretical innovation was unnecessary, because the implications of familiar principles seemed sufficient. The great heritage of the common law, the epic of parliamentary resistance to the Stuarts, and the abstractions of Algernon Sidney and John Locke, provided ideas on which a Revolution could feed; but nostalgia for ancient liberty was also nourished by the intensely practical experience of wide suffrage, representative government, and recurrent disputes with local executives. Even when the Revolutionaries departed from legalistic argument and embodied an abstract philosophy in the Declaration of Independence, they did no more than give elevated expression to the commonsense of the colonial political system.

Accumulated ideas and existing practice may well be more powerful than claims to break loose from past and present, and in many ways the American Revolution was a stronger movement than nineteenth-century revolutions, which took their cues from France. They failed to produce stable political systems but gave birth to revolutionary traditions which revived in each subsequent generation, leaving radicals as their heirs but also stimulating a live and vigorous counter-revolution. Other revolutions arose within old states, or in new states with strongly developed systems of class and privilege, and inevitably divided society into sharply antagonistic streams; the American Revolution took place in societies which were both simple and sophisticated, where "the establishment" was weak, the indigenous defense easily overcome, and no rhythm of attack and defense set up. Moreover, if the colonies were old their union was new, and the nation which evolved was based exclusively upon the Revolution. The American nation was the product of the Revolution, and Americans could not deny its principles without repudiating their loyalty.

The American Revolution, like all revolutions, was the work of a minority; but it was a minority which did its work in literate societies where government by discussion was already established. Social and political facts made the American Revolution a broad-based movement in which the gap between leaders and led could never be wide. The American Revolution could not have anticipated the Russian model and concentrated power in one party and political direction in a minority; to do so, it would have first been necessary to defeat a politically conscious majority. The United States born of the Revolution has not experienced the excitement of radical movements on the French model, nor has it seen the vision of society remade by rational intelligence, but it has achieved a stable society in which the principles of the Revolution have become political orthodoxy.

If one makes social upheaval the criterion of revolution, the American Revolution was incomplete. Leaders who backed the wrong horse were replaced by others who had seized the right opportunities; but most new men belonged to the same social and economic class as the old. The crisis saw mob violence and popular agitation, but turbulence subsided when the objectives of the Revolution had been achieved. A number of minor social changes followed in the wake of the Revolution, but they might well have occurred without it. Levelling enthusiasm was necessarily restrained in a society of property holders who preferred stability to the doubtful benefits of social revolt. Moreover, though the American Revolution rejected the idea of a hereditary elite, it took place in an age when government was expected to remain in the hands of those who had the leisure and education to conduct it. The American states enjoyed wide suffrage, but representation did not mean social upheaval. The American Revolution can be minimized by a critical examination of the changes which it effected in social relations and social assumptions. But the importance of an event is not necessarily proportionate to the disturbance which it causes, and the new philosophy of government was all the more durable because it was not associated with the disruption of society.

The real core of the Revolution was the assertion that authority over the people came from the people themselves; war, independence, and the organization of government proved that this was a workable proposition. For centuries it had been assumed that when St. Paul declared that the powers that existed were ordained of God, he thought only of the kings, princes, and governors; but now divine ordination was to be manifested in election by the people. The fundamental proposition of the Revolution was that governments derived their just powers from the consent of the governed; this statement was more significant than social revolutions which never materialized or ran into the sands of frustration.

The epic of the Revolution was the discovery that people organized for resistance—even in small and remote colonies—could defeat a great power deploying professional soldiers and the greatest navy in history. This example was to ignite and inspire revolutionary enthusiasm elsewhere. Less spectacular, but of even greater significance, was the demonstration that men need not choose between efficiency and freedom; centralizing tendencies, which were prevailing in Europe, were called in question, and undivided sovereignty was not seen as the only alternative to anarchy. The Revolution was literate, legalistic, and philosophical; innovation was veiled in precedent, abstract rights were presented as legal rights, and it was assumed that questions of political organization would answer themselves if approached in a rational way. But the conservatism of the Revolution was merely a veneer upon boldness in improvization and fertility in adaptation. The approach to revolution was cautious and often unwilling, but the consequence of revolution was a society unlike any that had previously existed. In the eighteenth century, a country without kings or hereditary aristocrats, with authority derived from consent, wide suffrage and frequent elections, and a deliberate division of sovereignty between local and national government, was a startling novelty. Some of these elements had existed in colonial society, but there was all the difference between political eccentricity in small colonies, which lay outside the main stream of events, and a new nation which claimed equality with the powers of the world and superiority in political wisdom.

The initial problem was whether small colonial societies could win autonomy within an imperial system; when this failed the major problem was whether independence would work. Concurrently major questions were raised about the nature of the Constitution, the character of and safeguards for individuals rights, and the source of authority in a political society. If it had been possible to satisfy colonial demands at the outset the deeper questions might not have been raised; but once raised they acquired a dynamic life of their own, influenced all future developments, and acquired immediate force when the breakdown of traditional authority made it necessary to write down in plain words what the new governments should be. Much was taken over unchanged from the old, but decisions to retain were as much acts of will as deliberate innovation. For the first time since the semimythical foundation of the ancient Greek states men sat down to decide what kind of government they wanted for themselves; the simple quest for colonial autonomy thus led to consideration of fundamental political problems and to unprecedented experiments in the making of states.

These novel demands crowded in upon one generation of Americans. Just over twenty years separated the first crisis, occasioned by the Stamp Act of 1765, from the making of the Federal Constitution in 1787; men who were enthusiastic youths at the beginning of the period were barely middle aged when it ended; many men who were already mature leaders at its outset lived to see its conclusion. These makers of the Revolution differed in temperament, interest, and regional affiliations; but they shared common traditions, responded to external and internal challenges in similar ways, and on most occasions found more points of agreement than of disagreement. The typical leader of the Revolution belonged to the Protestant middle class, owned considerable property—which might be in land or in movable wealth—and was most likely to have had some legal training even if not a professional lawyer. He was well-read in the history of England and in ancient history. The Middle Ages he ignored, or tended to regard as a dark age, except for such lights as the Magna Carta shining through the gloom; he regarded Great Britain as his mother country but felt more affinity with the seventeenth than with the eighteenth century (when he suspected that luxury had corrupted the British people). Many merchants supported the Revolution, and so did the large majority of planters in the South. In Northern towns the most enthusiastic supporters of the Revolution were drawn from the ranks of storekeepers, clerks, craftsmen, and small property owners, but there was no sharp stratification in revolutionary society and opinions and manners spread in a smooth blend from rich to poor. This resulted mainly from the absence of great masses of laboring poor, and the overwhelming preponderance of farmers of moderate property. The common legacy of experience and ideas, and the lack of class conflicts, gave solidity and unity of purpose to the revolutionary movement; there was little social upheaval because it was already a revolution in depth, and the major problem was not to impose solutions or even to educate opinion but to provide new government for a society which already satisfied most of its members. Dissenters there were—as witnessed by the very large Loyalist migrations—but the very fact that opponents of the Revolution either removed themselves or acquiesced meant that there was no material out of which to form a counter-revolution.

Thus the task of the Revolution, once Independence had been agreed, ceased to be ideological and became organizational; the problem was now to translate rhetorical victory into military success and viable political institutions. No "jacobin" movement developed to push ideology to its logical conclusions and political links between the people and the leaders remained strong; no dictatorship of the right or left was necessary, and familiar methods of political procedure remained adequate for the situation even while the philosophical justification of political institutions underwent a profound change. What resulted was a solidarity and uniformity of political belief which has since remained one of the wonders of the political world. This solidarity was achieved in the face of material and regional interests which could not be easily reconciled, and was built around allegiance to ideas which Americans came to regard as "self-evident." Despite the desperate practicality of the Revolution, its inner significance was ideological; it created a new society and a new system of ideas to sustain it.

*   *   *

The materials out of which Americans constructed their world view were varied and complex in their operation. British constitutional practice was itself the outcome of centuries of political evolution, and even in the eighteenth century its principles were not clear to those who lived under their operation. The fundamental proposition was that authority should be limited by law and its actions regulated by law. Law protected subjects by recognizing rights which belonged to them by nature but should be made secure in the course of living in society. Representation was a pillar of constitutionalism because it gave the right to influence law to those who were affected by it; so was the freedom of judges to administer the law as they understood it because this meant that no man, not even the ruler, could be judge in his own cause. More subtle in concept but firmly embedded in the constitutional tradition was the idea of checks and balances. Admitting that every force in society might attempt to enlarge its power at the expense of others the theory demanded that every political authority should be matched by another with power to restrain its operation. The most effective form of check and balance was found in a "mixed government" in which social forces were each given their niche in the constitution while none could act without the concurrence of others.

Trained to venerate the supposed harmony of mixed government, Americans could observe with some bewilderment the emergence of a new school of theorists who emphasized the need for undivided sovereignty. In every system, however complicated, it was held that there must be some authority capable of giving decisions which were final and alterable only by itself, and in the British system this authority could only be Parliament. Theory demanded such a concentration of power, politicians embodied it in the Declaratory Act of 1766, and practical considerations were adduced to explain the necessity for an ultimate authority to adjudicate and adjust the many interests involved in the imperial system. This was not the Constitution as the Parliamentarians and common lawyers of the British seventeenth century had understood it, and that eighteenth-century Americans believed they had inherited. Their Constitution knew no sovereign but only the majesty of the law which, in some mysterious way, embodied universal principles of justice and right, and consisted of a great network of customs, charters, statutes, and principles of natural justice which combined to protect the rights of the subject against arbitrary interference. The legalistic appeal to the Constitution thus implied a belief in a higher sanction behind the Law, and transition from legal precedent to self-evident truths was easily made. The Declaration of Independence asserted that men were created equal and endowed with certain inalienable rights; this highly abstract statement parted company with the long train of arguments used to demonstrate the limits of Parliamentary power, but for most Americans it was merely another way of saying the same thing. Equality under the law, and rights recognized by law, had been the core of their Constitution; it required no theoretical somersault to move from the rights of subjects in a single country to the universal rights of man.

Colonial experience was a powerful auxiliary in the development of this constitutional heritage. The Declaration of Independence asserted that governments existed to preserve individual rights and enumerated among these rights the pursuit of happiness. In the context of the European *ancien régime* these were startling statements, but to men bred in the colonial environment they were no more than commonsense. If governments had not existed to preserve rights, why had they been instituted? If colonists had not been permitted to pursue happiness as they saw fit, how could the colonies have grown? To Europeans, American independence involved the repudiation of a whole system of ideas and loyalties; to Americans it was no more than a reasonable deduction from their colonial experience.

The colonial background would affect the future in still more direct ways. Theorists might deplore divided sovereignty, but Americans had had ample experience of sovereignty which was divided in practice if not in name. All law should emanate from a single source, but Americans had lived all their lives under conflicting laws—Parliamentary statutes, colonial laws, charters, common law, and admiralty law—and it was not the confusion but the attempt to unify which had produced disaster. Indeed the colonist had wanted to make the confusion greater by cutting down the imperial power to disallow colonial laws and thus give scope for even greater divergence. Men might say that they could not live under two laws, but colonists knew that it was possible and that administrative inconvenience was inadequate ground for the reduction of individual freedom. From this haphazard system of colonial law in the imperial sytem it was comparatively easy to move to a pluralistic legal system in which men would live under state constitutions and state statutes, the Federal constitution and Federal statutes, constitutional law and common law.

Other novelties (according to the general experience of civilized nations) were easily acceptable because their workability had been demonstrated during the Colonial period. First and foremost was wide suffrage which Europeans (and even the British) regarded as the first step toward anarchy, but which colonists knew to be a stable and fairly conservative institution. It was a commonplace in the colonies that a Governor could be made or broken by the elected assembly, but this was not a symptom of anarchy. Assemblies had this power because of their election by the people and because they were indigenous to the society which they represented. Colonial assemblies were not always models of rectitude or enlightenment but they reflected with some accuracy the virtues as well as the vices of their constitutents; and frequently they seemed to stand for stability and common sense against the capriciousness of distant authority or the folly of its local representatives.

The authority of the representatives of the people was thus contrasted with the authority of those who represented no one. In the hardheaded world of colonial life everyone knew that, in order to get some things, it was necessary to seek the aid of the royal officials and to give something in return; but in most colonies men came to draw a distinction between the men who had to serve themselves or their constituents in this way and those who committed themselves permanently to imperial authority in return for privilege and office. The favored families of the Colonial period fathered the perennial American dislike of any elite which does not depend upon popular choice and, perhaps, too easy an acquiescence in wrongdoing by men who can win or manipulate elections.

Legal theory and colonial experience blended with the pervasive authority of the Bible, especially in its Puritan interpretation. In Europe the Bible taught submission, obedience, and a cheerful acceptance of suffering on earth; in America it taught how chosen people had not only the right but the duty to free themselves from unjust rulers, how prophets had spoken to kings with the higher authority of God, and how men under Providence could make society as it ought to be. Long experience had convinced the Americans that magistrates and assemblies were "powers ordained by God" and entrusted with the protection of the people under their charge. As the Revolution gathered way the rhetoric picked up many overtones from common knowledge of the Bible: here was a promised land, and here were the people in it; their duty was not to a single monarch but to God and mankind, theirs was a glorious destiny under Providence, in their new society men could be both free and good.

Less obvious but still influencing all notions about this better world was the classical heritage. Every educated man was familiar with the Latin authors, and classical examples remained with men when grammar was forgotten. Greek was less common and neither John Adams nor Thomas Jefferson read Plato's *Republic* until late in life (and were shocked by what they read), but Republican and Imperial Rome were full of apposite lessons for colonial revolutionaries. The greatness of Rome had begun when hereditary rule had been overthrown, and the moral and territorial growth of Roman power had been sustained by "republican virtue"; imperialism had brought an extension of conquest but also ostentation, with attendant corruptions, and Christianity had come too late to arrest a moral decline which was the true cause of disintegration. Across the Atlantic was another imperial power which had grown to greatness while her people were simple and vigilant, but which was now threatened with the dissolution of former glory from the corruption generated by luxury.

The idea of the Revolution as a regenerating process was put into secular and contemporary form by Tom Paine in *Common Sense* which had a decisive effect upon opinion in 1776 and left a firm imprint upon the American political mind. "Society in every state is a blessing," wrote Paine, "but government, even in its best state is but a necessary evil. . . . Government, like dress, is the badge of lost innocence; the palaces of Kings are built upon the ruins of the bowers of paradise." The implication was not that one dispense with government, any more than one should dispense with clothes, but that one should take a low and practical view of its functions. A government existed to remedy certain defects in human nature, to provide security against violence, to protect property against envious attacks, to uphold the law and punish crime; it should be responsible to the society which it served and in no way be superior to it. All forms of government were subject to a utilitarian test, and aspects of government which performed no useful function could be discarded without hurt to anyone except the kings and courtiers who derived personal advantage from them. "England, since the conquest," said Paine, "have known some few good monarchs, but groaned beneath a much larger number of bad ones; yet no man in his senses can say that their claim under William the Conqueror is a very honorable one. A French bastard, landing with an army of banditti and establishing himself King of England against the consent of the natives, is in plain terms a very paltry rascally original. It certainly hath no divinity in it. However it is needless to spend much time in exposing the folly of hereditary right; if there are any so weak as to believe it, let them promiscuously welcome the Ass and the Lion, and welcome. I shall neither copy their humility, nor disturb their devotion." Paine's attack upon hereditary right repudiated privilege derived from descent and a right to rule based upon status; it did not touch the right to inherit property. The United States started its national existence as a classless society, but its concept of class was framed in a pre-Marxian era; Americans repudiated class based on birth, not the existence of rich and poor. The opportunity to become rich was an essential part of the pursuit of happiness.

A by-product of the Revolutionary period was the rejection of a national established church. This was a necessity at the outset—because there were already separate churches established in the various states—but soon became a virtue. Everywhere in the old world established churches were bastions of the existing order, and the idea of "one state, one church" had not been entirely destroyed by the growing toleration of the age. Even in Great Britain a dissenting Protestant could not hold office under the Crown and was excluded in law, though not always in fact, from local office; only members of the Church of England could receive degrees from the ancient English universities (or of the Church of Scotland from Scottish Universities) and severe laws (not always enforced, but remaining as a statutory threat) treated Roman Catholics as an alien and subversive minority in much the same way as Communists are treated in twentieth-century America. This official marriage between national government and established church was disavowed at the time of the Revolution; though tax-supported churches lingered on in several states, the course was set towards a complete separation between secular and religious authority.

With these principles in mind, the American colonists had to make new governments for themselves, and the novelty of their task has not always been appreciated. One had to go back to the history of ancient Greece to find the making of new constitutions regarded as a normal process in the establishment of states—and even there the fundamental law was declared by a lawgiver rather than by deliberative action. John Adams, leader of the Massachusetts delegation at the Continental Congress and generally regarded as the most influential man in that body, was prone to exaggerate his own importance, but his account of events has the ring of authenticity. In 1775, before independence but after the breakdown of royal authority in most parts of the country, several members of Congress asked his advice on procedure.* How should governments be made to replace those of kings, governors and nominated officials? Adams replied that they should be made in conventions elected by the people. If there was doubt about the acceptability of a new constitution it should be referred to the people for approval. Here was an emphatic assertion of the implications of government by consent which anticipated the Declaration of Independence: The people must first decide who should make the constitution and then decide whether they liked what had been done. It was this process of election, convention, debate, and ratification that would give legality to a government, and the process could be repeated or reversed if the people grew dissatisfied with what had been established.

Of central importance in the new political system was the constitutional convention, and the history of the word "convention" in-

---

* John Adams recorded this in his *Autobiography* which he wrote many years later; it may therefore record an old man's recollections rather than a record of what actually happened.

dicates what lay behind the idea; it had been used occasionally in British history to describe a body which was parliamentary in form, and which could therefore claim to speak for the people, but which lacked royal authority or consent. The most famous and most recent example had been the convention Parliament of 1688 which arranged for the deposition of James II, the accession of William and Mary, and the presentation of the Bill of Rights to the new sovereigns. A convention might be similar in form to a legislature, but it was not a normal legislature; it opened a new era, and wrote the first chapter, but its authority was then at an end. Not all states would adopt this mode of procedure immediately, but in course of time all did and the word "convention" would also be extended to other bodies—such as special party gatherings—which performed vital and specific functions. Still later "convention" would come to describe the national meetings of business, professional, or fraternal associations, but even in this form a convention remains a body called for a special purpose, not to make law to bind other men but to make proposals to those whom it represents. The convention is one of the distinctive institutions of the American political system, and a potent legacy of the Revolution.

The process of constitution-making was to be vividly illustrated in John Adam's own state of Massachusetts. In September 1776 the House of Representatives of the General Court proposed that they, with the Council, should make and enact a constitution and form of government. This was referred to the towns who received the suggestion critically; some maintained that this task should not be done by the ordinary legislature, and many proposed that a constitution be submitted to the towns for comment and approval before enactment. In May 1777 the General Court tried again with a request that the towns elect as Representatives to the Legislature men whom they would entrust with the making of a constitution and promised that the result would be submitted to the people. Boston objected that the constitution should be made by an entirely separate body elected for that purpose alone, but the Court proceeded to act as a convention and to draw up a constitution. This was reported to the towns, and after debate it was rejected by a majority of them. One of the most frequently discussed clauses was that which restricted the right to vote to white males with property worth sixty pounds, and some remarkably clear expositions of democratic theory were presented from remote rural communities. The town of Lennox asserted that "all men were born equally free and independent, having certain natural and inherent and unalienable rights," and went on to ask "how can a man be said to be free and independent, enjoying Life, Liberty and protecting property, when he has not a voice allowed in the choice of the most important officers in the Legislature?"* The town of Sutton declared that the suffrage provision was repugnant "to the grand and fundamental maxim of Human Rights; viz. That Law to bind all must be assented to by all," and went on to protest vigorously against the exclusion of Negroes.

In 1780 a third attempt to draw up a constitution was made; this time a special Convention was elected and the document which they prepared was fuller and more explicit than the unacceptable constitution of 1777. A restriction on suffrage remained (freehold worth three pounds a year or any estate worth sixty pounds) but discrimination against Negroes was dropped. The towns submitted this constitution to a searching examination and many criticisms were made in detail, but enough support was shown for the document as a whole to warrant its adoption. There is no better evidence than these Massachusetts town meetings that the Revolution was indeed a revolution in depth; no doubt discussions were guided by local ministers, lawyers, or prominent property owners, but the participation of the people was manifest. Outside America no people had ever made their own government in this way, and few countries have since enjoyed a similar experience.

However, men of the revolutionary period made a sharp distinction between democracy—meaning direct majority rule or the concentration of power in a single elected assembly—and republican government or popular participation in a "mixed government." A majority of the whole might be required to ratify a constitution, but it was expected that this constitution should limit the power of the majority in ordinary legislative matters. Eighteenth-century men were realists who knew that the best institutions could be destroyed by that mixture of emotion, selfish design, prejudice, and fear which they called "passion," and they expected the machinery of government to allow an appeal from the people drunk to the people sober. This view of constitutional limitations is sometimes seen exclusively as a means of protecting the rich minority against the poor majority, but the men of the Revolution intended "mixed government" to secure stability in a much wider sense than this. In 1775 John Adams was shocked to find that many of his colleagues in Congress had no idea of government "save one which united all the powers in a contemptible single assembly." He used his powers of persuasion to argue for governments on the British model, with two legislative houses, a separate executive, and an independent

---

* This and the other quotations which follow from the Massachusetts discussions are taken from Oscar and Mary Handlin (eds.), *The Popular Sources of Political Authority: Documents on the Massachusetts Constitution of 1780* (Cambridge, Mass., 1966).

judiciary; subsequently he brought his ideas together in a letter to George Wythe of Virginia which was published under the title *Thoughts on Government* and which must be regarded as one of the seminal works in American constitutional theory.*

Adams argued that "a people cannot be long free, nor ever happy, whose government is in one assembly." The executive should be separated from the legislature and given a limited power of veto, the legislature should be divided into two houses, and judges should be appointed by the Governor with "the advice and consent" of the upper house. Other civil and military officers should be appointed in the same way as the judges, or perhaps through joint election by the two houses. So far Adams gave advice which was to be followed by most states and subsequently incorporated into the Constitution of the United States, but in several ways he stressed the popular element more than the men of 1787. The upper house or council should be elected by the lower house, and the Governor by both houses jointly; but all elections would be annual so that even officers who were indirectly chosen would remain conscious of their dependence upon the people. Government servants should serve for three years only, though they might be eligible for reelection. Judges on the other hand should hold office for life and could be removed only by impeachment. A constitution should contain provision for the establishment of an educational system "especially for the lower class of people" because this was "so extremely wise and useful . . . that no expense for this purpose would be thought extravagant."

The symmetry of the balanced constitution concealed difficulties in its composition. In England mixed government had matched the social forces of the country: continuity, hereditary succession, and the practical need for unformity in policy were represented in the monarchy; the aristocracy, landed property, and the established Church were represented in the Lords, and the people (at least in theory) in the Commons. Each part of British government depended upon a different social force, but in the new United States the consent of the government was the only source of authority. How then could one obtain the balance of forces required by the theory of mixed government? Adams proposed election of the Governor by the two houses jointly and of the upper house by the lower, and indirect election commended itself to a number of states. Others included in their constitutions special qualifications for membership of the upper house or for the people who elected them. As the Massachusetts convention

---

* A convenient collection of the writings of John Adams is Adrienne Koch and William Peden (eds.), *The Selected Writings of John and John Quincy Adams* (New York, 1946). *Thoughts on Government* was written in January, 1776.

explained, "the house of representatives is intended as the representatives of the persons, and the Senate of the property of the Commonwealth," and this was secured by making three hundred pounds freehold or six hundred pounds personal property the qualification for election to the Senate while the representatives required only one hundred pounds freehold or two hundred pounds personal property.* The towns seemed to accept this distinction. In other states the representation of property was secured by a special electorate for the upper house with a higher property qualification than that for the lower house. In New York, for instance, the electorate for the lower house consisted of all males who had been resident for six months in one of the counties of the state, possessed freehold property valued at twenty pounds, or rented property with forty shillings annual value, and had paid taxes: but senators were elected by men holding freeholds valued at one hundred pounds. The lower house was elected annually, the upper for four years with one quarter of the senators retiring each year. The Senate was fixed at twenty-four members, while the Assembly at not less than seventy; here, as elsewhere, the combination of higher voting qualifications with larger constituencies was intended to make the senators representative of property in a region rather than of the people in a district. The governor was chosen every three years by the senatorial electorate on a statewide vote. Thus the principle of balance was obtained by giving the two houses and the executive different electorates, different tenures, and different constituencies. "Mixed government" was an interlocking structure in which numbers and property, legislative and executive functions, were matched against each other.

The Revolution raised many questions about the nature of the right to vote. All were agreed that the political people need not necessarily be the whole people, but there was a break away from earlier ideas that the right to vote should be given only to those with a substantial stake—and preferably a freehold stake—in the country. Who then should be excluded if the special claim of freehold property were abandoned? A useful distinction seemed to be the exclusion of those whose votes were likely to be controlled by others, and on this ground women and slaves were disenfranchised without argument. But what of laborers without property, shiftless men, and transient migrants or seamen? The Massachusetts Convention pointed out that the property qualifications which it proposed would exclude only young men living with their parents, men just starting in business, and those "whose idleness of life and profligacy of manners will forever bar them from acquiring and possessing Property." This might seem acceptable in seaport towns with large numbers of laborers,

---

* Oscar and Mary Handlin, *Popular Sources of Political Authority*, as cited above.

seamen, and recent arrivals, but the exclusion of the honest poor did not commend itself to many of the inland towns of Massachusetts, and the suffrage provisions attracted more criticism than any others. It was a story which would be repeated many times: once a clear line between freeholders and the rest had been erased, there was ultimately no stopping place short of adult male suffrage and though every state discriminated in some way against men without property, or with very small property, the Revolution did mark a decisive stage in the history of suffrage.

Was the right to vote something which belonged to a man much as the right to life, liberty, and property belonged to him, or was it a right which could be given or withheld by political action? The Revolution gave no clear answer but the tide was towards the former interpretation. During the next fifty years the property qualifications imposed in the Revolutionary constitutions were eroded away, until nearly all white adult males could vote; the battle was to be fought again over the right of Negroes to vote and once again when the enfranchisement of women was proposed. Even when the major battles for extended suffrage had been won, the idea of denying the vote to men who were illiterate or had not paid certain taxes remained as theoretical and occasionally as practical possibilities; and all states denied the right to vote to men who had not resided for a statutory period in the state. Naturalization was not completed for five years and immigrants were usually denied the right to vote until the end of that period. Thus despite the surge forward in widening the suffrage, states retained the right to discriminate against some who were deemed unfit for membership of the political people.

With this qualification the Revolution, by making consent the basis of authority, helped to change the idea of representation. In the past the dominant idea had been the representation of communities with the representation of interests superimposed; but the United States was moving toward the representation of numbers and toward basing power upon the mass of the people rather than the people organized into communities or joined together in interests. This uniformity of representation made it more difficult to decide who was representing what in a "mixed government," for if all were chosen by the same people what right had any part of the government to check any other part? The theoretical difficulty remains, though it is not much noticed in practice; the will of the people flows upward through various channels, and the people in the mass provide the means by which their wishes can be thwarted in detail.

During the Revolutionary period most states saw a contest between those who wanted more or less power for the elected assembly, and this has sometimes been seen as a struggle between radicals and conservatives. In practice the terms are anachronistic and confusing; both groups regarding themselves as Revolution Whigs, accepting the necessity and justice of popular participation and some form of mixed government. There may have been men who would have preferred a more drastic limitation upon popular authority, but they were not publicly articulate; there may have been others who wished for a social revolution by popular assent, but they were not politically influential. The inner political conflicts of the states were concerned with the distribution of power within a framework of constitutional government, and common ground was always larger than the area of dissent. If the Declaration of Independence had declared that all men were equal, this did not endow all with equal education, capacity, or achievement, and most of the time it was assumed that men in authority would be drawn from the minority who were wealthy enough to afford the luxury of public service. The ladder was there for any man to climb into this minority, but it was not expected that many would do so; the opportunity was present for voters to choose as their representatives the poor or inexperienced, but for most of them this would defeat the purpose of representation. The aim was to choose a man who had the ability and reputation to hold his own, not one who would be smothered by the greater experience of others. The purpose of political participation was not to transmit majority will into positive action but to protect individual rights, serve the interests of constituents, and prevent the abuse of power by the men who governed.

This concept of the purpose of popular participation was acceptable because society remained comparatively stable, despite the gusts of political change. It is a common fallacy to believe that the mass of the people are always pressing forward to exert power for themselves; it is more usual for people to wish to be governed well, while leaving authority in the hands of those who have been accustomed to exercise it. The Revolution removed from the American scene a small number of families who had enjoyed favor and influence during the Colonial period, but their places were taken by men of similar social and economic status. If the elite in Colonial America had been composed of large landowners, successful lawyers, merchants with long-established wealth, and ministers of religion, the new elite contained the same ingredients; there were new men in power but not new classes. At the same time the overthrow of groups which had long enjoyed prestige, and whose position had seemed assured, did occasion some social restlessness, while the experience of popular agitation and organization sowed the idea that political activity could generate policy from below while reinforcing the dependence of rulers upon consent. The social fabric remained intact, but important questions were raised about the relationship between wealth, status, and the task of government. If the American Revolution was not a social revolution, it showed that one might be possible.

Colonial society had already been remarkable for more social mobility than any European society, and it is doubtful whether the Revolution accelerated this process to any marked degree. It was hard to rise up the social ladder, but the obstacles were understood and they were not insuperable. Broadly speaking a man rose by success, and high birth could not protect him against the consequences of failure; abundant land and growing business opportunities made mobility a practical experience, and colonial society honored both "first families" and the owners of newly acquired possessions. Equally accepted was the existence of idle or incapable men who never rose, drifted into subsistence farming, or joined the small class of property-less town laborers; no one made serious proposals to alter their condition. These facts were not changed by the Revolution, and no one proposed a leveling movement which would confiscate property at the top and distribute wealth among the men at the bottom. What the Revolution did do was to increase the awareness, among the men in the middle, of their political strength. Stable farmers, small merchants, superior craftsmen all knew how important their opinions, actions, and arms had been, and flattery of their wisdom and sound sense made it difficult to relapse easily into a condition of apathy. There was no social upheaval, but there was a slow flood of political change which touched every home and every bastion of society. The Revolution did not produce a demand that the poor should rule, or that the rich should be sent away empty, but it did make clear that men who ruled must render account for their stewardship, and that the people could change stewards when they wished to do so. Different issues would come into the political arena at election time; in the past local interests had been served by electing the men who seemed most likely to advance them, but for a decade and more American electors had been called upon to discuss major questions of wide immediate significance and profound philosophical implications. The experience would not be forgotten, and from the time of the Revolution politics took on a more ideological tinge; local affairs were not forgotten—even today European observers are surprised by their prominence in national elections—but links between the particular and the general had been forged and were ready for future use. If the Revolution challenged few social assumptions, and acted upon no new economic theory, its political consequences were enormous. The American Revolution created the climate of democratic politics, and its revolutionary character is underestimated only because so much which it set in motion has become commonplace in the modern world.

The measure of the Revolution for contemporaries may be expressed in this way. In 1763 the ordinary educated American expected that his Colony would continue as a part of the British Empire, and that he himself would die a subject of the British King. He thought that the Imperial Parliament would continue to exercise responsibility for defense and for the trade of the Empire, and that in this indirect way his daily life would be affected by the laws of Parliament. He believed that a body of ancient law (which the lawyers understood) called the British Constitution protected his personal liberty, but he did not anticipate that any special effort would be necessary to secure these constitutional rights. He had no knowledge of any type of colonial government save that by a governor representing the King (or in two colonies representing the proprietor with the assent of the King), and expected that the most important officials would continue to be nominated at Westminster; with a few sporadic exceptions he was not greatly troubled by this situation and may well have thought it a positive advantage that ultimate authority was divorced from local conflicts and intrigues. He believed that his elected house in the Legislature had an important task to fulfill in preventing the abuse of power and in acting as a watchdog over colony affairs; he believed that the representatives drawn from the substantial members of the population had the most to lose from disorder or from interference with property, and were therefore the natural guardians of personal liberty. He did not believe that anyone would find it necessary to resist an Act of Parliament, nor, for that matter, did he believe that Parliament would ever pass an act which could arouse this degree of opposition. He was glad to belong to the most successful political power of the eighteenth century, and he hoped that British glory would shine yet brighter still. He looked forward to a future in which past progress and present harmony would be indefinitely prolonged.

The man who thought this way when he came of age in 1763 had grown into a different world and a different future before he was forty. In 1776 he had ended his allegiance to George III and had then supported a long war against British forces. The independence of his country had been recognized first by foreign countries and finally in 1782 by the beaten mother country, and the idea of living in tutelage, or having major questions settled by external authority, had become abhorrent. The British Constitution had failed him, and he had been forced to recognize certain universal and self-evident truths as the real foundation for his rights and freedom. Almost without arguing the point he had accepted the propositions that monarchy was wrong, that authority must be indigenous, and that the people were its only source. He had seen this authority act in setting up

new governments for the states, and had been led to think deeply
about the problem of who should govern, and upon what principles;
if his conclusions were cautious, the experience was novel and far
removed from most European countries where the mass of the people
had no concern whatever with government. He had suddenly discovered loyalty to an entirely new political entity—the United States—
in whose name royal authority had been defied and an arduous war
had been fought. The political activity to which he had been accustomed in the past acquired a new significance; as a voter he was
a part of the only sovereign which America knew, and upon him
and his fellows rested responsibility for this strange new organization
which was already familiarly called "The Union."

The Revolution and success in war generated enthusiasm. Americans were not merely free but in a new situation. Nothing like this
had ever happened before and the secrets of social happiness were
suddenly unlocked. The men who had beaten the most successful
power in the world could afford to brag a little, and to turn with
confidence to the comparatively simple tasks of peace. It was perhaps
well for these new Americans that they looked forward with hope
that extinguished doubt and with confidence that justice and reason
could easily prevail.

CHAPTER III

UNION AND NEW GOVERNMENT

The Revolution produced a Union of States, which was destined to become a great power, and in 1787 came a Federal Constitution which is now the world's oldest written constitution. Yet on the morrow of independence hostile observers found a close parallel to the condition of America in the Holy Roman Empire, with its multitude of petty states, powerless central authority, and predatory princes advancing their interests at the expense of their neighbors. Men who prided themselves upon their foresight assumed that the United States could be safely ignored in world politics, and that the experiment of republican federalism was bound to fail; but the survival of the Union opened the vista of a continental domain offering the blessings of freedom and the prospects of national power. The psychological effects of this success story were as important as its immediate political consequences. Americans became confident of their own wisdom and of the justice of their institutions; the Union and the Constitution became symbols of achievement and promise; they ceased to be merely political institutions and became focal points for loyalty, national pride, and individual well-being.

Historians have often stressed the contrast between the weakness and confusion which followed peace in 1783 and the order and vigor of the years after 1787. Not everyone would agree, and it has been argued that an inevitable postwar depression was followed by rapid recovery, and that a new period of expansion had begun before 1787. This may be true; but it does not follow that political reform was unnecessary, for if the people were in good heart the government set up under the Articles of Confederation (proposed in 1776 and finally accepted in 1781) was very weak. The authority which fought the war on behalf of the United States was a Congress in which each state cast one vote (the size of the delegations varying from two to seven), without power to levy taxes, regulate trade, or coerce recalcitrant states. When the necessities of war gave way to the easier times of peace the incentive for agreement and action diminished, and by 1785 Congress had virtually ceased to govern.

The acceptance of the Constitution of 1787 gave a special flavor to American life. No other people have lived under a document in quite the same way, and if the ancient Jews had been the people of a Book, the Americans have become the people of a Document. Political argument has tended to concentrate upon constitutional interpretation, and solutions to difficulties have seldom been sought outside its provisions. If this limited the range of political discourse it also emphasized the American determination to live under the law and to submit their difficulties to rational arbitration. Even the catastrophe of 1861 did not dispel faith in the Constitution, though it did demonstrate that constitutional logic was no substitute for political wisdom. In retrospect some foreign critics have claimed that the Constitution inhibited growth by legal rigidity, tempted men to take refuge in legal quibbles rather than to face reality, and gave undue weight to obstructive minorities; but for Americans in 1788 the adoption of the Constitution released new energies and acted to liberate rather than to restrain. Without it the Revolution might have been no more than the prelude to lost opportunity, but as events transpired the decade after the winning of independence must be counted as one of the most decisive and constructive in world history.

The struggle against Great Britain brought two political emotions to birth. Men in their states saw emancipation from remote authority as the greatest gain from the Revolution, but equally strong was the knowledge that without union this freedom would have been impossible. The antithesis between local autonomy and union is false, because most Americans wanted both; but there was always the danger that the new and fragile loyalty to the Union might be smothered by events, and that if the needs of war had made union necessary the disputes of peace would compel separation. During war the objective was clear and disagreement had to be resolved; in peace the aims might become controversial and arguments over detail explode into major conflicts.

The Revolution had not originated as a national movement but as a series of protests in the separate colonies, and the discovery of common grievances had preceded collective action. The Stamp Act Congress of 1765 assumed no executive responsibilities and was never intended to do more than to provide a forum for protest and a show of strength to impress the Imperial Government. Action included the endorsement of retaliation against British trade in some colonies and recommended similar actions to others, but there was no suggestion that economic interests might be brought under a single direction and still less that Congress should assume any responsibility for internal affairs in the separate colonies. This Stamp Act Congress therefore provided precedents for collective protest but none for an American government. When the major crisis developed in and after 1773 there were therefore no precepts for common government and not much enthusiasm for the idea; the powers which Congress assumed came as a direct response to circumstances and were not inspired by theoretical arguments for central government. The logic of events meant that Congress had to plan political and military strategy, sanction inter-colonial organizations, direct the raising of armies, borrow money, and enter into relations with foreign powers; in this way Congress assumed some of the responsibilities of a national government, but in a haphazard way and without formal authority until the Articles of Confederation, proposed in 1776, were accepted by all the states in 1781. In this accidental manner a government for the Union was launched upon the world, and contemporaries hardly realized that a new form of political organization had been born. Foreigners saw an inefficiently organized government that rejected the principles of centralized authority which had turned the weak European societies into national states, while behind the facade of legality were turbulent people, riotous elections, and the promise of anarchy.

Americans may have been little aware of derogatory criticism and could have answered that colonial experience proved that local autonomy and loose central organization need result in neither disorder nor injustice. The Federal idea was not seen as a great step in the dark but as an empirical extension of colonial experience, and it seemed unnecessary, in the heat of conflict, to define the principles of the new development. This lack of definition would lead, in course of time, to one of the least constructive arguments in history. Future states' rights men maintained that the states had been sovereign before they delegated powers to the Federal government, and future nationalists maintained that the states had moved directly from being colonies under royal authority to being states in the Union. States' rights men replied to the nationalist argument that it played with names and fictions: the colonies and the states had been identical political societies, and the delegates of these political societies had agreed upon union and transferred the necessary powers. Nevertheless, replied the nationalists, they *had* agreed to join with others in creating a new government, and collective action could not be undone without collective agreement. As Lincoln was to say, "No State upon its own mere motion can lawfully get out of the Union."

The argument can be resolved if one admits that states' rights provided a somewhat better description of the Revolution while nationalists had a truer perception of what happened during and after the War of Independence. A great political event is not a legal contract to perform given actions in return for stated considerations, and once the Union was in existence it acquired a life of its own, attracted loyalty, gathered attachments of sentiment and interest, and acquired obligations different from those of any one state. If in the course of conflict a state had made peace with Great Britain, there can be little doubt that the United States would have admitted neither the legality nor the morality of the betrayal. In 1776 it had still been open to any colony to stand aside (as did the colonies of British North America) but this was no longer true once all had embarked upon a war for independence with all the mutual obligations which this entailed. The Union of 1783 was not the Union of 1776; experience had created a new political organization, and whatever the difficulties men were loath to dispense with its benefits. The Union had ceased to be a piece of political mechanism designed for a single object and had become the focus of ideas about the future of America: This, rather than anything else, was the force behind the movement for a stronger government.

The Articles of Confederation have sometimes been represented as the triumph of democracy over centralizing authority, but there was nothing very democratic about this form of government.* There was no direct representation of the people and no principle of decision by the majority. One state could block an amendment to the Articles, and the opposition of four could veto important measures. Delegates represented their states and in practice this meant the states' dominant groups, while minorities had no means of influencing congressional policy. The new Constitution gave direct representation to the people, and election by districts greatly improved the opportunities for minorities to participate in national government. The Constitution of 1787 was not, as has sometimes been maintained, "antidemocratic." It was, rather, a new variation upon the Revolutionary theme of power derived from consent. The question was complicated because the most articulate minorities in the states were the commercial and planting interests most likely to be frustrated by majorities chosen by small landowners, and it was therefore possible to represent the move for a stronger central government as a conspiracy of the few against the many, of the rich against the poor. The endorsement of this view by historians, however, has contributed little to an understanding of the Constitution. What happened in 1787 was not the outcome of an "antidemocratic" conspiracy but transference from a simple to a complex form of republicanism.†

As Americans understood it, a "republic" was a political system based upon consent, allowing for popular participation through frequent elections, and functioning as a "mixed" or balanced government. The concentration of all power in a majority was as dangerous to liberty as its concentration in the hands of a despotic sovereign; indeed, John Adams argued that it was more dangerous—a single despot could never go far against the wishes of his subjects, but a majority could

---

* The strongest argument for the democratic character of the Articles was by Merrill Jensen in *The Articles of Confederation* (New York, 1948); the real issue is whether one regards centralization as opposed to democracy. The Articles were certainly a victory for state autonomy against those who wanted a stronger government at the center.

† The argument that the Constitution was "antidemocratic" was put most forcibly by Charles Beard, *An Economic Interpretation of the Constitution* (New York, 1913). It has influenced many writers. Merrill Jensen in *The New Nation*, modifies Beard's argument but is in sympathy with the view of the Constitution as a counterrevolution against democratic influence.

crush opposition at the grass roots. When Elbridge Gerry, a delegate to the Federal Convention of 1787, said (in a much-quoted phrase), "The evils we experience flow from the excess of democracy," he did not mean to attack representation or consent but the lack of sufficient checks upon simple majorities in the states. The will of a majority was temporary and could be swayed by emotion; a Constitution should ensure that the people had time for consideration and should safeguard permanent interests against passing anger or scheming demagogues. The same speaker at the Convention said that "he had been too republican heretofore: he was still however republican, but had been taught by experience the danger of the levelling spirit."

James Madison, architect of the 1787 Constitution, put this in a more abstract way. The danger of popular government lay in the violence of "faction," by which he understood "a number of citizens, whether amounting to a majority or a minority of the whole, who are united and actuated by some common impulse of passion, or of interest, adverse to the rights of other citizens, or to the permanent and aggregate interests of the community."* Jean Jacques Rousseau had reached for the same distinction between what people appeared to want and what they would want if they understood the real good of the community, when he made the "general will" the unchallengeable sovereign but distinguished between the general will and the will of all. The people might, for instance, approve a war which was unjust and, in the long run, damaging to the community as a whole. Rousseau's *Contrat Social* was probably unknown to most Americans, but the distinction between what people appear to want and what they ought to want is fundamental to an understanding of American constitutionalism. Any constitution is a restraint upon power, and a democratic constitution restrains the power of the people while recognizing their ultimate sovereignty. This restraint is only justifiable, in abstract terms, if one thinks that the long-term interests of the community are thereby preserved. On the other hand the power of a minority to protect itself against a majority should not enable it to impose its will upon the country; the principle of constitutional balance should preserve the rights of both minorities and majorities.

The men who feared "excess of democracy" in 1787 stressed external weakness, social disorder, and damage to property. Their arguments were most likely to appeal to rich men, engaged in foreign trade, and discontented with their state legislatures; conversely they appealed least to men of small or no property, engaged in subsistence

---

* *The Federalist*, Letter X. Madison's whole argument in this letter deserves close study; its main purpose was to refute the thesis that free government was possible only in a small society.

farming or producing only for a local market, who expected their elected representatives to protect them against creditors or commercial exploitation. Between these two extremes there existed a wide range where the effects of change upon personal fortunes were difficult to calculate. Here political considerations were likely to be uppermost, and especially the need to preserve the Union, prevent social disorder, and present a bold face to foreign powers. Cutting across these general attitudes was a specific problem which was part economic and part political: the war had been fought on borrowed money, but neither Congress nor a majority of the states seemed likely to repay their debts, and public securities had fallen to a fraction of their face value, while currency had depreciated even more sharply and varied in value from state to state. Trade rivalries among the states added to the confusion as some tried to relieve landed property of taxation by levying customs duties, while others tried to undercut their neighbors by offering more favorable terms to importing merchants. Boundary disputes among states, and the uncertain future of western lands, added to the impression of weakness and confusion. Again these difficulties were likely to be seen most clearly by men with international concerns, or with interests crossing several state boundaries, but they could also be understood by a much larger body of men who were indirectly affected and aware of the danger that the Federal Republic would fail at the outset. Against this were a large number of small farmers, mainly engaged in subsistence farming, who valued their freedom from restraint and were unaffected by the difficulties of the times, and office-holders who had a vested interest in state autonomy. The political problem of making a constitution was to satisfy articulate interests while recognizing that any change must commend itself to a majority of the people; the immediate need to win ratification was reinforced by the knowledge that a working government must be a popular government.

Thus the movement which eventually produced the Federal Constitution of 1787 was not a simple current which moved towards a predestined conclusion; still less was it a conspiracy of the few against the many. It was rather the convergence of several tides of emotion, fear, interest, and political ideals. By 1787 there was wide agreement that some change was necessary, but uncertainty about the kind of change which would be most desirable. At one end of the spectrum were men who wanted to keep the organization of Congress unchanged but to give it increased powers to tax, regulate commerce, and prehaps (in some diluted form) the power to coerce a recalcitrant state. At the other end of the spectrum were men (of whom Alexander Hamilton was the most articulate spokesman) who wanted a strong national government on a completely new model, with an independent executive to provide purposeful direction, and a semipermanent upper house to preserve property from attacks; direct representation in the lower house would provide the new government with authority while the President and the Senate would curb the effects of popular emotion. Paradoxically the first plan might, in the long run, have produced a stronger central government on the parliamentary model. Congress under the Articles exercised both executive and legislative powers, and recent developments in its committee system had pointed to something like the British Cabinet, responsible to Congress and composed of its members; if this system had been strengthened at one stage, it might have been strengthened again, and any national crisis would have led to a further concentration of power. Hamilton's plan offered a more immediate prospect of national strength, but a struggle for power between an independent President, a property-conscious Senate, and a House representing the people, would have set the stage for a paralysis of government. Hamilton believed that he was copying the British model, but the need for definition (in contrast to the unwritten conventions which guided British practice) would have closed the door upon the British evolution towards party government, the supremacy of the Commons, and the concentration of power in the cabinet.

The choice of alternatives would be influenced by experience. In part this would be experience from the remote past, and several of the delegates who assembled at Philadelphia in 1787 were well versed in the history of ancient republics and of federal experiments; but these ancient examples served as warnings of error rather than as models to be copied, and their principal effect was to throw back the delegates upon that form of government which had already found favor in the separate states. At least half and perhaps more of the delegates assumed that mere amendment to the Articles would be insufficient and that a new pattern of government was required which would nevertheless embody the tried institutions of bicameral legislatures, separate executives, and independent judges. They believed that representation of the people in the national government would add strength and justify the direct operation of national authority upon individuals, but that the familiar principle of separate powers must set limits to the action of representatives. There were therefore many sympathetic hearers when Edmund Randolph, on behalf of the Virginian delegation (which reflected mainly the ideas of James Madison), proposed direct representation in the first house of a bicameral legislature, the election of the second house by the first, and election of the executive by both houses jointly. Indirect election would remove executive and upper house from the influence of the hustings; but as the apportionment of representatives to states would be in proportion to population the larger states would preponderate in both houses. The executive (to consist of a council, not a single person), together with the judges, would form a Council of Revision with the power to veto legislative acts, though this veto could subsequently be overridden by Congress.

No attempt was made at this stage to define the legislative powers of Congress, except that it could veto state acts and use force against a recalcitrant state. This plan provided a first draft for discussion, but after two weeks of debate William Paterson of New Jersey voiced the fears of the smaller states and proposed that the structure of Congress under the Articles should remain unchanged (with each state entitled to equal representation) but that the powers of Congress should be increased, that the laws of the United States should be the supreme law in the separate states, and that Congress should choose a separate executive without a veto. "If the sovereignty of the States is to be maintained," said Paterson, "the Representatives must be drawn immediately from the States, not from the people; and we have no power to vary the idea of equal sovereignty." There seemed to be a wide gap between the large and the small states, but in fact there was more room for agreement than appeared on the surface. Paterson was arguing about the composition and authority of Congress rather than about its power, and he reminded the convention that two small states, New Jersey and Maryland, that had been the last to join the Confederation, had not delayed because the Union was too strong but because it had insufficient power over commerce and western lands. What the small states really objected to was the disposition of the larger states to have it both ways: to obtain more central power for purposes which they approved while using their voting strength to prevent any interference with their own interests.

The compromise which led the convention out of the deadlock added a distinctive characteristic to American federalism by giving direct representation in proportion to population in the lower house and equal representation to each state in the Senate. Every two years every member of the house had to retire or seek reelection but only one third of the senators had to, and (until 1913) the latter were not directly elected but chosen by their state legislatures. The implications of this compromise in the composition of Congress are well known, but what often escapes notice is the change effected in the character of "mixed government." Hitherto it had been assumed that the function of the upper house in a bicameral legislature was to represent property; but there was no reason to suppose that the senators chosen by the states would be better representatives of property than anyone else. Indeed, in the early years of the new government, a man of wealth was more likely to represent a commercial town than to be chosen by a state legislature where farming interests normally predominated. What the Senate did come to represent was political success, and the one real qualification for membership was an ability to emerge as a leader of a party in a state. More secure than the representatives, gaining prestige from their constitutional role as guardians of the states and influence through their share in executive appointments, senators could become political magnates in their own right. The makers of the Constitution had expected the House of Representatives to be the dominant power in the new government, and at first it played this part; but the logic of the situation would eventually make senators the world's most powerful and independent legislators. Checks written into the Constitution to keep the power of representatives within bounds, helped to increase the stature of the upper house while depressing that of the lower, and American constitutional history has seen an almost continuous accretion of power in the Senate at the expense of the House. Ironically this could not have happened if the exponents of mixed government had succeeded in their first intention and made the Senate the bastion of property. Its powers would certainly have been whittled away by equalitarian tendencies (as were those of state senates so long as they were based upon the special representation of property), and the power of the House would have increased proportionately.

Before the composition of the Congress had been fixed, the Convention had decided to vest the executive power in a single person. Some delegates may have shared Hamilton's belief that executive vigor should be the mainspring of government, but most of them probably thought of it as essentially subordinate to the legislative power. The President was given some freedom of action in foreign affairs, and was obliged to render account to Congress only in an annual message on the state of the Union, but his principal function was to faithfully execute the law. For this task there were obvious advantages in centralizing power in a single person, rather than diffusing it in a council, but if delegates could have foreseen the towering importance of the President in the future they might well have hesitated before trusting so much latent power to an individual. They looked at the President primarily as an administrator and as an official head of state, not as a national leader, an initiator of policy, or the focal point of the whole political system. In this, as in other respects, the makers of the Constitution built for their day with recent experience in mind, and might have decided differently if they had possessed the foresight with which they have sometimes been credited.

This is not the place to discuss in detail the provisions of the Constitution, but rather to sketch its general influence upon political manners. It was written to be understood by ordinary citizens in the plain, dignified, and literary language of the eighteenth century. A lawyer's document would have been more precise, more cluttered with detail, and as comprehensive as possible in its consideration of contingencies. The more general language of the Constitution has proved to be an element of strength, because it has allowed change and growth in response to the changing needs of two centuries; but with so much dependent upon interpretation it has also allowed for cross-purposes and some conflicts. A good deal of American history has turned upon the interpretation, and upon rival interpretations, of this eighteenth-century document. Even within the brief which they drew up for themselves the makers of the Constitution left some gaps which may have been deliberate, may have been unintentional, or may have reflected merely a weariness of the flesh at the prospect of reopening controversy on hot summer days. The executive and the judiciary were both left with very bare bones; the initiation of policy was left in a void between the making and the execution of law, and it was not made clear whether the Supreme Court could or could not invalidate Federal laws. The powers of Congress were enumerated in some detail, but the list closed with the "sweeping clause" that it could "make all laws which shall be necessary and proper for carrying into execution the foregoing powers, and all other powers vested by this Constitution in the Government of the United States, or in any department or officers thereof." Nor were all the enumerated clauses very precise, and one of the most important—on the power of Congress over commerce—was particularly vague. The power conferred was that "to regulate commerce with foreign nations and among the several States," but "regulate" was an imprecise word, and "among" was an odd one which could mean either "between" or "mingled with." "Commerce" was often used in the eighteenth century to mean economic activity in general, but it could be strictly interpreted to mean the physical transference of goods. Was this a deliberate way of leaving the door open for a much wider implication of the commerce clause than some delegates would have accepted? The later interpretation of the clause justified a broad power to regulate all economic activities that affected more than one state; but many who accepted it must have thought of it as no more than the power to prohibit trade barriers among states and to impose uniform rules for navigation. In this, and in other matters, the silence of the Constitution was as significant as its provisions.

It would be possible to add other examples of ambiguity or lack of precision, but the great and remarkable strength of the Constitution remained. In a huge country, with several scattered centers and strong traditions of local autonomy, it did provide a government for the whole which a majority could accept; and even those who opposed the Constitution's acceptance preferred acquiescence to agitation once it had been ratified. Almost as soon as the new government was in operation arguments over its merits were abandoned and were succeeded by controversies over its meaning and application which have gone on ever since. The Constitution remains the framework for most political argument. Until 1850 it was expected that the answers to most problems could be found if one understood correctly the principles of the Constitution and the relationships which it established. In 1850 John C. Calhoun argued—for the first time publicly—that the Constitution should be amended if the Union were to survive, but even after this, controversialists in the growing quarrel between North and South assumed that constitutional logic would support their case and convert their opponents. After the Civil War the Constitution was amended, though in a way contrary to that proposed by Calhoun; new responsibilities were assumed by the national government, and a new relationship with the states was established. More has been done by interpretation than by amendment, and today an authority never envisaged by the "founding fathers" rests upon the clauses penned by them. Yet in spite of growing flexibility in the past century Americans are distinguished from other peoples by the respect still given to a now venerable Constitution.

In part, the durability of the Constitution can be explained by the immediate solution provided for so many difficulties. It provided an assurance that the Union would continue, that it could be defended against external enemies, and that economic weakness need not be the price of freedom. The restraints imposed upon the states checked inflation, prevented trade rivalries, protected property against confiscatory or retrospective legislation, and gave hope that the credit of the country would be restored. All this it did while retaining, and indeed reinforcing, the great principle that the people were the source of all authority.

The main burden of attack in the ratifying conventions was framed in language that now seems archaic or unrealistic. Would the President become a monarch? Was the Senate an aristocracy? Why was there no provision for trial by jury? By what warrant did the makers of the Constitution claim to speak for the people, when their authority had clearly derived from the states? Was the new Constitution federal, or was it really intended to consolidate power at the center? To calm some of these fears, rather than to introduce new principles, the first ten Amendments or Bill of Rights were added after the Constitution had been ratified. These amendments recapitulated the rights which individuals and states believed that they had inherited from the past or won at the Revolution. The First Amendment forbade the establishment of religion by Congress, thus writing into law for the first time the separation of Church and State. The Second to Ninth Amendments enumerated rights which Congress could not abridge. The Tenth Amendment affirmed that powers not given to Congress by the Constitution were reserved for the states or the people respectively; this clause was to be of importance in the many arguments over the division of national and state powers, but its principal significance at the time was to ensure that criminal jurisdiction remained with the states.

The Constitution appeared to achieve a nice balance in giving strength to the Union and security to property, while limiting its impact upon individuals and leaving the states as the governments most concerned with the day-to-day life of the people. Within the central government it achieved an equally good balance between the different branches, and if the distribution of function remained uncertain, the principle of checks and balances was clearly asserted and intricately devised. Men who had grown fearful at the prospect of disorder, were gratified by the creation of national checks upon state autonomy, but for anxious republicans, jealous of losing their revolutionary independence, the satisfactory thing was the concept of limited power. If it was not easy to say in precise terms what President or Congress could do, it was possible to say what they could not do. Within a short time after the establishment of the new government a debate developed about the extent of powers allowed by the "necessary and proper" clause; but even the widest claim for Congress retained the principle that power was limited at some point, and while arguing that Congress might have discretion to choose the means, admitted that it could not pursue aims outside the Constitution. Finally, to men who were anxious about the threat to state power, the Constitution proved far less dangerous than anticipated. What was surrendered was specific; what remained with the states was broad and general. There was no limitation at all upon the rights of states to punish criminals, to keep law and order, to regulate economic life within their borders, or to undertake whatever social legislation they might deem proper. In the South it was of particular importance that domestic slavery remained entirely under state jurisdiction.

The Constitution therefore became the institution upon which many currents of satisfaction converged; it gave a great deal, without inflicting perceptible damage upon anyone. There were no interests sufficiently offended to provide a nucleus for an anticonstitutional movement. It bred no counterrevolution, and even the vested political interests in the states—which had most to lose—found that the relative diminution in their political authority was offset by economic growth and increasing responsibilities. In politics success breeds success; the longer the Constitution survived the more generally was it regarded as the only possible solution to America's political problem and as an enduring monument to American political wisdom. Accepted by some with reluctance, by some with active dislike, and by many as a doubtful experiment, the Constitution soon became the inviolate expression of national unity and purpose.

In part this success was caused by underlying economic factors in the society. The new government was launched when the postwar depression and dislocation were giving way to an upward trend. The economic storms might have cleared in any case; but prosperity and expansion were inevitably associated wth the new Constitution, and in a very real way the Constitution stimulated both short- and long-term growth. It set up, in the United States, a free-trade area—the first in the world to cover so wide an area and such diverse resources—and traders could look forward to carrying and selling their goods wherever in America profit might be made. Agriculture and industry could think of a national market. Large property owners, no longer in fear of discriminatory state legislation, could invest with confidence. The psychological effect of expanded activity stimulated confidence, and the enormous areas to the west, awaiting exploitation and settlement, fostered a new continental vision. Thanks in part to the unseen influence of economic cycles, and in part because of its side-effects upon enterprise, the new Constitution rode forward on a wave of well-being.

Early America was a society of property owners, and one might expect that a Constitution made by their delegates, and ratified by its conventions, would express their aspirations. True, it is no accident that the Constitution was most specific when it prohibited those state activities which might interfere with property, but to suggest that this required a conspiracy is absurd. "Life, Liberty and Property" had been the slogan of the Revolution, until the Declaration of Independence made it "Life, Liberty, and the Pursuit of Happiness." In the event, Americans would quarrel about the benefits of security—and who should receive them—but no one went behind the social assumptions of the age to suggest that men should not be sovereign over their property. Locke had described the preservation of property as both the incentive and the justification for government among men, and, if a Constitution went out of its way to preserve property, this was accounted a virtue.

At the same time, the durability of the Constitution was explained by its recognition and formalization of popular government. The House of Representatives was based on wide suffrage, and elected every two years; the nearest approach was the British Commons who were elected by a tiny fraction of the adult male citizens and might remain for seven years. Elections for the President and Senate were indirect—

through the Colleges of Electors and the State Legislatures respectively —but in England no one had suggested even an indirect share for the people in the choice of a King or a House of Lords. This comparison, with the most similar government elsewhere, indicates the great stride forward in the principles and practice of popular government made by the Constitution of 1787. It was not only a question of numbers but also of size; after the inception and survival of the new government one heard no more of the axiom that "free" republics could exist only in small states. The "Great Experiment" would be an experiment in popular government on a huge scale, and it was this which inspired broad-based allegiance throughout the country. It was seen not as the betrayal of the Revolution but as its fulfillment.

The Constitution is a framework for government, not government itself. As has been already noted the administrative functions of government were passed by, and the policy-making function was ignored. The written Constitution provides the base, fixes the limits, and specifically orders some arrangements in detail; but on this foundation is built a huge edifice of law and interpretation. The American Constitution is more formal than the British Constitution (where informality has led to the disappearance of whatever safeguards the subject once thought he possessed); but the American Constitution as it exists today contains much that can be found in the written document only by strained and tenuous interpretation. The process of Constitution-making did not end in 1787; a new phase began with the first session of the first Congress, many of whose decisions have acquired the same sanctity as the Constitution itself.

The tasks were formidable. Working under considerable pressure— because little could happen, even in the most elementary field of government, until the basic laws had been passed—Congress discussed and passed twelve Amendments to the Constitution (ten were ratified), set up the national judiciary, established the departments of government, authorized the civil service, made important decisions about the relationship between President, Cabinet, and Congress, as well as settling its own rules of procedure and indulging in the first sharp discussion over slavery.

When Congress assembled in December 1788 it had to settle the relationship between the executive and the legislature, and produced answers which were to affect permanently the political character of the United States. The delegates at the Federal Convention, and participants in the state ratifying conventions, had had no single concept of the presidential office, and the wording of the Constitution allowed for a good deal of latitude. The President could be what he eventually became—head of state, party leader, and active head of government—

but many expected him to stand aloof from "faction" and to preside over government rather than direct it. The King of England was the head of his government with a complete theoretical control over its composition and policy, but to an increasing extent his choice of ministers was limited to those who were members of Parliament and approved by a majority in the House of Commons, while no policy rejected by Parliament could succeed. The King did not preside at the Cabinet, and if the Prime Minister had not then the commanding position which he now holds, he was certainly the key figure in any administration and the principal architect of its policy. The American President might have occupied a position comparable to that of the King, with reserves of power for use when things went wrong, but with day-to-day political responsibility resting with the Cabinet. Paradoxically Alexander Hamilton, who was the principal advocate of executive vigor, seems to have thought of the constitutional position in this way, and, after his appointment as Secretary of the Treasury, expected to act as a Prime Minister. Washington's own views attempted a compromise between a constitutional "limited monarch" and an active head of government. He gave Hamilton a free hand to initiate far-reaching proposals from the Treasury, but he also kept Jefferson (who was the chief critic of Hamilton's policy) in office as Secretary of State; he did not rebuke Hamilton's attempts to interfere in the business of other departments, but allowed him no overriding authority, and did not permit the chain of command to run to him through the hands of his powerful Secretary of the Treasury.

In England the gradual swing of authority from monarch to ministers was set in motion because the dual responsibility to King and to Parliament created a situation which could not endure, and in the long run responsibility to Parliament prevailed. The Prime Minister emerged as the commanding man in the Cabinet and was able to insist upon collective responsibility and to end independent relations between separate ministers and the King. In the United States there was no dual responsibility; a cabinet minister held office because he had been chosen by the President, not because of his acceptability to the legislature, and Congress could neither compel his resignation nor demand his retention. Cut off from any independent support in Congress, ministers were inevitably subordinate to the President; neither a separate office of first minister nor a doctrine of collective cabinet responsibility developed. The President could select whom he chose, could retain rivals in office if he wished to do so, and acted both as the arbiter between conflicting views and the director of policy.

It is often assumed that this was an inevitable outcome of the Constitution, but the first Congress had it in its power to set the trend in another direction. Of first importance was the President's power to appoint and dismiss. The Constitution provided for the "advice and consent" of the Senate in making appointments to federal office and said nothing about dismissals; some assumed that this meant the Senate would act with the President as a council of appointment and that the same procedure would govern dismissals. A few assumed that the silence of the Constitution on dismissals meant that appointments to office should be for life or until retirement, and that removals could only be made by impeachment for misconduct. The first doctrine would have made the cabinet partly responsible to the Senate, and a cabinet minister with the support of a majority in that body could have defied the President, with far-reaching consequences for the balance of the Constitution. The second doctrine would have strengthened cabinet and Congress against the President and perhaps, in course of time, made impeachment the normal means of changing a ministry, equivalent to a vote of no confidence in the British Parliament. It would also have set the Federal civil service on a firm footing, and prevented the later abuse of patronage for political purposes. Against both positions, Madison, speaking with all his known authority as the architect of the Constitution, argued that executive authority included the whole range of governmental powers which were not legislative; the Constitution specifically removed some executive powers, and modified others, but where it was silent one must assume that the full executive authority remained in force. The power to appoint was modified by requiring the advice and consent of the Senate, but silence on dismissal meant that this was left entirely to the President and could be exercised at his discretion. A majority in Congress accepted Madison's argument, and in so doing made the President master of his administration. In making appointments Washington chose his men and then submitted their names to the Senate for ratification; with a lesser man in the Presidency the Senate might have stood out for prior consultation, but from Washington this procedure was accepted without question. The Senate has often made difficulties over ratification, and occasionally rejected nominees to cabinet office, but the President has the initiative and his cabinet nominations are seldom refused even when the majority in the Senate belongs to the opposite party. In appointments to the lower ranks of the federal service the Senate has managed to maintain more control, but the President dominates the nerve center of government.

There is no doubt that many supporters of the Constitution expected the Congress, and particularly the House of Representatives, to be the mainspring of government. Congress would decide what laws should be enacted, and the President would "faithfully execute" them. This somewhat simple view of the initiation of policy underestimated the difficulty and the importance of consideration in detail by large deliberative bodies; at some point in the process measures must pass through the mill of discussion by a small group in full command of the materials and in agreement on the main outlines of policy. It was within the competence of Congress to create something akin to a congressional cabinet, but the House left deliberation to the whole body and set up committees to consider specific questions. In course of time the committees would become the channels through which all legislative proposals would go before consideration in Congress; but they came to act as autonomous units, each going its own way, and the lack of collective responsibility prevented the development of any coherent policy-making body in Congress.

Alexander Hamilton, as Secretary of the Treasury, believed that initiative should come from the executive, and that the proper procedure was for departmental heads to present legislative proposals to Congress in the form of reports which could then be worked out in detail. Hamilton hoped to present these reports to Congress in person, but, jealous of their own policy-making function (for which institutional machinery did not exist), congressmen decided that the secretaries should report in writing, when asked to do so. They feared "executive influence" upon the more tractable congressmen, but if cabinet officers had appeared on the floor of the house they would also have been open to cross-examination and forced to reply to criticism. Congress feared the development of ministerial corruption, whose malign effects had been one of the legends of the Revolution, but the procedure suggested by Hamilton would probably have added to its stature. Conversely the procedure adopted by Congress contributed still further to presidential authority; though Hamilton presented reports directly to Congress, when his friends had obtained a resolution that he should do so, most future cabinet ministers would avail themselves of the one statutory communication between the executive and the legislature—the President's State of the Union message—rather than wait for the uncertain outcome of congressional debate before presenting reports and proposals. Thus the President became the one recognized initiator of policy; there was no guarantee that his proposals would become law, but he was the one person in the country whose institutional position enabled him to say what he wanted.

The rapid rise in presidential authority was greatly aided by the personality of Washington. The President had every quality which could be desired in a constitutional monarch, and long-acquired habits of self-discipline had flung an aura of superhuman authority around a man who had started life with the normal enthusiasms, ambitions, and emotions. The experience of a war in which the main task was to maintain confidence when open encounters with the enemy were likely to end in defeat had imposed upon him a reserve which could be impenetrable and a caution in judgment which could be mistaken for slowness of mind. The public figure had long ago swallowed the individual; formidable in physique and in manner he was not the man to encourage gossip or familiarity; but he was an excellent administrator, who knew how to deal quickly with business, to delegate where necessary, and to establish a clear chain of command. Hamilton, whose department included by far the largest number of federal officials, was equally clear and decisive in administration, and both men insisted upon a standard of public spirit which epitomized the idea of "republican virtue." Between them they gave the new United States a civil service which was the best in the world both for its efficiency and its code of behavior. Thus Washington bequeathed to his successors an office which was dignified yet active, and already the focal point of the nation's political life.

In many other ways the first Congress provided a pattern of government and initiated trends which were not likely to be reversed. When its first session ended the United States had departments of government, a fiscal structure, and a revenue service, and Congress had worked out its own methods of doing business which were to be the foundation of future developments. The Senate had devised and Congress had passed a Judiciary Act which created a system of federal courts and laid down the relationship between federal and state courts. By the end of 1789 the United States had a government in being, one that was capable of assuming responsibility for all its constitutional functions. It was a remarkable achievement, and one which left an indelible imprint upon the future.

The institutional framework of the new government has been investigated, described, and analyzed by subsequent generations of lawyers, historians, and politicians. Time and again it has been necessary to take controversies back to the text of the Constitution and the intention of the various measures of the first Congress. The Revolution provided a tradition which was powerful but also ill-defined; the broad statements of the Declaration of Independence can inspire faith but are unlikely to provide answers to specific problems. Historians may see the government of the Union in its Revolutionary context, but when rights of individuals and powers of authorities have to be determined, lawyers prefer the firm ground of the written word. A conventional view of the relationship between the Revolution and the Constitution might suggest that the first supplied inspiration and ideology for the new nation, while the second provided the stability and balance without which enthusiasm would have wasted away and North American civilization would have become fragmented in the same way as Latin American civilization. A second view sees the movement which began in 1787 as a counterrevolution, as a restoration of the social order which had been threatened by the Revolution. A third view would see 1787 as the fulfillment of the Revolution; not as the antithesis to 1776 but as the synthesis between authority imposed from outside and authority proceeding from the people.

These abstract analyses of the relationship between the centrifugal forces of revolution and the centripetal forces of union can have important consequences for political understanding. The Constitution and the constituent acts of the first Congress require interpretation, and interpretation implies a philosophy. Is the philosophy supplied by the promise of equality and the premise of equal rights; or by the requirements of order? Or was the promise of the Declaration—that men had the right "to institute new Government, laying its foundation on such principles and organizing its powers in such form, as shall seem to them most likely to effect their Safety and Happiness"— superseded by obligations established under the Constitution? Much subsequent controversy was to revolve around answers to these questions. Their implications for the great debate between states' rights and nationalism, which reached its great crisis in the Civil War, are obvious.

A more subtle conflict is found between particularism and universality. The Revolution and the Constitution were made by a politically conscious people for their own ends; at the same time the Revolution claimed a political philosophy that belonged to all men. The politically conscious people were, by a vast majority, white, Anglo-Saxon, and Protestant; Negroes had no part in the great movements of the time save as spectators, as servants living under absolute authority, and occasionally as very humble participants; generations yet unborn of Jews, Latins, Slavs, and non-Protestants had no part in it. Were the achievements of the Revolutionary era to be interpreted as the heritage of the chosen people who had made them; or were they offered to all peoples who might come under American jurisdiction? The question would be most pertinent when the status of Negroes in the nation became a question of urgent concern.

It has been suggested that the Revolutionary ideology was a real promise of equality and rights to all men and that it was seen in the Northern states (where slavery was already withering away), and by some enlightened Southerners, as a blow against slavery. The later abolitionist, William Lloyd Garrison, was to condemn the Constitution as a proslavery document and to suggest that it was adopted and sustained in order to protect slavery. Garrison's view has found favor among modern writers of the "New Left" school, for whom the Constitution has become the symbol of a revolution betrayed and its hidden motive the fears of Southern slave owners prompted by slave revolts, the Revolutionary promise of equality, and the repudiation of slavery in Northern states.* This argument is attractive, but it has little to do with the facts of history. The Constitution was not made to preserve slavery though it was made in a world in which Negro inferiority was axiomatic. It did not occur to any Northern Revolutionary leaders to suggest that Negroes formed a part of the political people; fears for the future of slavery played a very small part in Southern calculations in 1787, and Northerners who disliked slavery were quite content to leave its future for determination by the states. A conviction of white superiority was one of the bonds of union in 1787 and no one suggested racial equality. American liberty was conceived as white liberty, and the promise held out to the black race was only that they might benefit indirectly from the improvement of their masters, but this was so much a truism that no one thought of questioning it. When Garrison attacked the Constitution as a proslavery document there was some ground for thinking that the Union protected slavery against the tide of antislavery sentiment mounting in the world; but it is unhistorical to argue that the circumstances of 1787 were the same as those of a half-century later.

Of more immediate importance was the consequence of the Constitution for democratic processes. Hitherto the whole experience of the American people in elective representative government had been in the separate states. Delegates to Congress had been chosen by state legislatures, and the state governor had been the highest executive functionary directly chosen by voters. The inauguration of the new government superimposed a new range of electoral activity upon the existing machinery. Qualifications for suffrage remained the responsibility of the states, but they could not impose different qualifications for federal and state suffrage in elections to the directly elected assemblies. "The times, places, and manner of holding elections" were to be decided by the states, though Congress had an overriding power to make or alter such regulations by law. The purpose was clearly to use, so far as possible, the existing suffrage and methods of election, leaving the states to make whatever additional regulations might be necessary. Nothing was said in the Constitution about the size or character of constituencies, and the states were left discretionary power to divide their territory into electoral districts or to hold general elections for the whole state. Only the number of representatives apportioned to each state was fixed, and this would be subject to alteration after each decennial census.

* The argument about slavery is made by Staughton Lynd in *Class Conflict, Slavery and the United States Constitution* (Indianapolis, 1968).

The Constitution therefore initiated no new expedients in the representative system, and the states were left wide powers which they exercised freely; but despite this cautious approach the institution of congressional elections provided a whole new sphere of democratic activity. At first, and in some states for years to come, elections to Congress were regarded as ancillary matters of secondary importance to state elections, and many ambitious men would prefer to make their careers at home rather than venture upon the hazardous and unknown field of congressional politics. Moreover the state legislatures made numerous decisions which affected the daily lives of the people, while Congress dealt with comparatively few questions, many of which were remote from their experience. Nevertheless the magnetic attraction of federal office, and congressional seats, steadily drew interest, excitement, and ambition. Political organization, maneuver, and calculation would soon be geared to national questions and before long to national parties.

The states remained the political units, but within these units more and more men would look to alliance with men in other states. The formal machinery of union would be supplemented by a web of informal contacts and understandings. The constitutional principle that the authority of the House should be derived directly from the people went a long way towards creating a political nation which transcended state boundaries. Senators were chosen by state legislatures; this did not mean that state politics were infused into national politics but the reverse. In terms of prestige of office, a senatorship became equal to or greater than a governorship; the latter office enjoyed temporary distinction but the tenure was short and most states limited the number of possible reelections; a Senator began with six years, and there was no legal barrier to successive tenures. Naturally the choice of United States senators became one of the most keenly contested events in state politics.

Thus the adoption of the Constitution set in motion processes which would harness state politics to national politics. Democratic activity was raised to a new plane, and new fields of endeavor and organization were opened up. The Constitution which was once erroneously described as "an antidemocratic document," marked a decisive stage in the evolution of modern democracy. Democratic organization was shifted away from local affairs in small societies to national affairs in a very large society, and the Constitution heralded mass democracy in the modern world.

CHAPTER IV

THE FORMATION OF GREAT TRADITIONS

The Constitution created a new government; the great question facing the country was how it would be used and for what purpose? Within ten years two answers had been given and two rival traditions had emerged. On the one hand was the ideal of a purposeful national government, vigorously pursuing chosen objectives among which economic development was preeminent, guaranteeing social order, squeezing every ounce of authority out of the Constitution, and reducing the states to the role of agencies for the performance of specified tasks. On the other hand was the concept of states as the active elements in government, with Congress held strictly to the powers enumerated in the Constitution; the national government would perform the tasks which the states separately could not perform—such as defense and the regulation of commerce—but could claim no right to enlarge its authority by interpretation; the Union was a compact among the states, and the individual states retained the right to act if they deemed that the compact had been broken. As well as having differing views about the Constitution the two traditions were identified with different views about the future of America; the first envisaged a country growing strong through economic success, the second a country remaining free by resisting oppression and the influence of concentrated wealth. The architect and prophet of the first tradition was Alexander Hamilton; of the second, Thomas Jefferson.

Alexander Hamilton, born of an obscure West Indian family, had become one of the favored children of fortune in the Revolutionary era. As Washington's military secretary he had risen rapidly to become a colonel at twenty-four; a brilliant career in law had followed, with marriage into a wealthy New York family, and then in 1789 appointment as Secretary of the Treasury. An extraordinary lucidity of mind, an ability to grasp both the essentials and the details of complex problems, and a clear, vigorous mode of expression made Hamilton the ideal man to bring order into the finances and to set a new pattern of administrative efficiency. In one respect only did he lack qualification for leadership in the new Republic: he had never fought for election and had neither understanding of nor respect for the people.

Thomas Jefferson belonged to a patrician Virginian family, but he had been brought up in the western part of the state where sturdy yeomen farmers outnumbered large planters, and throughout his life Jefferson would have more respect for the instinctive wisdom of these simple countrymen than for the experience of their "natural" leaders. Not that Jefferson was a sunny optimist trusting in the goodness of men; rather he thought it probable that wealth and privilege would corrupt. Men could resist tyranny, but they could not resist riches or flattery. Jefferson's greatest contribution to political thought was the preamble to the Declaration of Independence, and throughout his life he continued to act on the principle that governments derived their just powers from the consent of the governed. But to make consent effective the governed must be wary, suspicious, and ever on guard against those in authority. Jefferson was no anarchist and spent the greater part of his life in public office; the right precept was to accept responsibility and to act responsibly, remembering that the people were the masters. Jefferson is rightly regarded as a prophet of democracy, but hardly of mass democracy; he disliked cities and believed that independent judgment could never be exercised in a crowd; his best hope for America lay in the abundant land to the west which would ensure that farmers remained the most numerous part of the nation.

Hamilton would have preferred a government which was more remote from the people than that of the Constitution, and one which had greater freedom to act for the general welfare. He feared and distrusted the dominant groups in the various states whom he regarded as narrow-minded and selfish: He believed that strength in the states meant weakness at the center, and many of his ideas were directed to correcting this centrifugal tendency in the American system. His views were too strong for the convention, and his only important speech was not well received. As a pamphleteer, however, he joined forces with John Jay and James Madison to produce in *The Federalist Papers* not only a forceful plea for the new Constitution but a permanent contribution to political argument. As Secretary of the Treasury Hamilton intended to be the moving spirit and directing force in the new government. He was to succeed in his immediate aims, fail in his long-term plans, and leave a controversial heritage for the future.

Hamilton's special contribution to American political tradition was forging a link between social conservatism and economic dynamism. In Europe the conservative temperament was linked with large landowners, established churches, aristocracy, and monarchy; in America it was to be joined with economic enterprise, expansion, and the profitable exploitation of American resources. Yet though Hamilton neither respected nor understood popular politics, the partnership which he envisaged—between government and economic enterprise—had to exist in a wide suffrage society. Hamilton could not solve this political equation, but the inheritors of his tradition would discover how capitalism could exist and prosper in a democratic society. Hamilton joined the quest for national prosperity, and individual opportunity, with the search for social status and the defense of an elite against popular pressure. The combination was powerful and has never lacked adherents. Radical tides, inspired by equalitarian aims, have shaken every ancient institution, and destroyed most of them, but monied men have remained resilient, and, as Marxists have come to admit, popular approval sustains capitalism wherever the test is fairly tried. First among modern nations, the United States reconciled capitalist power with democratic aspirations, and for this Hamilton (who thought that democracy would destroy itself) was partly responsible. American conservatism was riding the winning economic horse, and popular approval followed its success.

Hamilton's immediate objectives were the restoration of credit, the creation of strong financial institutions, and the attraction of vested interests to the federal center. The funding of national and state debts at their face value, with a guaranteed interest, would restore confidence and encourage future investment, while a national bank would act as the government's banker, regulate the currency by setting a uniform standard for exchange, and utilize the government deposits as the base for commercial credit. Hamilton turned his eyes to English experience of the later seventeenth century and hoped that his funded National Debt and Government Chartered Bank would serve both to advance the prosperity of the country and win the support of monied men for the Government. Eighteenth-centurly British governments had discovered efficient ways of using large private savings for public purposes, but Hamilton's America had little accumulated capital, and he therefore proposed to build private enterprise on public revenue and government securities. On this base bankers could raise a credit structure, while the government created an atmosphere of confidence which would encourage enterprise, and remedy by public policy the shortage of private assets. With one eye Hamilton looked to strengthened government at the center and with the other at the diffusion of prosperity throughout the nation. Beyond this was a sturdy patriotic ambition to see the United States solvent, strong, and truly independent as the happy result of an alliance between masterful administration and forceful capitalism.

A policy conceived in such positive terms could not be executed without benefiting some and damaging others. Even without political implications, a program of economic growth would cause dislocation and some resentment, and, when Hamilton appeared to claim the less attractive consequences as blessings, political questions were bound to be asked. Policy could not exist in a political void (as Washington and Hamilton seemed to imagine); the consequence of positive proposals was a political explosion that reverberated through subsequent history. When the National Debt was funded at face value the national creditors reaped a large profit; when the debts of the states were assumed by the national government, more creditors made speculative gains, many property owners looked to the federal rather than to the state governments, and states with low debts, or repaid debts, resented the obligation to rescue less provident neighbors. Most state debts had been incurred to fight the Revolutionary War, but Hamilton did nothing to ease the burden of private debt to foreign merchants, a fact that weighed heavily in the plantation states, so that the assumption of state debts could be represented as a bonus to speculators at the expense of honest agriculturalists. The National Bank brought together three convergent streams of disquiet: popular dislike of a monied elite, fear of the states yielding further power, and the belief that commercial and financial interests were being deliberately favored.

The man who took the first step to formulate an opposition was James Madison, architect of the Constitution and collaborator with Hamilton in *The Federalist*. Madison had been largely responsible for persuading suspicious Virginians to ratify the Constitution, and in the first session he was the leading man in Congress. Later Hamilton was to confess to Washington that he would never have undertaken the Treasury if he had not assumed that Madison would lead for the administration in Congress; but the difference between the two, if not inevitable, was predictable. There were contrasts of temperament between Hamilton, the favorite child of New York Society and Madison who like Jefferson was a Virginian landowner, and had had to surmount the rough conflicts of popular politics; by nature Madison was secretive, subtle, reflective, and patrician, but the facts of political life in eighteenth-century Virginia made him sensitive to public opinion and aware of violent currents beneath the surface of politics. For Hamilton the major impetus for a new Constitution was the need for vigorous government; Madison, though anxious for a more forceful foreign policy, saw the main domestic need as the correction and limitation of "faction" without the sacrifice of popular government. The domestic function of the central government was to harmonize, moderate, and face factions with the choice between compromise and impotence. For the central government to favor faction—which was what Hamilton appeared to do when he aided monied men—was for Madison the reverse of its proper function. In Congress Hamilton's supporters had a majority and showed a disposition to force through his policy; faced with this situation the only remedy was to bring into play the one great remaining check in a republican government—the organization of the people.

At this stage a new and powerful factor entered the situation. In 1789 the French Revolution began, and in 1790 and 1791 it moved rapidly from a movement of constitutional reform to the establishment of a revolutionary and democratic regime; in 1792 war broke out between France and her continental neighbors, and in 1793 Great Britain joined the alliance against France. These European events imposed an unusual and unexpected strain upon the new American nation, and the repercussions of the French Revolution cut deep into the American political mind. France was the ally of the Revolutionary War and was now herself committed to Revolution; to many Americans these considerations combined to forge the strongest possible moral obligation. Americans should welcome this further blow to the *ancien régime*, should regard the French movement as an extension of their own, and should give whatever aid was necessary in the struggle against reaction. On the other side many Americans of British descent retained strong feelings of friendship for Great Britain, and throughout the period of Revolutionary experiment the British model of government had been claimed as the best the world had known before American independence. Conservative Americans had clung to the concept of mixed government, checks and balances, and constitutional restraint; but the French Revolutionaries, now claiming to speak with the voice of the people, would sweep away all law and disrupt the social order. If America was bound to look with sympathy upon the spread of republican institutions, this did not imply condonation of the Terror, of Jacobin dictatorship, or of class warfare waged against the old aristocracy.

Instinctively Hamilton's sympathies were thrown against the French Revolutionaries; for a man whose vision was dominated by the idea of economic growth in a politically stable society, the plea for the renewal of revolutionary ardor was dangerous and repulsive. Even more relevant to Hamilton's mind were the probably disastrous consequences of a breach with Great Britain, which was the best market for American products, the best supplier of manufactured goods, and the principal source from which he hoped to draw capital for American investment. During and immediately after the Revolutionary War the emotions of independence seemed to dictate an economic breach with Great Britain, but the American peace commissioners showed the ambivalence of the American position by pressing for an Anglo-American treaty of commerce which would produce the freest possible trade between the two countries. The treaty was never obtained, but even so the majority of American merchants showed themselves as ready and anxious to resume their relations with British merchants as were the latter to reenter the American market. The Americans wanted British goods and valued the accumulated expertise of British merchants in handling the complex problems of transoceanic trade. In particular they could obtain from the British, and from no one else, very favorable credit terms which, in effect, went far to remedy the American shortage of working capital. If all these advantages were to be thrown away in order to pursue an ideological war alongside revolutionary France, merchants and monied men predicted economic catastrophe.

While appearing to be pro-British—or "Anglomen" as their enemies preferred to call them—the majority of the country's economic leaders claimed that their major concern was with American prosperity.

Washington was even firmer than Hamilton about the need to avoid involvement in the European war, and neutrality—leaving the existing economic association intact—necessarily favored the British. With no reason to respect or admire the British, Washington realized more clearly than most the consequences of a quarrel with them. Remembering their recent defeats, the British were unlikely to launch another land war, but, with their great North Atlantic fleets and bases in British North America and the West Indies, they could cut off the trade and harry the coast of the United States. Even more disastrous than the material impact would be the emotional impact of a conflict which would range American against American, interest against interest, and state against state. The Union would hardly withstand the shock, and great parties would arise committed to the support of rival European powers. In 1796, in his Farewell Address, Washington stressed this theme:

> The nation which indulges toward another an habitual hatred or an habitual fondness is in some degree a slave. It is a slave to its animosity or to its affection, either of which is sufficient to lead it astray from its duty and its interest.

Posterity was to pay more attention to Washington's isolationism—embodied in the advice "to steer clear of alliances with any portion of the foreign world"—than to the argument on which it was based. Emotional hostility to a particular nation would often be the bane of American political attitudes; national interest could be rationally calculated, but conviction that another power could do no right drastically limited this freedom of choice.

Against the views of Washington and Hamilton, a growing opposition maintained that if America had no duty to fight for France at least her neutrality should be benevolent. There was more in this than moral obligation to an ally or identification with revolution; it symbolized a deep-seated conviction about the kind of society that should develop in America. The Revolution had stressed the claim of freedom and the mission of America in making freedom possible, and the enemy had been monarchy, aristocracy, and the corrupt Commons of England. Now that the political channels, through which the menace of power could flow to America, had been stopped, there remained the more insidious channels of trade and wealth. The links with Great Britain provided the means for transplanting old evils; an American commercial aristocracy would grow strong on British money, seek to extend its power over the continent, and make free men slaves to economic power. Attitudes toward Great Britain worked round in a circle to join with distrust of the monied men who benefited from Hamilton's financial policy, and if Hamilton argued that prosperity was the key to real independence, his critics believed that the agents of his prosperity would drag Americans back into the orbit of power from which they had freed themselves by the Revolution.

Thomas Jefferson had accepted the office of Secretary of State and served for a time in the same administration as Hamilton, but his hostility was manifest and privately he encouraged the opposition. He believed that Hamilton's incautious and contemptuous references to the people betrayed his true intentions, and that his apparent readiness to sacrifice American to British interests was proof of his antirepublican design. Where Madison thought that Hamilton was disturbing the balance of the Constitution, Jefferson believed that he aimed to establish a monarchy with the support of a favored class. Suspicions were increased by the kind of men who gathered around Hamilton and by their anxiety in forcing through Congress measures from which they would derive personal profit.

In practice events in Congress illustrated one of the perennial truths of American politics: The separation of powers and the exclusion of ministers from Congress meant that a Secretary with a policy had to win the support of a majority, so that the incentive for the formation of a party came from the executive. The idea of a coherent group in Congress, representing the country's major interests and winning support in the country through influence, fitted in well with Hamilton's social and political ideas and, for a time, the Federalists (as they were called) could command a majority in the country. They succeeded in this because large numbers of voters identified Washington's government with the cause of union and stability; but as the Hamiltonian Federalists became more committed to a policy of strong government and hostility to France their voting base crumbled away. Their real weakness, however, lay less in policy than in their attempt to organize from the center rather than in the constituencies. At the outset the Federalists hoped to be the leading men in their districts, winning support through example; in most parts of the country they would end as leaders without followers.

The Anti-Federalists—or "the Republicans" as they soon came to be called—adopted a quite different structure. Madison's efforts failed in Congress, and he turned to organize opposition at the lower level of society. Republican leaders were as much members of the ruling class as the Federalists, but they looked for support to local and popular organizations. The "self-created" Democratic Republican Clubs provided the nucleus, but what emerged was the first tentative experiment in professional politics. The leaders of the new party cultivated the pose of amateurs, and Jefferson in particular lamented with frequency the extent to which public life separated him from the delights of pastoral and patrician existence; but this amateurism was proclaimed rather than real. Jefferson and Madison both spent the greater part of their lives in legislative or executive office, and their experience was longer and broader than any of their Federalist rivals (with the single exception of John Adams). At the lower level the resources of patronage were not yet sufficient to provide a livelihood for rank-and-file politicians, but the majority treated politics seriously and regarded it as their major occupation, even though they might earn their keep in other ways. Newspaper editors were frequently in evidence and conducted propaganda which helped both their party and their circulation. Philip Freneau, the most distinguished of the Republican propagandists, found employment in Jefferson's State Department, from which he attacked with impunity the Secretary of the Treasury.

Republican politics not only looked toward professionalism, they also forecast the typical balance of power within an American party. The Federalists were cohesive and purposeful at the center, but loose and imprecise in the constituencies. The Republicans never had much organization, discipline, or agreed policy at the center, but locally they were tightly organized and closely identified with local interests. This kind of party could flourish much better by being opposed to something than by adopting a positive policy for itself; its heterogeneous elements could build upon common fears, while an attempt to draw together their various aspirations could only have a devisive effect.

The Republican party arose in response to Hamilton's policy and the Congressional strategy of his supporters; but a durable political movement cannot live upon opposition alone. What gave the Republican party a notable future was not only its adoption of a structure well-suited to a wide suffrage society but also its identification with a new political tradition. With all his economic foresight Hamilton was limited and sometimes obtuse as a political thinker: he tried to adapt British models when they were not adaptable; he attempted to ignore the implications of wide suffrage when this was the salient fact of the new American society; he expected influence to operate when the mass of the voters were independent freeholders and not susceptible to pressure from landowners or monied men; and he never came to grips with the idea that the power of government depended upon the consent of the governed. Posterity was to demonstrate that the "executive vigor," which Hamilton admired so much, was compatible with democratic society; but the mandate for vigor would have to come, at least in appearance, from below. If Hamilton lacked understanding of a democratic society he was equally insensitive to the limitations and possibilities of a federal society. With great clarity he saw that the development of the nation depended upon strength at the center, but he continued to act as though the states, either voluntarily or through pressure, would become silent allies in the steady accumulation of central power. He saw one side of the equation —that state autonomy was a danger to the Union—but he ignored the need to find within the Union a balance of power in which the states would contribute to the general strength. Whatever happened, the states would continue to exist as political entities, retaining many governmental functions, and able to draw upon funds of local patriotism; the states could not be exorcised by appeals for strength in the Union. They had been persuaded that their future depended upon closer association in the Union and in giving great powers to the federal government; but concession did not mean abdication, and it was Hamilton's great error to believe that the states' power could be reduced by congressional decision, constitutional argument, or executive pressure.

Hamilton's policy depended upon a loose but not unreasonable interpretation of the Constitution. The Constitution conferred powers upon Congress but did not specify how they were to be used; there must be "implied powers," otherwise there could be no authority to set up the departments of government, create a federal service, or arrange for the collection of revenue. From these precedents Hamilton argued that the power to tax, borrow money, and pay debts would be facilitated by the establishment of a national bank, and that it was clearly within the right of Congress to choose this method of carrying out its constitutional tasks. There was no need to hold the Federal Government down to a narrow interpretation of the law, for a national act had large objectives and should be judged by its contribution to the general welfare. Against this Jefferson admitted that Congress could pass laws "necessary and proper" for carrying out its functions, but claimed that this phrase should be strictly interpreted to mean "essential," not "convenient." A revenue service was essential and therefore "necessary"; a bank was merely convenient and could not, therefore, be justified on the same grounds. Moreover the right to charter corporations was a familiar act of government, and if the Constitution had meant to confer this power upon the National Government it would have said so. The silence of the Constitution did not mean that additional powers could be given to the national government: it meant that the power in question was reserved to the states.

Jefferson's rule of "strict construction" became an essential part of the developing Republican philosophy, and behind it lay Jefferson's profound conviction that all men with power would encroach upon liberty if allowed to do so; his argument was brought into focus by

Hamilton's Bank, but it contained a general theory for judging and limiting the powers of *all* government. In application it might lead to a loss of efficiency, but expediency could be the enemy of justice. Hamilton's grand concept of a planning government and invigorating leadership might attract men with weak minds or with strong minds but a weak attachment to liberty; but properly understood it was the essence of a constitutional, federal republic to sacrifice immediate efficiency for the long-term rewards of a strict limitation upon the exercise of power.

The other major contribution to Republican theory came in 1798 when a Federalist majority in Congress passed acts against undesirable aliens and seditious persons. The Sedition Act gave the President authority to institute prosecutions against persons who endeavored to subvert the Constitution by speech or writing, and its advocates maintained that any government must have power to protect itself against its domestic enemies. The states had taken repressive measures against Loyalists during the Revolution and continued to punish seditious libels. It could therefore be argued, said defenders of the acts, that these powers were inherent in every government. But, replied their critics, the government of the United States was not an ordinary government. It was a government of limited powers which divided sovereignty with the states, it exercised no power not transferred to it by the Constitution, and the right to punish sedition was among those reserved to the states by the Tenth Amendment.

If the Alien and Sedition Acts were unconstitutional, who had the right to say so? The Federal courts had jurisdiction over "all cases arising under the Constitution," but the strongly Federalist sympathies of the Supreme Court made this solution unacceptable to Republicans. Was it not, then, logical to suggest that the states, as parties to the Constitutional compact, had the right to say when it had been broken? This claim was made by Madison, in resolutions written for the Virginia Legislature, and by Jefferson for Kentucky. If the legislature of a state should declare an act to be unconstitutional, what was the next step? Could a state refuse to obey one act, while remaining in the Union for all other purposes? Or was it necessary to withdraw from the Union? And if it did so, had the other states any right to insist that the seceding state fulfill its obligations to the Union? It was undeniable that no state had been compelled to join the Union, and two states—North Carolina and Rhode Island—had maintained an independent existence outside the Union for a short while. Was it therefore logical to argue that the decision to join was irrevocable and that there was a perpetual undertaking to obey all the acts of Congress? The difficulty was that the Union which existed was never the same as the Union which a state had joined; when a state added its people and resources to the Union it entered into agreement with all the other states, and a contract made by several parties could not be abandoned by one of them. Thus, the claim that a state could decide when an act of Congress was unconstitutional raised all kinds of questions which no one—including Madison and Jefferson—could answer with assurance.

Yet for all their theoretical and practical difficulties, the argument of the Virginia and Kentucky Resolutions had a powerful appeal and helped to gather votes behind the Republican banner. In popular debate the emphasis lay less upon the the action that an aggrieved state might take than upon the dangers inherent in the Federalist doctrine that the National Government could advance into areas where the Constitution was silent. The states had ample authority to punish sedition and to exercise all other forms of criminal jurisdiction; if the National Government could assume this power merely by passing a law in Congress then an essential characteristic of a federal republic would be lost. This argument from the Resolutions of 1798 became embedded in the emergent tradition of the Jeffersonian Republicans—and later of the Democrats—and became for them a fundamental principle.

The issue raised by the Virginia and Kentucky Resolutions was not settled by constitutional debate but by the decision of the electorate when, in 1800, they elected Jefferson over John Adams. Was it then arguable that neither the Supreme Court nor the states were the ultimate judges of constitutionality? Some Jeffersonians pursued this thought and argued that every executive officer and legislator, being bound by oath to observe the Constitution, must be trusted to observe it to the best of his ability; it was for the people to decide when the Constitution had been broken and to rebuke those who had offended by refusing them election. This would have brought constitutional issues into popular debate and might have destroyed the idea that the Constitution stood above politics.

In 1803, in the celebrated case of Marbury v. Madison, Chief Justice John Marshall staked the claim for the Supreme Court as the ultimate tribunal for deciding the validity of congressional acts; though he did not explicitly deny the other theories that had been advanced, the clarity of his exposition left little room for other claimants. The Constitution, he argued, was the supreme law of the land; the Supreme Court was bound to decide according to the Constitution; if a congressional law was inconsistent with the Constitution the Court must declare it void. The Constitution itself had not said as much, and the Supreme Court would not invalidate another law of Congress until 1857; but Marshall's logic was persuasive and is rightly regarded as the cornerstone of the Court's right to review federal statutes. Thus the ultimate solution to the problem posed by the Virginia and Kentucky Resolutions was to give the Supreme Court greater authority than the judges of any other country.

The Supreme Court can act only when a case comes before it on appeal from a lower federal court (save in the very few cases when it acts as a court of first instance). Normally there will be a long interval between the passage of an act and the moment that it is tested in the Court, and decision by the Court does not provide the quick ruling on constitutionality that the sponsors of the Virginia and Kentucky Resolutions would have liked. A more difficult question is raised by the wide discretion allowed to the judges, for the issue is seldom so clear-cut as Marshall's argument implied. The Court can often use technical reasons for avoiding consideration of a statute, either by refusing jurisdiction over a case or by doing justice on grounds that do not touch the challenged law. On the other hand, the Court can equally well decide to consider the constitutionality of a statute even though a case could be decided without doing so. Sometimes the result will depend upon the skill of lawyers in bringing a case to a point at which it cannot be decided without consideration of a federal law, while at other times both they and the Court may be anxious to avoid such a confrontation. Moreover, if the Court does decide to pass judgment on a federal statute, the relationship between it and the Constitution will seldom be clear. For the most part the judges will have to consider the interpretation of the Constitution rather than its wording alone, and once interpretation is introduced the political philosophy and social assumptions of the judges- are brought into play. The ideal of an Olympian court administering a Constitution that stands above political conflicts of the day has remained a dream; this suggests that the Court has always been as much a political as a judicial body. Judicial review finally prevailed as the only means of deciding the meaning of the Constitution because there were greater objections to every other proposal.

While controversy over constitutional interpretation led to an impasse, the more general aspects of Jeffersonian tradition struck deep roots in the fabric of American life. Jefferson's reaction to Hamilton had been partly personal, partly concerned with immediate issues, but also touched upon deeper problems of national character. What kind of society should exist in America? Unlike Hamilton, Jefferson had visited Europe, and the experience had made him distrustful of men with power and privilege, compassionate toward the humble, and fearful of vicious urban mobs. The cultivators of the soil, could, he believed, be restored to purity once relieved from the injustice of privilege and hereditary oppression; but the city dwellers would forever remain victims of their environment. Hamilton based his faith for the future in the potentiality of economic growth in a land of abundant resources, but for Jefferson the social consequences of commercial and manufacturing prosperity were as disastrous as the privileges of a landed aristocracy. Indeed a new aristocracy of wealth would not even be redeemed by the paternalism of the old. It followed that the new society which had rejected the vices of the Old World must also resist the temptations of capitalist prosperity. The first deprived men of an inherent freedom, but the second corrupted their inner being. Fear of power and corruption were fitted by Jefferson into the eighteenth-century concept of checks and balances; the constitutional right of the people to rebuke their rulers, and to choose others, was the safeguard of liberty; but this alone was not enough, for the people themselves might become corrupt. The least liable to corruption were the independent farmers who had nothing to gain by giving power to others, had no avaricious designs upon their neighbors, and stood to lose the most if freedom were diminished. One could not rely upon men to resist temptation, and even the favorable environment of America was no guarantee that freedom would remain inviolate; but the paradox of the Jeffersonian system was that people must build their own world while the guiding wisdom of the patrician order perished along with its vices. A statesman could avoid encouraging the forces of corruption but ultimately he could do no more than follow the tides of public opinion and make the best of what might be a bad job. Within the limits thus set by his dependence upon opinion the art of politics consisted in choosing the least dangerous course, and this could be discerned with reference to a few fixed principles. It is in these principles, more than in anything else, that the fascination of Jefferson for successive generations has lain. The great principle was that of unalienable right and freedom. A person was born with rights that could not be removed—even with his own consent—and at the heart of these rights was freedom of choice. The more others encroached upon free choice, the less freedom a man enjoyed; supernatural wisdom might dictate the right choice, but what mattered was not so much the conclusion as the right to reach it by one's own road. Or, to put it in less abstract terms, the Revolution had declared men's emancipation from traditional authority, but had not intended them to fly into the arms of commercial authority; the very essence of the Revolution was freedom from all unessential authority. The creative forces in society were found in individuals, no one had a natural right to dictate to others how these forces should be used, and neither birth nor wealth justified authority.

Jefferson's individualism was not equalitarian. The poor man was as good as the rich man, but the former would not become better by appropriating the wealth of the latter. There was no inherent virtue in wealth and socially superior status, but covetousness remained a cardinal sin. The best way of thinking of social order was still that of a rural hierarchy in which each class performed certain functions for the good of the whole. When Jefferson designed an educational system he did not act upon an equalitarian principle, but upon a selective pattern which would recruit the upper ranks of society by drawing the most able from the lower ranks up an educational ladder. "The rubbish would be raked over" and the valuable elements taken out; the less able would continue to perform the laboring function for which nature had equipped them. At the sàme time ability did not provide any grounds for moral superiority and laboring farmers should retain their freedom to choose their rulers and criticize their superiors.

Thus Jefferson drew upon the revolutionary rejection of traditional authority but did not contemplate a society in constant flux and change. It is true that he said (with reference to the alarm created by Shays' Rebellion),

> Calculate that one rebellion in thirteen States in the course of eleven years, is but one for each State in a century and a half. No country should be so long without one.

But, as with other Jeffersonian statements, this is capable of various interpretations. In the same letter he went on to argue that increased authority vested in government was no guarantee against insurrection, and the best hope for order lay in education. "Educate and inform the whole mass of the people. Enable them to see that it is their interest to preserve peace and order, and they will preserve them." Jefferson thought that upheaval was a necessary consequence of injustice, but he believed that stability would be the normal condition of a free and educated society. He saw Hamilton's initiative as a threat to social balance, and his own countermove was to restore equilibrium. In later years Jefferson would speak of his own election to the Presidency as "the revolution of 1800," and this gives a clue to the way in which he understood the revolutionary process. What happened in 1800 was an election, conducted in full accordance with the law and the Constitution, that resulted in the repudiation of one set of politicians and the elevation of another. For Jefferson the intellectual gap between himself and the Federalists was wide and important, but his "revolution" called for no violence and no social upheaval.

Jefferson was, therefore, as much a believer in "checks and balances" as John Adams or any other theorists of mixed government. The difference lay in his abandonment of the purely mechanical features of balance, and his reinforcement of the checks with all the humane aspirations of mankind. Where Adams thought that authority and property must be given protection against the tumultuous inclinations of the majority, Jefferson believed that authority must be kept within proper bounds by giving full weight to the decent instincts of mankind. If every mortal man were liable to corruption, there was greater safety in serving the aspirations of simple men than in giving more freedom of action to the talented or wealthy few. It is this, rather than his formal contribution to political ideas, which makes Jefferson one of the patron saints of modern democracy. John Adams was a more lucid political theorist; Alexander Hamilton had a much clearer perception of the economic and administrative needs of modern society; but Jefferson was stronger than either in his realization that the quest for a better life, on the part of ordinary men, would be a mainspring of political action in the future. In 1801, in his first inaugural, he put into words his concepts of the ideas, principles, and political forces which would be at work, and should be fostered, not deplored:

> Equal and exact justice to all men, of whatever state or persuasion, religious or political; peace, commerce, and honest friendship, with all nations—entangling alliances with none; the support of the state governments in all their rights, as the most competent administrations for our domestic concerns and the surest bulwarks against anti-republican tendencies; the preservation of the general government in its whole constitutional vigor, as the sheet anchor of our peace at home and safety abroad; a jealous care of the right of election by the people—a mild and safe corrective of abuses which are lopped by the sword of the revolution where peaceable remedies are unprovided; absolute acquiescence in the decisions of the majority—the vital principle of republics, from which there is no appeal but to force, the vital principle and immediate parent of despotism; a well-disciplined militia—our best reliance in peace and for the first moments of war, till regulars may relieve them; the supremacy of the civil over the military authority; economy in the public expense, that labor may be lightly burdened; the honest payment of our debts and sacred preservation of the public faith; encouragement of agriculture, and of commerce as its handmaid; the diffusion of information and the arraignment of all abuses at the bar of public reason; freedom of religion; freedom of the press; freedom of person under the protection of the habeas corpus; and trial by juries impartially selected—these principles form the bright constellation which has gone before us, and guided our steps through an age of revolution and reformation.

The modern age has grown less sympathetic to Jeffersonian rhetoric, and it is easy to point to the limitations of Jefferson's principles in practice. The apostle of equality remained a large (though indebted) landowner, and the champion of freedom died the owner of many slaves. If the Federalist concentration of economic power was rejected, a great deal of vigorous and aggressive capitalist growth went forward during the Jeffersonian ascendancy. The believer in "peace, commerce, and honest friendship, with all nations," pressed his country to the brink of war with Great Britain, leaving Madison, his friend and successor, to take the last decisive steps into conflict. The champion of states' rights tried to coerce states as a part of his policy of economic embargo in defense of national maritime rights. The strict constructionist used a power unauthorized by the Constitution to purchase Louisiana. These points, which can be made with varying degrees of irony or anguish, do not affect the central core of Jefferson's political creed. He was the last man to believe that the world was perfect, or to deny that he himself shared in its imperfections; he was also well aware of the limitations that all theories encountered in practice and of the qualifications which must be attached to all principles. He hoped that he had done something to keep America free from the dangers of European society, but at the end of a lifetime of achievement he thought that things were more likely to get worse than better. The principles in which he believed were simple, but they were exceedingly complex in operation; and the more sophisticated and vigorous were the interests of society, the more difficult it became to keep the principles alive.

The best precept for statesmen was to keep government "wise and frugal." Wisdom lay in performing constitutional duties firmly and efficiently, but not in claiming superior authority over areas in which individuals or local governments were the best judges of their own interests. In American terms this meant that not only the daily problems of law and order, but also care for economic progress should be left to the states. The states were best fitted to provide what little direction and regulation might be required by the dynamism of private enterprise; and, if this failed, it deserved to fail and should not be rescued by the exercise of national authority. The plea for efficiency and progress could be the most insidious enemy of freedom. The colorless appearance of Jefferson's domestic administration was intentional and did not prevent the early years of the nineteenth century from being a period of economic expansion and social development.

One aspect of Jefferson's career which often escapes notice was his success as a politician. Despite his frequently declared preference for retreat from public life, the greater part of his active life was spent in office. As a member of the Continental Congress, Governor, Minister to France, Secretary of State, Vice-President, and President, he acquired an unrivaled knowledge of national affairs. John Adams,

like Washington, had hovered uneasily as President between the aloof-
ness of a head of state and the partisanship of a head of government; his
dealings with Congress were generally unhappy and he neither restrained his friends nor conciliated his critics. Jefferson had no doubt
that it was the duty of a President both to govern and to give tone
or direction to public affairs; but he got his way with Congress without
arousing resentment or suspicion of executive influence. He was aided
by the decline of the Federalists, which left his supporters with large
majorities in both Houses; later Presidents, however, would often
find that a supposedly friendly majority, which felt too safe, was as
hard to manage as one with a narrow margin. Characteristically
Jefferson made no outward claim to leadership or demonstration of
authority, but exercised his influence in easy and informal discourse
with select congressional leaders. At the same time he was open to
all and did not appear to give his confidence exclusively to any.
Harmony in the party was maintained while congressional business
was conducted with remarkable efficiency. In this way Jefferson set
a pattern for crossing the divide created by the separation of powers,
and he showed how a successful executive could get his own way
without appearing to do so.

The way in which the Jeffersonian tradition was molded by
circumstances had far-reaching effects upon the American future.
The democratic principle of equal rights and majority rule was linked
with the centrifugal principle of states' rights; when democracy came
in later years to European states it coincided with greater centralization, and majority rule accelerated the tendency to greater governmental authority. In America the democratic impulse was allied
with the rights of local government, while the relationship between
national and local majorities remained an enigma. Elsewhere majority
rule treated local majorities as minorities in the nation and required
them to acquiesce in national decisions; in America the right of local
minorities to refuse acquiescence was an article in the Jeffersonian
creed. The theoretical explanation was that a state government, being
closest to the people, was most responsive to their needs and most
likely to protect their rights. In practice the right of a state might mean
the right of whatever faction or interest was predominant in the state.

Jeffersonian tradition also endowed American democratic tradition with a negative aim. The purpose of popular political activity
was to defend existing rights against the abuse of power, not to provide
a mandate for policy approved by the majority will. Again there is a
contrast with those European countries where universal suffrage came
late and was regarded as a means by which the people could obtain
social benefits through positive action. But perhaps the most significant,
and most disturbing, aspect of the Jeffersonian tradition was the way

in which it identified liberal and humane values with rural society. It has been noted that Hamilton harnessed social conservatism to economic dynamism; Jefferson harnessed liberalism to the ideas and institutions that were bound to suffer defeat under the impact of economic revolution.

CHAPTER V

DEMOCRACY

The history of the United States as a nation has spanned a political revolution which has entirely altered the aims and assumptions of all modern societies. Seven separate forces have been involved in this revolution: rejection of traditional authority (in religion and in learning as well as in politics); the claim that men have the right to accept or reject the government that is offered to them; the belief that the will of the people is the source of authority; the claim that people have the right to govern themselves in matters that concern them alone; the idea of majority decision; the idea of majority rule; and the aspiration of men to be free from constraint. These major forces have been associated with other ideas—some derived from the past and some the product of new humanitarian or scientific attitudes—and the whole complex of ideas are often grouped together under some generic title such as "free society."

The various elements in this political revolution have combined to produce sharply conflicting results. The revolt against traditional authority has produced an equalitarian urge which regards social differences as being harmful *per se*, while the quest for freedom leads to economic inequalities and the replacement of hereditary power, based on land and status, with power based an industry and acquired wealth. The principles of consent and self-government can lead to fervent claims for the rights of minorities to protect themselves against the force of the majority, while the principle of majority decision (and the idea of will translated into authority through a "mandate" given to government) can lead to the intensive concentration of power at the center. The revolt of the Confederacy during the Civil War against the wishes of a national majority, and the dictatorship of the Communist party in "peoples" democracies, are equally products of the democratic revolution. There is no doubt that the preservation of individual rights was a mainspring of this revolution, but modern democratic states—even the mildest of them—have done far more than traditional governments to regulate human behavior. Though it is possible to claim that a humane and rational attitude to social problems is a consequence of democracy, it is not possible to prove it; and it is possible to cite occasions on which majorities have sanctioned unnecessary wars, the persecution of minorities, and extreme forms of anti-intellectualism in politics. Many people seem to equate the rise of modern democracy with the smooth and continuing transition from darkness to light; a less kind interpretation would attempt to prove that the slow advance of enlightenment against obscurantism—which marked the eighteenth century—was rudely interrupted by the "democratic revolution," and that the world still suffers under its heritage of violence and emotion. Both views are partial, extreme, and misleading; the truth is that democracy has given rein to all kinds of human impulses and instincts, and if it has sanctioned violence in the name of the people, it has also fostered tolerance and the advancement of knowledge.

Almost every statement which can be made about democracy can be contradicted by historical evidence. Over a century ago, Alexis de Tocqueville drew attention to the paradoxical nature of many such statements. Conservative critics of democracy argued that it was unstable and tended to anarchy; Tocqueville argued from American experience that it was stable and likely to be conservative. Liberal admirers claimed that democracy was the handmaid of freedom; Tocqueville showed that freedom was most in danger when exposed to the "tyranny of the majority." If traditional governments could oppress individuals, the liberties of churches, corporate towns, and aristocratic privilege provided bulwarks against the fury of arbitrary rule. In a democracy, government might "derive its just powers from the consent of the governed," but the individual would find little defense against the enormous weight of social pressure toward conformity.* Since de Tocqueville wrote, experience has proven, in hundreds of ways, the complex and contradictory nature of the forces at work in democratic society, and the one practice to be avoided is the use of the word "democratic" as a simple term of approval equated with "the good society"; a society is not a better society because it is "more democratic" than its neighbor. The true test is what kind of behavior has been encouraged and what kind of energies have been released by the democratic forms of government. It may also be necessary to ask whether the democratic society belongs to one or another of the main forms of democracy. Is it the purpose of democracy to provide a framework of representation and consent, within which legal security and social justice can be preserved? Or is it the purpose to provide the machinery by which the will of a majority of the people can be translated into political action?

The tangled skein of democratic history is rendered more complex by the coincidence between political, scientific, and economic revolutions. What were once the frontiers of knowledge have been broken down, and scientists seem to hold keys to the knowledge of good and evil which were once the exclusive possession of priests. Economic change has revolutionized communications, provided goods on a scale never before envisaged, and made economic power as potent, and as much sought after, as was political power in the past. In the present context it is idle to speculate upon the relationship between

---

* There are many editions of Alexis de Tocqueville, *Democracy in America*. Volume 1 was first published in 1835 and Volume 2 in 1840. The argument about the tyranny of the majority is found in Vol. 1, Part II, Ch. 7.

democracy and these other changes; since these changes have been running together for some two hundred years, the causes and consequences of one change cannot be considered without reference to all the others.

Inaugurated as a nation on the threshold of this new age the United States formed, from the start, a politically modern society. Hereditary status went with the Revolution. The idea that government ought to be vested in an elite (of talents, education, and wealth) did not survive much longer. Social aims were comprised in the right to pursue happiness, and the utilitarian urge to judge institutions by their effect upon individual well-being was implicit in the revolutionary situation even though not enunciated as a formal philosophy. Americans also had, from the start, both a respect for practical things and a willingness to experiment that furnished keys for the new age of economic opportunity. It has often been remarked that the United States had no feudal past, and was free of the institutions that obstructed change in other countries. There were both advantages and disadvantages in this situation: It was healthy to reject the claims of hereditary landowners to control the destinies of humble men, but along with this went a rejection of the culture which intelligent aristocrats had done so much to preserve; it was healthy to insist that men had the right to enjoy whatever position their talents could secure, but this might lead to an unhealthy veneration for wealth. Respect for "republican virtue"—a new spirit of devotion to the public good— yielded enormous dividends, but it could degenerate into a jealous contempt for everything that aimed to maintain standards above those of the common man. Respect for the rights of ordinary men was a valuable and dynamic innovation, but in its more foolish manifestations it could lead to suspicion of everyone who was not ordinary.

The political revolution of the age varied in impact and intensity in different parts of the United States. If the rejection of traditional authority was universal, and if one consequence was the spread everywhere of the idea that one white male should have one vote, the implications were not uniform. A major difference was the survival in the Southern states of a ruling class based on land ownership and slave labor. Elsewhere the well-educated and wealthy tried to cling to the right to rule, but only in the South did they have the economic basis which made this possible. There was more wealth in the North; but though merchants and financiers might pull the economic wires, they could never attain the social and political influence of the large planters. The Southern gentlemen were not hereditary aristocrats, but land and servile labor gave them some attributes of a land-owning nobility. Collectively they had the leisure, training, and inclination to carry out the tasks of government—from the county magistracy to major state offices—and individually they possessed the economic status to live as independent men. Nor were they challenged from below, for one of the virtues of Jefferson's cultivators of the soil was a willingness (under normal circumstances) to elect into office the men whom "nature" had marked out for responsibility. Southern society became, and remained, an instructive example of an un-challenged ruling class in a wide suffrage society; and, almost alone in the family of democratic societies, the South produced no element of social revolution, no pressure toward economic change, and no demand for a more equal distribution of wealth. There was political reform, but usually of the mildest kind; minor adjustments in suffrage qualifications, in the apportionment of legislative seats, and in the powers of upper houses were hardly comparable to the great political upheavals which shook other societies under the impact of democratic revolution.

The Northern and Western states developed differently from the South. Both societies felt the influence of capitalist enterprise, and both offered status and prestige to material success; but these influences were more obvious in the Northern states and still more so in the Western states. Large landowners existed in these states, but they were few in number, lacked influence, and were suspect to a majority with an inbred fear of aristocracy. In the West political pressure was exerted against the greater landowners, and discriminatory tax-ation, combined with public hostility, brought about the breakup of the greater landholdings and their dispersion among smaller owners. In the South a plantation automatically earned its owner a place in the ruling class and brought with it prestige and respect, but in the Northeast wealthy men remained attached to the banks, commercial activities, or manufacturing establishments, in which they had made their wealth. A house in the country was a place of relaxation, not the center of their lives. In the West the ownership of land gave a man a stake in the country, but ambitious men tended to move to the towns and set up in business or law. Thus the social rhythm of success became quite different in the South and in the North. The Southwest took over the social pattern of the Old South; the Northwest became a more fluid society in which mercantile or manufacturing enterprise, the legal profession, and politics were the keys to success.

The political implications of these social variations were profound, though difficult to measure. In all sections most adult white males could vote by 1830, and by this test the whole of the United States formed a democratic society. But in the South and the Southwest the planter gentry became the centerpiece of political life, and around their aspira-tions and interests revolved all the elements of the Southern political universe. In the North political control lay with the voting majority and with the politicians who could guide and manipulate the people. The voice of the South was the voice of its ruling class, modified by the recurrent need for explanation to an electorate. The voice of the other sections was that of politically successful individuals, dependent on majorities, and modified by the need to cooperate with economic interests. In the South political, economic, and social influence was fused together in the planter class; in the North politics became professionalized, and business became a way of life. Despite its democratic form the Southern political society retained many characteristics of the rural, hierarchical, paternalistic society of the past; in the North and West the society in the making foreshadowed many features of a modern democratic state.

The political mood of the democratic South was defensive. The electorate of small farmers defended themselves against excessive taxation and domination by the upper class. The upper class defended its status, its political power, and its labor system against criticism and pressure from below. The whole section defended itself against interference from outside. In the North the defensive aspects of the Jeffersonian tradition were not entirely shed, but more positive attitudes were abroad. The purpose of politics was to get things done, and inevitably this meant competition between groups wanting different things. Protective tariffs, stable banks, sound but flexible credit formed the core of one set of aims—identifiable by 1824 as National Republican and after 1834 as Whig—bound together by common agreement that government was duty-bound to foster private economic development. Against this set of aims the Republicans and later Democrats required minimum activity on the part of the central government, autonomy for the states, and economic initiative in the hands of local entrepreneurs rather than in the great commercial centers. But the negative, Jeffersonian, aspect of this Democratic tradition was compatible with the lively activity of an expanding society; it was not anticapitalist, but thought of economic development generating among individuals rather than fostered at the center. If the theme was sometimes presented in defensive rhetoric—as the need to resist the encoachment of government—the purpose was to unfetter the positive forces at work in an expanding society.

These social and economic differences between North and South were to assume tragic significance in American history, but in the present argument they demonstrate the folly of generalizing about "democracy" without considering how the democratic processes are being used and what opinions they are propagating. The long term consequence of democracy, combined with the revolution in transportation, was to reduce differences among peoples; but in the short run it might exaggerate differences, and federal democracy on the American pattern was particularly liable to do so. There is a common and fallacious belief that government by consent and discussion leads to agreement; in fact the tendency is usually to encourage disagreement, rivalry, and the formation of parties. The art of democratic politics does not lie in the pursuit of some fictional consensus, but in ensuring that the triumph of one party is not achieved in such a way that the verdict cannot be accepted by the minority. In the American system a safety valve for outraged feelings was the autonomy of states; men who lost in the nation could remain hopeful of winning in their state. This remedy, however, allowed local peculiarities to become entrenched without salutory exposure to criticism or competition.

A small but important example of this was seen in the history of education. By tradition primary education was the responsibility of the local community, and in the Northern and Western states (largely inspired by the Puritan example) education flourished under local guidance. There was no need to invoke aid from the Government, for, even if this had been constitutionally possible, the local communities managed to maintain and extend the best system of elementary education in the world; but the same principle of local autonomy allowed the ruling class of the South to govern a society in which the majority of whites (and, of course, nearly all Negroes) went unlettered to their graves. If the Federal Government had possessed the right to encourage education this could hardly have happened. If the white majority of the South had been aware of what was done for their countrymen to the North internal demands might have forced state government to act and planters to pay. As it was, states' rights and rural isolation kept ignorance a way of life and multiplied differences between North and South.

Less obvious but equally important were the variations in law from state to state, fostered not only by different legislation but also by different attitudes toward the common law inherited from England. Throughout the first half of the nineteenth century there was a running argument between conservative jurists, who believed that the principles and precedents of the common law were the necessary symbols of natural justice, and legal reformers, who found it laden with technicalities and obsolete procedures appropriate to a monarchical country but unfitted for American conditions. State courts varied considerably in their response to this argument, so that as a litigant waded through a mass of cases and precedents only local experts could tell which had been accepted or rejected. A more obvious contrast was the existence, in every Southern state, of legal codes regulating slavery, and their absence in the North; but even from state to state in the South there were marked differences in the codes.

Federal structure fostered these differences, and American democracy was also complicated by working within the constitutional framework of checks and balances. It was never enough to ask what the majority thought, for President and Senate participated in law making, and the Supreme Court might have the last word. The early nineteenth century saw an acceleration of the tendency for the President and the Senate to gain in authority at the expense of the directly elected House. At best election to the House was a step in a career, and only a minority remained long enough to establish themselves as public men. Many, probably a majority, of representatives during the nineteenth century sat for not more than one or two terms, and the party line had to substitute for accumulated experience. The speaker remained one of the most important men in the nation, and the frequent and fierce contests over election to the office kept interest alive; but even he hardly played the part of second man in the nation, which had been designed for him. The decline of the House should not perhaps be exaggerated; it was still an essential part of government, and the influence of individual representatives was often much greater than one might infer from the noisy and hurried proceedings. The greatest influence accrued however to those who could survive frequent elections, and this usually meant the men from districts where, for one reason or another, their party was dominant.

A representative must be resident in the state that he represents and by convention resident in the district for which he is elected. This local orientation has its healthy aspect, but it also means a limitation on the independence of representatives; a man who pleases an administration, serves a party, or even votes according to his conscience, but loses favor with his constituents has committed political suicide. In practice this has meant that representatives often prefer to serve the special interests dominating their districts, or the political machines that get out the votes, rather than to entertain national views. At the same time their success will depend upon their ability to extract favors and patronage for their districts, so that dependence upon their constituents does not necessarily mean independence of the executive. These factors help to explain why the great debates of the nineteenth century took place in the Senate, and why ten senators acquired national reputations for every one representative known outside his own district and the walls of Congress.

The growing importance of national policy stimulated efforts to direct and control it. In Great Britain political parties had originated at the center to gather support for governmental policies, but it has already been shown that the successful American pattern was to organize in the constituencies and converge upon the center. Some, at least, among the makers of the Constitution had thought vaguely of a no-party or one party state; but Hamilton's initiative had shown the vital importance of the executive in the formation of policy, and control of the executive became a major objective of the political process. The executive could be controlled only by the election of a President, and requirement that a successful candidate for the Presidency must have a majority of all the electoral votes made nation-wide alliances necessary. National parties to elect a President were thus a logical consequence of the political machinery set up by the Constitution; the same logic prevented fragmentation of parties and the establishment of a multi-party society. National policy was a magnet drawing men to the center, but the federal principle ensured that parties would aim at broad alliances. The Jeffersonians created such an alliance and were rewarded with success; the Hamiltonians failed to do so and dwindled into insignificance. The one-party system seemed to have returned during the long period of Jeffersonian ascendancy, but conflicts reemerged after 1820 and by 1840 a vigorous two-party system flourished. While popular government through the directly elected House declined, popular influence through democratically organized parties increased.

The Supreme Court was, of all the institutions of government, the furthest removed from the people and, under the Federalist John Marshall, seemed the least likely to make a significant contribution to democratic theory. Yet in the celebrated case of McCulloch v. Maryland Marshall elaborated one of the essential ideas in the evolution of modern democracy by arguing that the will of the people was not merely a check upon the abuse of power but the source of positive authority. A bridge was set up between democracy and power—between the mass of the people and the government acting of their behalf; a link had exsisted since the Declaration of Independence had asserted that government derived its just power from the consent of the governed, but with Marshall consent made government strong not weak. Marshall was a patrician, a Virginian gentleman who distrusted the people, and a Federalist who hated the democratic element in Jeffersonian politics; yet his argument provides the theoretical justification for all the vast powers wielded by a modern democratic government.

In McCulloch v. Maryland, decided in 1819, Marshall was asked to decide whether the State of Maryland could legally tax a bank incorporated by the United States. He used this opportunity to rebut the theory that "the powers of the general government are . . . delegated by the States who alone are truly sovereign." If this theory were true it might follow that states could resume their sovereign power if they deemed that Congress had exceeded its constitutional authority, but Marshall was determined to show that there was no ground for state interference with national laws. The authority of the Constitution derived from its ratification from the people in their conventions; they had met in their States, but one could not infer from this that their decisions ceased "to be measures of the people themselves or become measures of the State governments." Ratification "required not the affirmation, and could not be negatived, by the State governments," and "the Constitution, when thus adopted, was of complete obligation and bound the State sovereignties." But could Congress exercise unrestricted freedom in choosing the means to carry out its constitutional duties? Marshall answered this question by affirming that "the sound construction of the Constitution must allow to the national legislature that discretion, with respect to the means by which the powers it confers are to be carried into execution." The Constitution set the limits; it was for the judges to decide if a law of Congress overstepped constitutional bounds, and no subordinate authority could claim the right to do so. Thus the most complete theoretical statement of national authority rested upon the premise that "The government of the United States . . . is emphatically and truly a government of the people."

The decision of a court, even of the Supreme Court, does not necessarily convince public men and may pass unnoticed by the people at large; but Marshall's argument fed into the storehouse of ideas from which future generations would draw. Eleven years later, in a famous oration which became one of the most familiar pieces of rhetoric in America, Daniel Webster explained and justified the supremacy of the Union in language which might have been, and perhaps was, drawn directly from McCulloch v. Maryland. "We are here," he said, "to administer a Constitution emanating immediately from the people, and trusted by them to our administration. It is not the creature of the State governments. . . . This government . . . is the independent offspring of the popular will." If there was anything in the Constitution that should not be there, or any interpretation that should not have been made, "the people know how to get rid of it." The people had not given this right to the states; rather they trusted to the integrity of the men whom they had elected, to frequent elections, and to the courts to prevent breaches of the Constitution.

In this speech Daniel Webster added another ingredient to the association of democracy with strength. Political theory was of little force unless backed by conviction, and his peroration associated the philosophy of national power and popular will with the glory and benefits of the Union. "Every year of its duration has teemed with fresh proofs of its utility and its blessings . . . It has been to us all a copious fountain of national, social, and personal happiness . . .

While the Union lasts, we have high, exciting, gratifying prospects spread out before us, for us and our children." To those who claimed to support the Union but to place liberty first, Webster responded that his dying eyes would hope to see "everywhere, spread all over in characters of living light, blazing on all its ample folds, as they float over the sea, and in very wind under the whole heavens, that other sentiment, dear to every true American heart—Liberty *and* Union, now and forever, one and inseparable!"

The Jeffersonian concept of popular government had seen the states as the guardians of liberty, the people as the defenders of their own rights, and the Government with useful but limited and unemotional functions. The new ideas of the early nineteenth century saw the states as limited to their local functions, the people providing the sanction for positive government, and the idea of Union merging with a commanding appeal to loyalty and pride. This powerful alliance of ideas combined with the nationalism of the age to forge new attitudes, and, ultimately, to provide that devotion to the Union for which thousands would die. However, it did not move or convince everyone. All over the United States were men who believed in republican government but feared that the will of the majority might be used to justify excessive government. Also, men were devoted to the Union without admitting that loyalty must be undivided or unqualified whatever the Government did. For rhetoric about the will of the people did often mean, in hard fact, the will of the majority; and to many, an essential principle of a federal system was that the national majority should not rule unchecked.

The makers of the Constitution had attempted to remove the office of President from direct contact with the people and set up an elaborate system of indirect election. Thus, there was irony in the transformation of the Presidency into the most popular of government institutions, the instrument of the national majority, and the embodiment of democratic will. In 1796, and ever since, the leading contenders for the Presidency became nominees of a party and depended for success largely upon the solidarity of that party across the country. Indeed, during the ascendancy of the Jeffersonian Republicans nomination became almost as important as election. Republican presidential candidates were nominated by a caucus of party members in Congress; this was akin to the system now used to select a party leader in Great Britain, but it virtually confined choice to the "in-group" of public men who had been at the center of national politics for a long time. A political elite tended to choose a man whom they knew, and no outsider was likely to break through into the inner circle. By 1824 there were a good many "outsiders" pressing upon the gates: Westerners who resented the dominance of the East, younger politicians who resented the established cliques, and rank-and-file voters who displayed a healthy suspicion of men remote from the people.

Under these pressures the caucus system broke down, and in 1824 a new phenomenon appeared in the nomination, by the legislature of Tennessee, of Andrew Jackson, who failed to win a majority in the electoral college but received the largest number of popular votes. The novelty of the Jackson candidature was that, though a widely known general, his experience with national government had been confined to one undistinguished term in the House and a brief incomplete term in the Senate. He had more experience of public affairs than his rivals admitted, but every preceding President had served for years in national office before being elected. No one, of the four candidates in the field (Andrew Jackson, John Quincy Adams, W. H. Crawford, and Henry Clay), secured a majority in the Electoral College, and the election went to the House of Representatives where Adams was chosen.* The rejection of the candidate with the largest popular vote was widely criticized, and the subsequent appointment of Henry Clay as Secretary of State gave currency to the rumor of a "corrupt bargain" under which the Clay men had given their support to Adams. In fact the procedure in the House had been precisely that envisaged by the Constitution, which specifically avoided giving the office to the man with the largest vote when no one had a majority of the electors. Moreover the alliance between Adams, strong in the Northeast, and Clay, strong in the West and identified with a program of economic growth, was logical. Nevertheless, the events left a cloud over the reputations of both men and a long-lived distaste for the electoral procedure in the House.

Since 1824 there has been an unwritten assumption in American politics that it is in the national interest for one candidate to obtain a clear victory and much effort has been expended to secure this result. In the election of 1968, when some commentators foresaw that the decision might be thrown to the House, they spoke of it almost as a national calamity. The real danger was that supporters of the candidate with the least votes would hold the leading candidates to ransom and

---

* Article II of the Constitution provided that the electors, in their states, should vote for two persons. The candidate with a majority of all the votes cast became President and the second-highest, Vice-President; if no one had a majority the House, voting by states and each state having one vote, should choose one from among the five highest. The Twelfth Amendment required separate votes for President and Vice-President; if no candidate for President received a majority the House, voting by states, chose one from the leading three. The Senate would choose the Vice-President from the leading two.

extract promises which neither wished to give; the winning of the Presidency would become a matter of political bargaining in which minority interests would demand and secure unreasonable terms.

In 1828 Andrew Jackson won easily over Adams. This was not the consequence of a great upsurge of democracy, nor did it indicate the predominance of the West in national politics. The vote was higher than in preceding presidential elections, but the turnout in state elections had often been higher; and Jackson would have been nowhere without a heavy vote in the South and in the mid-Atlantic states. The Jackson movement owed more to efficient organization than to anything else, but the election indicated that professional politicians and voters were coming to regard the Presidency as the focal point of democratic politics, and candidates must in future be seen as the choice of the people and not of an elite.

There remained the argument that democratic processes should apply to nomination as well as to the election itself. In 1832 the Jacksonians (known by this time as the Democrats—though party labels remained confused for some time to come) adopted (from the minor Anti-Mason Party) the National Nominating Convention; delegates from the party in each state were summoned to nominate a candidate for the Presidency, and thus was born one of the unique institutions of American democracy. In 1836 the Democrats adopted the rule that a two-thirds majority was necessary in the Convention for nomination; this was confirmed in 1844 and continued until 1936. The opponents, organized from 1834 as the Whig party, also adopted the National Nominating Convention but allowed nomination by a simple majority of the delegates. In both parties the participation of professional politicians in National Conventions was more evident than direct representation of the people, but the public debates over nomination stimulated interest while the delegates themselves were acutely aware of repercussions in their own states and districts.

The makers of the Constitution had envisaged the President as the man who would execute the laws, and give vigor and efficiency to the administration; with Hamilton the role of the Executive in initiating policy became apparent, and though Jefferson had taken a lower view of executive responsibilities he exercised a great deal of indirect influence over Congress. Under Jackson there was a decided shift toward Presidential responsibility for national policy. The full impact of this was obscured because Jackson used his authority mainly to prevent things from being done; he vetoed an internal improvements bill and a bill to recharter the Bank of the United States, he removed government deposits from the Bank, refused to accept paper currency in payment for public land, and denied the right of a hostile Senate to censure his conduct. Nevertheless the negative aspects of his authority did not alter the fact that the President, rather than the representatives of the people, now claimed the last word on policy. In theory it remained true that Congress made the laws and the President executed them, but in practice no law was going to be effective or even passed if it had not the prior approval of the President. Early critics of the Constitution, during the ratification debates, had raised alarm over the "monarchical" implications of the Presidency; under Jackson executive domination over government became real, but not— as an earlier generation had assumed—because the President was remote from popular influences but because his authority was now firmly based upon a national vote of confidence. He was the one man in government for whom all the people had voted and the one man who could claim that his office was truly national. The strong Presidency was the product of democracy and not a counterweight to popular pressure.

The force of the new concepts of Presidential power was illustrated by the messages with which Jackson accompanied his vetoes. They were not abstruse arguments about constitutional law but straightforward statements of policy. Indeed the famous 1832 veto of the bill to recharter the Bank of the United States became an authoritative statement of the principles of Jacksonian Democracy. "There are no necessary evils in government. Its evils exist only in its abuses. If it would confine itself to equal protection, and, as Heaven does its rains, shower its favors alike on the high and the low, the rich and the poor, it would be an unqualified blessing." 'Equal rights for all, legislative privileges for none' was a slogan which put the fire of popular enthusiasm into the concepts of Jeffersonian democracy; limited government was now the means by which the common man could protect himself against the rich and presumptuous. "Many of our rich men," said Jackson, "have not been content with equal protection and equal benefits but have besought us to make them richer by act of Congress." In Congress these "rich men" might have their way, and it was the duty of a vigilant President to protect the people as a whole against the unhealthy policies of their representatives.

Andrew Jackson claimed the right to judge issues without acknowledging either past precedents or the Supreme Court. Madison, the great authority on the Constitution, had signed a bank charter bill in 1816, but this did not mean that Jackson was bound to follow suit in 1832; the Supreme Court had found the Bank constitutional in McCulloch v. Maryland, but, said Jackson, "The opinion of judges has no more authority over Congress than the opinion of Congress has over the judges, and on that point the President is independent of both." Thus the President stood alone and insisted upon his right to decide policy without reference to precedent, judges, or congressional majorities. The claim seemed acceptable when made by a popular President fresh from an electoral victory, and his triumphant reelection in 1832 smothered the attacks of his critics upon "executive tyranny"; but could this exalted view of Presidential authority be sustained unless linked with the will of the people? In 1841 John Tyler, elected as Vice-President in a landslide triumph for William Henry Harrison, became President when Harrison died. Tyler, who was out of sympathy with the majority of his own Whig party, proceeded to wreck by veto the principal measures passed in Congress. Tyler could hardly be said to have a mandate from the people, personally he was unpopular, and the party had just won a resounding victory at the polls. Was the exercise of Presidential authority justified under these circumstances? The question remained unanswered, and much subsequent controversy was generated by the failure to decide whether President or Congress had the initiative in policy or the mastery in politics.

Democracy existed within the framework of "checks and balances," and the will of the people had to be accommodated within a political system in which no institution had the supreme power of decision. The Constitution had imposed restraints upon the sovereign people and could be amended only by a cumbersome process, which gave minorities ample opportunity to obstruct. Two-thirds in both houses of Congress, three-fourth of the states, had to concur to amend the Constitution, and faced with these obstacles the Constitution remained without amendment during the long formative years of the nineteenth century. Not until 1865 would an amendment be made which touched an important principle and then only in the unusual circumstances of postwar reconstruction. On major questions of policy and change the will of the majority could not act, and democracy had to function upon the assumption that certain matters lay beyond the reach of popular decision.

Constitutional checks were not evenly applied and in certain fields operated less effectively than in others. In 1845 it is probable (though not certain) that there was a national majority in favor of the annexation of Texas, but a treaty would have failed because two-thirds of the Senate could not be mustered for ratification; President Tyler, however, secured annexation by getting each house to pass, by simple majorities, resolutions in its favor. The declaration of war against Mexico in 1846, and appropriations to carry on the war, required only simple majorities though the decision for war was of major importance. In 1850 decisions to admit California, allow slavery in New Mexico, and pass a tough Fugitive Slave Law were all made by simple majorities in Congress, although each was strenuously opposed by important minorities. In other words the checks and balances of the Constitution operated selectively; the will of the majority was allowed to prevail in some areas and on some questions, while on others it was blocked. The most crucial of these inconsistencies affected slavery. It would have required an amendment to the Constitution (which was quite out of the question before 1861) to end slavery in the states, but, until 1857, a simple majority could prohibit it in the Territories. In 1857, in the Dred Scott case, the Supreme Court decided that it was also unconstitutional to prohibit slavery in the Territories, and an amendment would have been required to surmount this obstacle.

During the first half the nineteenth century, tension developed between those who thought these obstacles to majority rule were too great and those who thought them too weak. Among the latter, the most influential by far was John C. Calhoun, whose attacks upon the power of what he called "the numerical majority" have commended him to modern critics of mass democracy. Calhoun was drawn into this argument by the attempt of his state, South Carolina, to defeat a protective tariff passed in 1828. In that year, the legislature made a solemn protest against the tariff and questioned the constitutionality of a measure passed against the interests of a large minority, and when a modified tariff of 1832 proved unsatisfactory, it took steps to "nullify" the revenue act. Calhoun met Marshall's argument on national supremacy, based on a grant of power by the people, by arguing that if the authority of the Constitution rested upon ratification by conventions in the states, the same popular action could challenge the authority of the National Government. Neither Congress nor the states, argued Calhoun, were sovereign; both were agents to whom the sovereign people had delegated certain functions, and a failure to recognize this had produced the heretical idea that an agent could determine what powers he possessed. If the National Government exceeded its powers, how could the people act? It was inconceivable that they had no remedy and absurd that no action was possible until all the people were agreed. Rather, logic seemed to suggest that the people could nullify in the same way as they had once ratified: that is, by conventions in their states.

Calhoun did not intend his system to produce anarchy. In his later *Disquisition on Government* he would argue that the local majority must be given this power to check the numerical majority; but recognition of this right would of itself produce harmony and, therefore, strength. Men were not constantly running into the brick wall of constitutional prohibitions, whose very existence caused them to plan their actions accordingly. The requirement for a "concurrent majority" might make the National Government weaker by imposing a further practical check upon what it could do; but it would make the Union stronger by eliminating the friction that resulted when a majority attempted to impose decisions which were unacceptable to the minority.

The theoretical attractions of nullification need not conceal its practical difficulties. If minorities have rights so have majorities, and it may be as logical to suggest that minorities must acquiesce at times as that majorities must sometimes abandon their objectives. If one State refused to collect the customs—thus opening a breach in the protective tariff wall—the remaining states would be faced with the choice of either placing customs posts around the frontiers of the nullifying state or abandoning the law entirely. What was at stake, therefore, was not merely the right of a single state to contract out of a federal law, but also to prevent the operation of a law passed by Congress and signed by the President. Andrew Jackson reacted sharply to nullification; so far as the cause of dispute was concerned, he leaned to the low tariff rather than to the high tariff, but on the constitutional issue, he was perfectly clear that a federal law must be enforced and was prepared to coerce South Carolina. Conflict was averted by a compromise tariff, which did not go all the way toward the South Carolinian position but provided for a progressive reduction of duties over a ten year period. At the same time, however, a good many Southerners who did not subscribe to the theory of nullification had been alarmed by the suggestion that a President could compel a state to obey by armed force.

Nullification raised other questions. A majority in a state might feel that they were wronged by a majority in the nation, but a minority in the state might feel equally aggrieved. During the crisis, the dominant nullifiers imposed a strict oath upon office holders, and more severe measures were contemplated against the "traitors" who were loyal to the Union; so that nullification denied both the right of national majorities to decide and freedom to local minorities who happened to agree with them. Moreover it contemplated giving a special right of obstruction only to a particular kind of minority, for many other minority interests across the country did not have this opportunity of organizing a majority in a state. This argument was made more pointed by the existence of the greatest of all minorities, the Negro slaves. It is possible that the nullification movement was motivated by a desire to protect slavery from federal interference rather than by the need to break a tariff law; at least it was argued that the stronger the defense of the Southern states against the national government, and the national majority, the better their prospect of keeping slavery.*

The preceding pages have explored some of the theoretical and practical difficulties, involved in reconciling democracy with constitutional limitations; yet these considerations had little influence upon the majority of Americans who remained profoundly satisfied with the institutions they had inherited. The Constitution defined the authority of people in a broad sense, and the governmental processes gave them ample opportunities for rebuking errors and preventing the abuse of official power. What was exhilarating was participation in political debate. All white male citizens could discuss, associate, organize, vote with great frequency, and participate in a great range of local decisions. Sensibly most of them realized that no one could expect everything in a system that encouraged argument and fostered compromise. The citizen might be remote from the national government, but he knew everything that went on in his county or township. Even the remoteness of Washington was offset by the knowledge that every two years congressmen would have to face criticism and satisfy local majorities before they went back for another spell. Under these circumstances it was natural to think of Congressmen as the agents of their constituents rather than as men sent to decide for themselves about great national questions. What mattered was a new road, the improvement of a river, the location of county government, and the way in which the local federal offices had been filled. Interest in national politics was most likely to focus upon the issues (such as protective tariffs and internal improvements) on which a national decision could directly influence local interests. Democracy was local, and it seemed unnecessary to bother about the power of a national majority when the political process was doing reasonably well in satisfying the local interests of a growing nation. And if government seems to have been remarkably circumscribed by modern standards, a great many men could get on as well as they wanted without its help at all. Jacksonian democracy opposed intervention by government in most economic activities, but this negative aim was highly attractive to a vast number of entrepreneurs who were making their way forward in every part of the country. Even the Whig opponents of Jacksonian Democracy, who did favor more activity on the part of government, were modest in their aims when compared with even the weakest of modern administrations. They wanted a national bank and a protective tariff; they favored federal subsidy for selected roads, canals, and harbors,

---

* The most recent study of the Nullification crisis by William W. Freehling, *Prelude to Civil War*. (New York, 1965), stresses the need to defend slavery as an explanation for South Carolinian attitudes.

but they never contemplated the national government as an agency for economic planning. They wanted to use the revenue from the public lands to help states finance improvements, but the nearest they got to welfare legislation was a short-lived, bankrupt act of 1841 which enabled small businessmen, caught in a serious depression, to compound with their creditors.

The experience of these years did bring to the fore certain other problems which would remain endemic in the democratic system. How could the democratic system control the machinery which was so essential for the continuous survival of a party? The emergence of professional politics was inevitable, for frequent elections made the business of organization a full-time occupation; there were more well-intentioned than unscrupulous politicians, but the first half of the nineteenth century saw the rise of bosses whose skill lay in the manipulation of a democratic electorate and whose profits lay in exploiting the power so gained to their own advantage. No real answer was found, and the problem would become more acute, and the scandals more dramatic, in the later years of the century. How, too, would democracy cope with the numerous private interests which sought to influence and bribe the politicians? Jefferson had hoped that "wise and frugal" government would so reduce the material advantages to be wrung out of politics that private individuals would not find it worth their while to put pressure on legislators. Yet even the most negative and parsimonious government was involved in decisions which would profit someone, and from early days there were pressure groups at work behind the scenes. The multiplication of activities touched by government increased the incentive for influencing government, and lobbyists entered the political stage, where they have remained ever since. Frequently politicians and businessmen on the make would find reason for cooperation, and democracy had few defenses against the private deal or even against the open advocacy of certain economic interests in return for favors received. The vast variety of local interests created a political jungle in which all kinds of predatory beasts could wander with impunity.

Yet if democracy fostered local activities, which were sometimes healthy and sometimes harmful, and encouraged men to look at problems through local eyes, issues were appearing which brought national politics into sharper focus and increased participation in national elections. The revolt against the caucus had been caused in part by reactions against the idea of a governing elite and a consequent interest in what would replace it. In spite of the frequent affirmations to the contrary, federal spending on internal improvements increased, and each appropriation meant that some areas and some interests had much at stake in the outcome. Jackson's veto in 1832 of a road improvement bill (the Maysville veto) attempted to draw a line between improvements that were truly national and those that were purely local, and from that time, opinion polarized between those who accepted and those who denied the distinction. Jackson's handling of the Bank question roused both enthusiastic support and indignant opposition, and again concern was widespread, and opinion divided into two camps. In 1837 the financial panic, followed by a deep depression, raised the whole question of governmental responsibility for economic well-being. National questions and national concern were incentives for the formation of new party alliances; no one planned it this way, but, without realizing what was happening, the American people were moving out of an era in which local questions had dominated their lives into one in which national questions would demand attention and divide men across the country. By 1840 a new two-party system had appeared, and party loyalty was superimposed upon easygoing diversity; but the new national party system was so important a feature in the development of American democracy that it deserves a chapter to itself.

CHAPTER VI

PARTY

At the height of Jackson's power Alexis de Tocqueville wrote, "America has had great parties; now they no longer exist. This has been a great gain in happiness but not in morality."* This comment should be seen in the light of a distinction, made by Tocqueville, between great and small political parties; the first represented great divisions among men upon the fundamental character of their society. "Such parties generally have nobler features, more generous passions, more real convictions, and a bolder and more open look than others." They could elevate the mind and inspire self-sacrifice, but could also convulse society. Small parties were based on material interests and "the selfishness of their character is openly displayed in all their actions." In America of his day he saw no great parties. The "Republican, or Democratic, party has gone on from strength to strength and taken possession of the whole society." Under the broad wings of Republicanism small parties (or what an earlier generation would have called "factions") existed, but they were based upon local and temporary interests rather than upon great ideas. America was happier without "great parties," because no one threatened to tear society apart, but the tone of public life had declined because politicians served material interests, not lofty ideals.

Within five years of the publication of *Democracy in America* there were two national parties in existence, each enjoying support in every state of the Union, each organized to fight every election, and together presenting the voters with a choice of policies, personalities, and basic social attitudes. It is doubtful whether either party would have qualified in Tocqueville's mind as a "great party," but looking even at the "small parties," he had detected an important principle dividing them. "When one comes to study carefully the secret instincts governing American factions, one easily finds out that most of them are more or less connected with one or other of the two great parties which have divided mankind since free societies came into existence. As one comes to penetrate deeper into the intimate thought of these parties, one sees that some parties are working to restrict the use of public power and others to extend it."†

Following Tocqueville's analysis one might therefore say that during the Jacksonian decade, various "small parties" based on regional and material interests coalesced. The Whigs came to embrace, in a general and ill-defined way, the principle that public power ought to be extended, while the Democrats defended the idea that it should be

---

* *Democracy in America*, Vol. 1, Part II, Ch. 2. The quotation is taken from the new translation by George Lawrence in the Fontana Library edition (J. P. Meyer and Marc Lerner, eds.).

† A. de Tocqueville, *op. cit.*, Vol. 1, Part II, pp. 219–29.

restricted. The united parties retained nevertheless the character of "small parties," failed to advance philosophical expositions of their ideas, fastened upon minor conflicts, and exploited temporary clashes of interest and emotion. The party battles of 1790 to 1800 had turned upon profound differences about the present character and future destiny of the United States; the battles of the 1840's were concerned with tariffs, banks, public lands, and the acquisition of new territories. The solution, one way or the other, to any of these questions would provide no more than minor variations upon a pattern that everyone accepted. As soon as a real and profound issue emerged—in the shape of the controversy of slavery—the national parties of the 1840's broke up.

Most historians have accepted this interpretation of the two-party system of this period, yet it is not wholly satisfactory. The parties may have presented hollow ideologies to the people, but they brought voters to the polls in numbers hitherto unprecedented in national elections. If historical wisdom sees that little of importance was at stake, this was not the view of contemporaries; for them there were real differences between the parties, and elections were fought with high excitement and a good deal of bitterness. Voter participation was very high in 1840 and 1844 (by the standards of any democratic society), and if the percentage participation fell slightly in 1848 and 1852 the actual number of votes cast increased. Party loyalty was as strong as it has ever been, and even on questions which were bound to introduce sectional considerations—such as territorial expansion and the future of slavery—the parties strove with some success to maintain their unity. The fact that emotions roused by these issues ultimately proved too strong has obscured the importance of this two-party system. The abandonment of the one-party ideal marks a turning point in the evolution of modern democracy and helps to explain the great divide which now exists in the democratic world. In approximately half the societies which call themselves "democratic" the existence of two or more parties, and of freely organized opposition to the government of the day, is regarded as one of the essentials; in the remaining "democratic" societies, the existence of organized opposition is regarded as a sign of weakness and as proof that antisocial forces are gaining ground. Therefore, the American experience of two parties, differing upon policies but united in support for the fundamentals of their society, is of crucial significance. It involves not only a philosophic distinction between what a majority wants and the good of society as a whole, but also a practical demonstration that sharp differences, freely expressed, need not destroy society. A two-party system cannot function without the tacit assumption that one set of men, who think that the aims of their rivals are erroneously conceived and damaging in their consequences, will not push their opposition beyond the boundaries set by the existing institutional framework. Continued stability despite internal dissension has been tested by experience; but the final assumption of the two-party system rests upon faith that the conclusion which emerges, after the public discussion of differences, will be stronger, truer, and more durable than that reached by any harmonious group however wise or experienced. Controversy may seem disruptive, but political education is its outcome.

In less abstract terms the emergence of the two-party system can be examined for its historical consequences. The pattern set by Whigs and Democrats remains that of modern American parties. The possibility of nationwide organization was demonstrated and ever after became the lodestar of political activity. Two parties became normal, so that the complete and permanent triumph of one party would be regarded as unhealthy even by its adherents. At the same period experience with two minor parties, the Liberty and Free Soil Parties, nourished the idea that the country should stick with two parties and that third parties were to be deplored; even the supporters of minor parties aimed to replace or capture one of the major parties not to perpetuate the multiplication of parties. Finally, despite vicissitudes and changes in emphasis, there is continuity between the parties of the 1840's and those of the present day. Though most Democrats have long since abandoned the Jeffersonian precept that the best government is that which governs least, they remain the direct descendants of the Jacksonians. Though the Whigs ceased to exist as an independent party after 1852, their Northern members were absorbed into the Republicans, and the party of Henry Clay and Daniel Webster is still recognizable in that of Eisenhower and Nixon. The Whigs were the first party with the characteristics of modern conservatism to win the approval of a democratic electorate. They were not to be the last, and in advanced industrial societies parties which combine respect for the existing social order with business dynamism have been remarkably successful in their appeals to the electorate.

For all these reasons, the emergence of the two-party system in America, and its acceptance as a normal and permanent feature of political life, is an event of great significance. It marks a new stage in the history of democratic societies, and sets up criteria by which Americans tend to assess political systems. The existence of a two-party system on the pattern set in the 1840's is one of the tests of a "free" society and monopoly by one party is taken as one of the surest indications of despotism. They are, perhaps, too ready to dismiss the fact that in the history of democracy, and in the majority of nations now claiming to be democratic, two parties are the exception and not the rule. In some of these countries, it is deemed absurd to foster the existence of a party which aims not to facilitate government but to represent its policies in the worst possible light, while in others a restriction to two parties is seen as an unnecessary restraint. The emergence of the two-party system in America was a phenomenon of abiding importance for the American political system, but it was not inevitable and deserves close analysis.

The major objective of any party is to provide a government. In a one-party system this is achieved by recruitment into the party of potential administrators, by training them at various levels in local and national affairs, and finally by promoting them to power by some internal party procedure. The single party operates in much the same way as a large business concern; there is no formal democratic process, but a continuous process of assessment and of promotion for efficiency. Like the business corporation, the party sometimes gives executive responsibilities to outsiders but real authority is likely to go to the men with most experience and fewest errors. The government so produced has the virtues and limitations of a good bureaucracy: it can be efficient and foster cooperation among men who have been trained in the same way in the same environment; it can also be ponderous, drift away from public needs, and foster intense jealousy among the contenders for power within the system. The coexistence of harmonious understanding and bitter internal rivalries is an apparent contradiction, but one that anyone who has worked in a large organization will understand.

In a two-party system rivalries are institutionalized and presented as mutually exclusive proposals for government. When a party wins an election the result will not be merely the replacement of a few key men, but a wholesale change in administrative personnel which will go as far as civil service rules permit; there are two organizations for the government of the country, of which only one is employed while the other is excluded, so far as possible, from all power and patronage. Compared with the one-party system, the two-party system is therefore wasteful in manpower (twice as many men are employed in politics as are necessary) and careless of efficiency. Moreover there is a tendency to exaggerate differences and to invent them if they do not exist. The great defense of the two-party system is that rivalry constantly brings discussion into the open, and every political proposal is subjected to intense criticism. Behind this lies the belief that in social and political affairs there can be no absolutes, and if the party conflict ends by neither having the whole cake, this is a virtue, not a failing. The more intensely a particular policy is desired by one party, the more reason there is to believe that its full satisfaction may be to the detriment of the public good. While both parties present distinct ideas, the long-term interests of the community are best served by compromise between the two.

Thus the two-party system adds another tier to the theoretical structure presented by James Madison in Federalist Letter X. Faction was the enemy of popular government, and the best way to neutralize faction was to combine in a federal society, in which no local faction could obtain ascendancy, and all would find their violence moderated by their need to join together. The two-party system offers not one association but two, and requires first agreement within a party and then rivalry between the parties with the consequence that a party seldom achieves anything without concessions to the opposition.

In a multi-party state, governments can only be formed by coalitions between small parties whose separate followings encourage their leaders to sacrifice stability in administration to independence. The consequences may not be so debilitating as is sometimes imagined, because frequent changes in government usually leave the professional administrators in positions of permanent strength. In foreign affairs, or in times of domestic crisis, however, the fluctuating alliances of a multiparty state can paralyze initiative and destroy confidence. Americans would claim that they have steered between the confusion of a multiparty state and the monolithic character of one-party states (or of two-party states in which party discipline has become rigid). The American system allows for a great deal of autonomy within the party, and though groups draw closely together in the quadrennial alliance for the election of a President, they exercise great freedom at other times. In the Senate this is reflected in the independence of senators who frequently pay scant regard to party loyalty. Stability is obtained by electing a President who is in sole command of the Administration for the next four years; flexibility is maintained by the independent action of politicians whose primary allegiance is neither to the Administration nor to the party leaders but to the local political organization on which they rely for support.

It would be idle to suggest that men engaged in the formation of parties during the early nineteenth century foresaw these subtleties. Parties arose because, all over the country, enough men were opposed to the existing political establishment to do something about it. The Jacksonian Democratic Party was fostered by the suspicion that, in politics and in economics, the country was being governed by an elite based on the Atlantic seaboard. The Whig party was formed because enough men were sufficiently alarmed by the trend of Jackson's policy to organize opposition, and it flowered when depression closed the Jacksonian decade and discredited the government. Neither party would have progressed without favorable circumstances, real grievances, interests aware of these grievances and hurt by them, leaders with strong personalities, organization, and a ready-made rhetoric which could be adapted to the situation. The polarization of political argument into two parties has been diagnosed in various ways: as a contest between interest groups, as a struggle for survival among professional politicians whose livelihood would vanish if their organization ceased to exist, and as the consequence of ideological disagreement. The first suggests an extraordinary strength for "interests," which can never have comprised more than a small minority; the second fails to suggest any reason why rational men should have entrusted so much to aggrieved professionals with a selfish interest in success; the third stumbles upon the failure of parties to explain what ideological issues were at stake. Above all, most explanations of party err on the side of simplicity and underestimate the capacity of men to agree on means while differing on ends, to share common aims while dividing on means, to join together for different reasons and for different objectives. It is also too easy to discount the imponderable fact that an association, once formed, acquires its own tradition, its own compulsive rhetoric, and a vitality which can defy rational reasons for its demise.

An American party is a very large and very complex organism. It is an alliance to elect a President, and though there is always continuity from election to election, there is also perceptible change. It is an alliance in which disparate elements combine, and a party platform is more likely to be distinguished by its skill in concealing differences than by its positive contributions to political debate; it indicates the permissible limits for variation within the party, rather than a policy which demands agreement. The loose character of the alliance is reflected in the amorphous nature of the central organization; central dictation is unpopular, and national leadership tends to confine itself to liaison and intra-party diplomacy rather than to leadership in any real sense. But the alliance does have as its purpose the election of one man to the White House, and the success of the President will set the tone and determine the prospects for the future. American parties can only run for or against the presidential record, and the more unpopular a President, the more difficult it is for his party to escape from the burden. Thus the party as a national alliance is amorphous in policy and organization, but precise in its purpose and crucial in its consequence.

A party is also a local organization for power. Here professionalism is likely to be paramount, for it is the men with offices and careers at stake who have an incentive for the perpetual task of political management. With national elections every two years, and with state elections often more frequent, the organization of a party can never relax, and it is usually continuous contact with the electorate that pays dividends. Nor can the local party afford to reflect the tolerance of the national party for internal dissidence; the party is at war with the rival party, and the dominant faction within a party is on its guard against competing factions. Local organization is therefore likely to be rigid, to insist upon party loyalty, and to make a great virtue of "regularity." The professionalism of the local party does not exclude the influence of economic and class interests; indeed, while the national party strenuously avoids identification with any interest or class, the local party may be formed along the lines of conflict in local society. Finally the local party has a special interest in patronage, and in extracting local favors from the national government. It is this, more than anything else, that unites the local party oligarchy with the national party. The great prizes are won from a national victory, but this concern with the mechanics of power may also make it desirable sometimes for the local organization to preserve itself by disassociation from national disaster. In other words, local bosses do not feel themselves bound by the rules of "regularity" upon which they insist for their subordinates. It is best for one's party to win the Presidency, but the worst thing is for the local party to be destroyed by national unpopularity.

A party is an association by which some men hope to achieve positive ends. They may be businessmen who want a certain economic policy, or an idealistic group that wants certain reforms. The uncertainties of American politics assure no men that they will get what they want, even after an electoral triumph; but any group with positive ends must make a choice, and then hope that the promise of support will give them bargaining power in the party and subsequently put pressure upon the government. The most noted alliances between an interest group and a political party have been those between protectionists and first the Whig and then the modern Republican parties, and, of recent years, between organized labor and the Democratic party. Here, however, the uncertainty principle of American politics comes into play: If one could have predicted that the Whigs or Republicans would always pass a protective tariff, and that the Democrats would always pass a low tariff, protectionists might have been uniform in their Whig or Republican allegiance; in practice some protectionists have always been Democrats, while some free traders are Republicans. Similarly, Democrats, since 1945, have not rushed to meet trade union demands while Republicans have been only mildly opposed to them. A member of an economic group who dislikes one policy of a party may well take the risk of voting against his apparent interest and rest assured that others like him will be working to keep the party away from this objective, or even combining with members of the other party to defeat the measure in Congress. Similarly, idealistic groups must make a rational choice and choose the party which is most likely to advance their general aims; they will seldom find a party which guarantees to enact a specific measure. These considerations may seem to nullify the importance of interest groups and ideological groups; in fact they do operate to prevent hard and fast socioeconomic alignments, but groups wanting to achieve specific aims remain vital to a party. They often have ready-made organizations and publications which can be enlisted, they provide an enthusiasm which is divorced from political professionalism, and they have money.

Groups with defensive aims may sometimes adopt similar tactics to those with aggressive aims. Indeed the same person may well be aggressive in one respect and defensive in another. This is particularly probable in America with its Hamiltonian association between social conservatism and economic dynamism. Even so it is worthwhile to distinguish between the two kinds of aim. Men whose major objective is to defend status, privilege, or economic advantage may occasionally become rabid and indulge in violence—as does the Ku Klux Klan in defense of white supremacy—but more often such men act as a conservative anchor in a party. Whereas the activists always want change, the defense groups always want to remain as they are. This conservatism has its attractive side, as its liking for existing arrangements leads to a respect for law and an insistence upon the need for social order. Except in a crisis they are not likely to be politically active, but they will supply a solid core of respectable citizens who redeem the party from a sordid alliance between professional politicians and men on the make. It should be added that this kind of conservatism is by no means synonymous with laissez faire, and that defense may sometimes require innovation. The Anti-Trust Act of 1890 can be viewed, in part at least, as a defensive move, against economic consolidation, on the part of small business; yet it opened an entirely new chapter in the history of government regulation.

Finally a party is a tradition. This move from hardheaded "realism" to abstraction may seem to be no more than a postscript to the analysis; in fact it is vital, and, in some senses, the most important thing about a party. The ordinary voter may have little interest in the fortunes of professional politicians and be only mildly concerned by the aims of interest groups, but the competitive instinct roused by a Presidential race must be reinforced by a conviction that important decisions are to be made. The loyal voter defends himself by pointing out that over a long period his party has adopted attitudes which are superior to those of the rival party. He probably has a rhetorical vocabulary to explain what this superiority is. The independent voter may explain his vote by saying that he subscribes to the support of neither party, but in present circumstances the attitudes associated with one party seem more useful, more productive, or more just than those of the other party. This general identification of a party with a traditional approach to politics is the magnet that draws most voters to the polls. Without it apathy may be the rule, and skilled politicians know that their success depends not only upon keeping the tradition alive but also in constantly demonstrating its relevance to contemporary problems.

These were the social mechanics of the two-party system that emerged after 1835, and during the next decade the features of party organization became crystallized in forms which they have since retained. Party politics came to focus on the Presidency, and there was a relative decline of interest in state elections. This was reflected in greatly increased voter participation in Presidential elections, rising steadily from 1828 on, reaching an unprecedented level in 1840, and from there remaining on a high plateau. Side by side with increased interest in national elections went a growing professionalism in political management. The rise of professionally organized "machines" was associated particularly with Martin Van Buren, but the rise of the professional was a response to the needs of a democratic society rather than the work of any one man. The fact was that in a society with wide suffrage and frequent elections, amateurism was not enough, and an elite which stood aside from the rough and tumble of constituency life was doomed to lose political influence. By 1840 there were party organizations, manned by men who devoted most of their time to politics, in nearly all parts of the country; but they were especially notable in those regions where there was no established ruling class. The existence of local political organizations provided an element of stability in what might otherwise have been a very fluid situation: the politicians both stimulated political participation and guided political energies into well-chartered channels. It is customary to speak of professional politicians as a useless, or even injurious, class, but no one suggests a better way of running politics in a country where frequent elections render constant activity necessary.

The popular and professional elements in politics both found their focus in the institution of a National Nominating Convention to choose the party's candidate for the Presidency. Composed of delegates from the states—most of whom were chosen at state conventions—the Conventions were meetings of professionals rather than of ordinary party members; but the publicity which attended the whole process, from the choice of delegates to the nomination of a President, meant that the Convention was exposed to all kinds of popular pressure. The emotional nonsense, ham oratory and backroom deals, which are so often associated with the Convention, should not obscure its significance as a democratic institution. Here, in the full glare of publicity, a political party is forced to decide how it will act and under whom it will act. Inevitably, the choices made are not acceptable to everyone, but usually knowledge of why the decisions were reached helps to reconcile dissenters and wins their support for convention nominees. The National Nominating Convention does not always work perfectly, but there are few occasions on which it has worked very badly. In no other country does so much discussion of issues, so many opportunities for the expression of minority views, or so large an element of popular participation attend the vital task of choosing a national leader.

More serious criticisms are raised when one considers the effect of party upon administration. The federal service created by Washington and Hamilton was the most efficient and least corruptible in the world, and the accession of the Jeffersonians did not alter its essential structure. Though Jefferson removed some active Federalist politicians, and was unlikely to appoint men who were not good Republicans, he resisted pressure to "purge" the federal service and acted generally upon the assumption that a man who had worked efficiently, and had not been an active partisan, had a moral right to remain undisturbed in public employment. By the end of John Quincy Adams's Presidency the federal service was still as good, or almost as good, as it had ever been. Its principal weakness lay not in submission to political pressure, but in the failure to provide any or adequate pensions so that kindly departmental heads were persuaded to retain elderly men in office. Jackson's arrival at the White House did not herald a wholesale removal of existing office holders, and the new President was not insensible to the claims of long service and good conduct. He did, however, nourish the fatal idea that the operations of government were essentially simple, that they could be carried out by ordinary men, and that long continuance in office led to the formation of a bureaucratic aristocracy. If administration was simple, and rotation in office desirable for its own sake, it followed that new men should be appointed whenever possible; and faced with a choice among new candidates, it was reasonable to select those with acceptable political recommendations. Professional politicians, hungry for the fruits of patronage, were only too ready to agree with this analysis; and the process of demoralization, which had already undermined administration in several states, now attacked the federal service. By 1840 the American civil service was becoming, if it had not already become, the least efficient and most corruptible in the world.

The error of Jackson and his supporters was initially responsible for this decline, but the party struggle accelerated and intensified it. When the Whigs gained the ascendancy, flocks of federal appointees, from postmasters, junior revenue officers, and departmental clerks upward, were dismissed and replaced by good Whigs. When President Tyler broke with the Whigs he made a further inroad by dismissing Clay Whigs and replacing them with his personal supporters. After Polk's victory in 1844 it was taken for granted that the new President would dismiss and appoint all federal officials on party grounds. The major problem of appointment was not to find the best men, but to share out offices so that no supporters of the party were alienated, while friendly factions within it received more favor than those believed to be hostile. The whole concept of a professional, nonpolitical civil service grew dim, at the very time when it was accepted in Prussia and France, and making slow advances in Great Britain.

It would be wrong to overestimate the effects of party upon administrative decline. There were other causes operating in the same direction, but it is true that in the United States organized political interests tended to debase the public service, while in Great Britain and elsewhere some pressure groups were working for its improvement. In America, administrative elitism was associated with discredited Federalism, and 'rotation in office' was associated with the equalitarian aspirations of democracy; in Great Britain administrative corruption was associated with Tory oligarchy, while administrative reform was one of the weapons used by Radicals to undermine the system of privilege and waste. The whole movement was inspired by Jeremy Bentham and his disciples—the Utilitarians—who applied the searching question "What use is it?" to all political institutions. One tendency of Benthamism was toward laissez faire; but another was toward administrative efficiency, and the idea of a professional service was nourished by the quest for ability, integrity, and public spirit. Security of tenure and promotion on merit were won at an early stage. Recruitment by competitive examination came more slowly and advanced against stiffer opposition but was finally successful. Impetus to the cause of administrative reform was given by British experience in India where it was imperative to build up a corps of dedicated public servants to preserve British hegemony. In the United States there was nothing comparable to the Utilitarian movement, and it was not until after the Civil War that criticism of public corruption and inefficiency generated a movement for civil service reform.

This may be seen as another illustration of Tocqueville's axiom about the moral influence of "great parties." In Great Britain the radical critics of aristocratic politics believed that their mission was not only to reform but to change the basis of political life and make fundamental alterations in the balance of social forces. It was a necessary part of their argument to present their world as materially and morally better. Conversely, their conservative rivals were compelled to meet legitimate criticism. Both parties were thus put into a position where they had to compete in providing the country with efficient and incorrupt government, and the greatest administrative reformer of the nineteenth century was Sir Robert Peel, a Conservative Prime Minister. This kind of conflict did not develop in America; both parties accepted the same fundamentals, and neither was committed to any basic reforms. The regular sequence of Presidential elections held out to each party an early prospect of controlling the patronage, and both were prepared to accept, if not to defend, political supremacy over public service. Scandals made good propaganda for the opposition, but the burden of complaint was not the system but the iniquity of Democrats (or Whigs as the case might be). Criticism of the patronage system was unwelcome to both parties, and all politicians rallied to its defense.

Agreement upon the constitutional and administrative structure of the state meant that party strategy was confined to a comparatively narrow field, and even here the need to ally diverse groups made clear commitments difficult. Nevertheless, within these limitations there were important differences between the parties, and it is absurd to suppose that the course of history was not affected by the electoral fortunes of one or the other. The circumstances of Andrew Jackson's ascendancy had committed the Democrats to a high view of executive power, but, unlike the earlier Hamiltonians, they thought that this power was essentially defensive. It protected the public against the predatory interests that could always find lodgment in elected bodies, and the major instrument was the veto rather than the power to initiate policy. The Whigs, in contrast, condemned "executive tyranny" and championed congressional government; they hoped that their Presidents would recognize the right of congressional discretion in matters of policy and would reserve the veto for the very rare occasions on which there might be infringements of the Constitution in legislative acts. After the unfortunate experience with President Tyler, Henry Clay proposed an amendment which greatly reduced the veto power of the President. This got nowhere, but the Whigs continued to stand for the superiority of Congress in policy making. The failure of the masterful Clay to win the Presidency never put the theory to the test, and the Whigs were able to criticize President Polk for committing the country to war with Mexico and for exerting unjustifiable executive influence upon policy.

Both parties were parties of the Union, although both included some Southern members who were devotees of states' rights. The Democrats, following the argument of Jackson's Bank Charter veto, maintained that attempts by the national government to force the country along a chosen road would foster sectionalism. Positive government inevitably meant that some men and some regions would receive positive benefits at the expense of others, and the consequent tension would weaken the Union. The Whigs believed that a government which remained passive and inert allowed the different parts of the country to drift apart and fostered sectionalism. The touchstone in the later 1830's was the reaction of the two parties to the Panic of 1837 and to the severe depression which set in after a brief recovery in 1838. The Democrats responded by urging a reduction in government expenditure, by rejecting indignantly the suggestion that the National Government should come to the aid of indebted states (even when the debts had been incurred to finance roads, canals, and railroads), and by establishing an Independent Treasury which made the government its own banker and segregated public funds from private business. The Whigs responded by proposing a new National Bank (which would support commerce and bring government to the aid of private credit), a protective tariff to help manufacturing interests, a national bankruptcy act to ease the difficulties of small debtors, and distribution of the revenue from public land sales to the states. Not all Whigs supported each item in this national program with equal enthusiasm, but the party as a whole would show a remarkable solidarity in Congress. Even when the program was ruined by Tyler's vetoes, they hung together and fought as a united party in 1844, and Southerners who had once been orthodox Jeffersonians resisted the lure of Tyler's strict construction and constitutional scruples.

The different attitudes of the parties toward national needs drew different interests into their party camps. The Whigs appealed to merchants and manufacturers; bankers were divided, and so were planters, but a majority in both classes were Whigs. The views of small entrepreneurs would vary greatly from region to region. In some areas, already well-favored by communication and with a traditional suspicion of Eastern interference, Democratic laissez faire had a strong appeal; in others, where internal improvements were popular and enterprise felt the need of capital, Whigs were in a majority. The same could be said of small farmers who (in spite of assertions often made to the contrary) divided their support between both parties. Often the choice of party was influenced by accident and history rather than by calculation of immediate interests: The back country of Georgia was solidly Democratic, that of North Carolina, where material needs were very similar, was predominantly Whig. Western New York, an area of farms and small towns, was solidly Whig. In Vermont only one county was occasionally carried by the Democrats, but neighboring New Hampshire had become a Democratic stronghold. Massachusetts was always Whig (with an active Democratic minority), but Connecticut was always a marginal state. Kentucky and Tennessee were carried by the Whigs in every Presidential election from 1840 to 1852, but Missouri and Arkansas were always Democratic. But despite these peculiarities of political geography, it is possible to say that the Whigs were strong where economic activity would flourish most with protection, internal improvements, and a stable banking system; this included some regions (such as Western North Carolina and Vermont) where poor communications hampered development and some (such as Northern Ohio and parts of New England) where enterprise was active enough to feel that it could do better. The depression brought strong reinforcements to the Whig ranks, and there was no shortage of groups positively committed to Whig nationalism as a whole and to one or more aspects of it in particular. This coming together of so many financial, mercantile, manufacturing, planting, farming, and small business interests produced something more than a mere bundle of disparate policies. Behind the specific proposals was a commitment to the idea of a national community of interest: states, sections, economic activities were not separate and hostile, but bound together in one national association in which the various economic interests were complementary to each other. A major bond of union tied cotton planting to Northern commercial and banking interests; cotton exports financed imports, secured interest payments on foreign investments, and provided a stable base for the whole credit structure. At the same time increased production by American industry would lessen dependence upon foreign imports and so release a larger proportion of the cotton earnings for domestic development. The greatest opportunities for development existed in the West, and, if Western agricultural produce could be brought easily into the world market, the general prosperity of the nation could be still further improved. Whigs who responded to Clay's nationalism were engaged upon a real effort to lead America away from the sterile concept that the great economic interests of the country were engaged upon an internecine struggle to divide national wealth.

Compared with these positive aims embodied in Whig policy the Democrats lacked a strong theme until 1844. From that time onward the party adopted territorial expansion as its major theme, and it attracted not only popular enthusiasm but also a larger share of major interest groups. Texas bondholders, speculators in Texas lands, and cotton planters anxious to move to virgin soil all played a significant part in the Texas controversy. The war with Mexico opened a magnificent opportunity for commercial speculation in the West, and on the Pacific coast. In the old Northwest, and especially in Chicago, aggressive enterpreneurial interests looked to the rising star of Stephen A. Douglas in order to realize the opportunities of Western expansion. Revived prosperity increased the attractiveness of laissez faire and low tariffs, while reducing the need for central financial institutions or federal aid for internal improvements. Under these circumstances the Democratic party recovered the attractiveness for small entrepreneurs which it had possessed in Jackson's heyday.

Both parties provided a defense mechanism for established interests and ideas. The Whigs were the party of order, piety, and respectability. No Whig could openly repudiate universal white male suffrage, but most of those who deplored its advent found themselves in the Whig ranks. Ministers of the older denominations, fearful of the decline of religion, were more likely to be Whig than Democrat. So were members of the wealthy and social elite in the larger cities. On the other hand, stable agricultural regions, which feared both financial manipulation and the competition of more enterprising agriculturalists tended to be Democratic; so did the backcountry farmers in several Southern states, where the Democratic party organization was largely a means of defending themselves against domination based on the larger plantations. Storekeepers, craftsmen, low-paid labor, and many immigrant groups supported the Democrats, but without a philosophy of social change their political aims were mainly defensive. In parts of the South the Whig party had a decidedly patrician air, with large planters defending their position as a ruling class against the attacks of the small farmers, and of established wealth against the poor back-country. Yet elsewhere the positive aspects of Whiggism appealed to entrepreneurs in the small commercial towns.

The national appearance of these parties could be amorphous and uncertain, but locally the lines of division were tightly drawn and corresponded closely to economic, geographical, and class differences. Through the party the participants in these local struggles learned to cooperate with others in different parts of the country, but the quest for local advantage often remained the spur for party activity. Parties were therefore performing two valuable functions; they fostered co-operation across the country, and they provided both an incentive and a restraint for local factions—an incentive because national success and access to federal patronage might turn the scale in local conflicts, and a restraint because these prizes could not be won without the cooperation of others in distant parts of the country. The effect was not, however, to modulate the tone of party spirit in all cases; it worked rather to give an emphasis to those issues on which there was a large measure of agreement within the party, and to condemn to silence those questions which were likely to be most divisive. Specif-ically the operation of parties tended to magnify the importance of banks and tariffs and minimize that of slavery.

The majority of ordinary voters responded to the appeal of a tradition rather than to interests or specific issues. In presenting and popularizing their tradition the Democrats had the easier task: They were for the common men and against businessmen; they were for limited government, the rights of states, and the freedom of individuals. They claimed to be the heirs of the Revolutionary tradition, the disciples of Jefferson, and the followers of Jackson. "Equal rights for all, privileges for none" was their great slogan. They were steadily opposed to the idea of an elite, and they proclaimed the virtues of self-help and the iniquity of aristocracy. These equalitarian sentiments were quite compatible with large social differences in wealth; it was not success, but the abuse of success, which the Democrats attacked. It was the party of Irishmen, recently immigrated Germans, and Roman Catholics, but also emphatically the white man's party: equal rights stopped sharply at the color line. All these characteristics gave the Democrats a ready-made rhetoric drawn from the Revolutionary era; and to incoming foreigners they seemed to embody truly American principles and practices.

The Whigs had a much harder job, and frequently showed the strain of a party believing in upper class leadership but using popular methods. The best that they could do was to compare their struggle with executive authority to that of the Revolutionary Whigs and to suggest that their opponents were the real Tories. But during the depression period from 1837 to 1843 they profited from being the party of change. As was to happen again ninety years later depression stimulated the demand for "action and action now." In 1840, it was as the party of change and improvement that the Whigs swept the country; and behind the emotionalism and nonsense of that campaign stood the solid fact that the Whigs coupled the desire for social stability with the quest for economic achievement. The formula has always been a powerful one, and the scorn with which some historians have dismissed the Whigs fails to do justice to the American marriage between conservatism and enterprise.

The two parties offered a choice to the voters, and personified different traditions, different approaches to national development, different attitudes to economic policy, and different concepts of the role of government. At the same time neither questioned the constitutional framework or social structure of the country: They were not, therefore, "great parties" in the sense used by Tocqueville, but they were certainly the prototypes of modern parties. Each party, within its ranks, sought to discover the greatest satisfaction that could be given to local and special needs, and each strove for harmony by moderating controversies which might reveal irreconcilable differences. The parties emerged as sensitive instruments for the satisfaction and reconciliation of small needs, and as the means for avoiding larger and more disturbing questions. In a static world there would have been no reason why the techniques of party management should not have become more and more sophisticated, efficient, and responsive. In a changing world the parties still offered great opportunities for adjustment and flexible development. The challenge lay, however, in the revolutionary currents moving in the North Atlantic world as a whole, and especially in the northern United States. Would the national parties keep pace with social changes which affected not merely the balance of economic interest, but also more profoundly ideas about the character and purpose of American society? This was the major question upon which would hang the future of the democratic and federal United States.

CHAPTER VII

DEMOCRACY
AND THE
FORCES
OF CHANGE

The first half of the nineteenth century witnessed bustling activity and sustained growth in every part of American life. Population increase, immigration, settlement, territorial expansion into the Southwest and to the Pacific coast, and the rise of cities, in the recently settled areas as well as in the old Atlantic colonies, were the most tangible signs of increasing national power. Americans became the most numerous representatives of the English-speaking races, and the cities of the New World rivaled those of the Old in size and wealth, though not in elegance. A vast agricultural revolution, harnessed to the British textile industry, made cotton the premier American export and the dominant crop of the Lower South. Improved roads, canals, and, above all, railroads released Americans from dependence upon sea and river for the transport of heavy goods and made possible the penetration of the great interior. Industrial production gathered momentum and moved from small enterprise to large plants with heavy capital investment, and if industry was still primitive by modern standards, both in scale and technique, its progress was sufficient to excite the wonder of observers.

The American born in 1800 lived through great changes in the manner and appearance of life, though men who experienced this transformation were least sensitive to its implications. Laudatory oration drew annual attention to American progress, but it remained difficult to understand the watershed that cut off the middle years from the early part of the century. Men of seventy-five in 1850 had been born before Independence, and at some point during their lives they had crossed the divide from a rural age of settled belief into the modern world of cities, industry, anxiety, and doubt. The old certainties had been swept away forever, but the experience of change on this scale was a new experience in human history and it is not surprising that men of 1850 continued to talk as though they still lived in the age of Jefferson and John Adams.

In some ways America was better equipped to absorb these changes, and to profit by them, than most older countries. She did not suffer from a social system that condemned much talent to lie buried in poverty, and her politics were designed to release energy rather than suppress it. First among the great modern nations, America had accepted as axiomatic the social fact that vigor and leadership would emerge from the masses, and the Northern and Western states first sought the ideal of an educated people. America was the child of rationalism, revolt, and enterprise and became the prototype of modernity in a modernizing age.

Novelty could inhibit experiment, and a country that depended upon the inspiration of a revolutionary past was not always the best-equipped to tackle changing forces in a new age. It was assumed that the answer to political problems could be discovered from the work and writings of "founding fathers," and that innovation was betrayal. In other countries going though similar transformations, one party assumed responsibility for a rearguard action, while another looked forward to a better world when all vestiges of the old had been swept away. In Europe traditions developed around the conviction that change must come, that institutions must be amended or ended, and that everything done by the establishment was probably wrong. In America both major parties agreed that any political change would be for the worse, and that criticism of political institutions was heresy. The United States grew up with a tradition of revolution but no party of reform.

In a country with so many other things to think about, political certainty yielded some important dividends. There were ready-made formulae to fit many situations that arose, and, as these formulae worked well in many circumstances, men were spared the agonizing controversy that would otherwise have occurred. A striking example of the value of an accepted pattern of political behavior was found in the government of newly settled areas. The Northwest Ordinance of 1787 laid down the stages by which a Territory could move from first settlement to statehood; from government by appointed federal officials, to a stage in which Congress retained overall responsibility but with representation and local self-government, to the making of a state constitution and admission to the Union. During all these stages individuals retained their rights as American citizens. It was a process of colonial evolution under which no "colonial" was ever regarded as "inferior," and equal membership in the Union was promised as soon as development reached the appropriate stage. Moreover, in constitution-making, the Territories were spared a great deal of pointless dissension because there were so many existing and excellent state constitutions to be copied. Political innovation was unnecessary and communities grew to maturity within an accepted and revered framework.

The stability of political institutions had great advantages for an expanding society, but there was always the danger that the forces of expansion would overflow the banks. The crystallization of political thought in the later eighteenth century meant that in the first half of the nineteenth men would seek to achieve major political objectives by interpretation; the letter of the law was unassailable and controversy concentrated upon its meaning. The Constitution was flexible, but was it flexible enough? There was scope for change within its framework, but the natural inertia of established ways worked to the advantage of vested interests while the forces of change built up behind the constitutional dams. Here then was the fundamental problem of

American life: Could a fixed and venerated political framework contain dynamic and divergent interests in an age of revolutionary social change?

Economic change worked for both unificaton and diversification. From one view the strength of America grew with economic specialization and a high degree of interdependence between regions. Economic analysis has revealed again and again the way in which less developed regions can leap forward when closely associated with more developed societies, while commerce, banking, and industry draw strength from association with productive agriculture. If the complementary activities of the United States had been planned as a whole by some economic lawgiver they could hardly have been improved. Yet specialization of economic function bred different attitudes, different social patterns, and different ways of life; so that the more efficient the national economy became the greater was the danger that the different regions would draw apart. The resentment and suspicion likely to ensue was increased by the operation of these forces within a democratic society. Merchants, financiers, and manufacturers had the most demands to make on government and had able spokesmen and direct access to the centers of power; yet they failed at the point where decision rested with the people or their representatives; Southern planters complained of waning influence but secure political bases and long experience gave them effective leverage in national affairs; small farmers and entrepreneurs across the country could decide politics at the grass roots but suspected that events at the center were settled by Southern gentry, by Northern businessmen, or by politicians subservient to one or the other. Thus tremendous economic advances fostered social differentiation and regional tension that political action seemed incapable of resolving.

A young nation depended upon others for many things. Manufactures and capital still had to come, for the most part, from external sources, and there was a danger that economic advantages would increase this dependence. Great Britain had a long start in the modernization of industry and was able to supply goods of higher quality and at a cheaper price than American industry. The huge capital required for the development of American resources could only be drawn from the money markets of Europe and particularly of London. It was the good fortune of America to discover, early in the century, an export crop which was itself harnessed to industrial growth and provided the foreign earnings to finance imports and borrowing. Cotton production and export played a vital role in American development, and it is difficult to see how expansion could have been financed without it. Cotton was produced in the Lower South, the trade was largely in the hands of New York and Boston merchants, and the whole process from production to market was financed by Northern bankers. The inflow of earnings from cotton sales provided the lifeblood for this whole complex of economic activities and kept the nerve centers of economic life in good health. At a later stage western wheat would come to play a similar and complementary function in American economic growth, but until the midcentury cotton was essential and unrivaled.

The importance of cotton in the development of Southern civilization was incalculable. The profits of cotton grown on fresh land acted as a magnet drawing settlement to the central uplands of Georgia and Alabama, to the southern Mississippi valley, and on into Texas. Much cotton was grown on small farms, but it was preeminently a crop for large-scale commercial production, provided that labor could be found for hard, monotonous, and disciplined work. Thus the expansion of cotton ensured that the dominant social pattern of the Old South—large plantations and slave labor—would spread to the New South, and areas that might have become the stronghold of a Jeffersonian yeomanry came under the control of a ruling capitalist gentry.

It is too large a generalization to say that the rise of cotton saved slavery from extinction. The hope that slavery would wither away with the advance of civilization was never founded on solid calculations, and the mass of Southern landowners clung fiercely to the institution however much some of their leaders might deplore it. Slavery met one of the basic requirements of commercial agriculture in a country with abundant land. Free labor would not remain tied to the plantations when an empty continent beckoned; labor had to be forced, or there would be no labor at all. Once the pattern of plantation and slavery was set, other powerful forces were brought into play. The plantation was the support for an upper class dependent upon slaves both for field work and domestic service, and planter gentry could not dispense with slaves without sacrificing their whole way of life. At the same time the presence of the black people introduced a racial tension which affected all whites whatever their social status. The white majority was unanimous in agreeing that Negroes were inferior and potentially dangerous, while slavery recognized this inferiority and settled the question of status. Few Southerners could contemplate a situation in which the Negro would be free and might press for equality. Violence, race war, ethnic amalgamation, and the debasement of white civilization were seen as the alternatives to slavery.

Southerners were mildly disturbed by the end of slavery in the Northern states, but they could console themselves with the thought that this was the result of expediency rather than conviction and that an agreement upon white supremacy remained as one of the bonds of union. It was not until the crisis produced in 1820 by the admission of Missouri as a slave state that Southerners realized the extent of Northern hostility to slavery. They realized that Northern objections were based upon fear of the effects of slavery on white society, rather than upon philanthropy, but this did not improve matters. The opposition by a Northern majority to the expansion of slavery towards the West was justified by the belief that the class structure, and social habits, of a slave society were incompatible with the spirit of American civilization. The Northern people wanted neither slaves nor slave-owners in the West. Land monopoly had been largely eliminated in the old Northwest, no class of large landowners had been allowed to develop, and the same kind of equalitarian society should extend to the West, providing a land of promise for the poor of the East and of Europe. This line of argument was alarming to the Southern gentry, for it implied condemnation not only of their labor system but also of their social role. If the Northern majority had their way, the Southern gentleman, who sought new opportunities and new land, would be forced to degrade himself to the status of a small farmer, while the ambitious yeoman would be denied the promise of achievement in a new land. The success of self-made planters in the cotton South could never be repeated if the transportation of slave labor were forbidden.

The Southern gentry dominated their states: they were educated when the mass of the whites were ignorant; they had leisure when small homesteads demanded continuous toil; and they monopolized public office. The law, the press, and business were either dominated by or dependent upon the planters. The ownership of land and slaves became the one certain ladder upward to this superior status. There was sometimes opposition to class rule among the more numerous non-slaveholders or small slaveholders, but their objectives were usually limited and local. In national debate the voice of the south was that of the planter gentry, motivated by the strongest possible social and economic interests to defend slavery and trained by law and custom to detect the implications of any development that might threaten the institution.

The Southern leaders did not all speak with one voice because their fundamental agreement to defend slavery could be expressed in several different ways. Southern Whigs worked upon the national community of interest and relied upon their social and economic affinity with the economic leaders in Northern society. Their support of Henry Clay's nationalism recognized that a society of primary producers, with weak commercial and industrial institutions, would benefit immeasurably by association with a more diversified society which was growing in mercantile skill and manufacturing proficiency. The United States formed a free trade area, and specialization of function was its natural pattern of development; but government power could legitimately be used to foster growth by providing stable monetary conditions, financial aid for selected improvements, and protection for industries. If Southern Whigs were not enamored of high or prohibitive tariffs, they were prepared to support moderate protection as part of a national program. Southern Democrats had an equal faith in national harmony but thought that this could be best advanced by allowing different occupations and different regions to pursue their own interest, and to adjust themselves to existing conditions, without federal interference. The selection of any particular activity or region for aid would create dissension without improving upon the consequences of unassisted enterprise, but if the case for public aid were clear, Democrats would prefer to see it provided by the state than by the Federal Government. Equally opposed to the enlargement of federal power, but far more rigid in their attitudes, were the states' rights men who flourished in South Carolina and were an active minority in other states. Many of them adopted nullification, and talked seriously about the prospects of secession. But whereas the objection of orthodox Jacksonians to federal activity was based upon dislike of taxation, suspicion of distant government, and faith in local enterprise, the nullifiers and states' rights men thought mainly of the implication of enlarged federal power for the slave-owning class. If an outright attack upon slavery was improbable there were many other ways in which Federal policy might be influenced by the antislavery stance of a majority. It followed that the interests of the slave owners depended upon drawing a firm line between federal and state responsibilities and then keeping it intact.

It was to be the tragedy of the South that the view of the nullifiers eventually triumphed. A minority of large planters, who happened to be in an economically vulnerable position, would prevail over the larger number of Whig planters, who believed in a national community of interest, and over the Democrats resting upon the numerical support of small farmers and committed to both limited government and Jacksonian nationalism. The presence of slaves, and all the attendant problems of a biracial society, provided Southerners with a common bond which proved stronger than the many differences between them and distinguished them from other Americans.

The truth of this generalization can be tested by examining relations between the Northeast and the nonslaveholding West. There seemed to be many reasons for tension between the Atlantic seaboard and the new Western "colonies of settlement." Despite the favorable conditions for political evolution, there was bound to be a period during which the new settlers resented both their remote situation and the attempts of Eastern capitalists to control their development. Expanding agricultural regions, much dependent upon credit for the exploitation of new land, were hardest hit in the financial panics of 1819 and 1837, and recovery was impeded both by the demands of old creditors and by the refusal of Eastern bankers to sanction new loans. Local banks were often eager to lend, but if they did so neither the Bank of the United States nor the great private bankers of New York and Philadelphia were likely to honor their notes. Differences in manners between rough Westerners and urbane Easterners demonstrated their apparent incompatibility and increased their distrust of each other.

A good deal of this resentment found political outlets, first in Jacksonian democracy, and then in the Harrison Whig movement of 1840. These political developments provided the Westerners with the sense of participation upon equal terms and lessened the friction between less developed and more developed regions. Like the South, the West divided between the two great parties, but both accepted the facts of nationalism and there was no hint of Western nullification or separatism.

This drawing together of West and East despite tension was partly the consequence of Western devotion to the ideals of an expanding society. The original pioneer might have gone west to escape, but escape could only be made good by success as a commercial farmer. Success depended upon communications, credit, markets, and the development of whole regions, and though Westerners might resent their loss of independence, their material aspirations easily justified their welcome to the instruments of capitalism. They might distinguish between the unnecessary intervention of distant "money power" and the useful activities of local merchants, but in time the differences were blurred and the old Northwest became the ideal environment for businessmen, big and small. The separatism of the West was extinguished when its dominant groups had the clearest possible reasons for cooperation with representatives of the older East, who could alone supply the means for sustained growth.

These economic bonds of union might have been broken if the West had had, like the South, strong sociological and emotional reasons for regarding themselves as a distinct people. In fact it was not only the merchant culture of the East that spread into the old Northwest, but also its educational, intellectual, and religious influence. If the initial result of western movement was the rejection of the older culture, this phase was of short duration; as soon as a community existed there were sure to be some men (or often some women) who would work to transplant both the superficial refinement and the deeper literary and religious elements of Eastern life. By the midcentury, the American from New England or the Mid-Atlantic States, who traveled in what had now become the Mid-West, found himself in an environment which was different yet familiar. There were the same ponderous but active businessmen, the same Ladies' Literary Societies, similar schools, colleges modeling themselves upon Eastern universities, religious denominations carrying familiar names, and pulpit utterances which were indistinguishable from those heard at home.

By contrast a Northerner who traveled to the South found much that was unfamiliar and unattractive. His journey south was marked by the progressive elimination of what was known and valued. Southern society, with its privileged classes and its masses of ignorant poor, its claim to superior culture and its economic backwardness, its contrast between great houses and small farms which lacked most amenities of comfortable Northern life, was strange, inexplicable, and disturbing. The forces of change that were transforming the North made it more difficult every year for the two sections to understand each other. Slavery was the most obvious symptom and perhaps the cause of these differences, and the changing climate of Northern opinion made slavery appear not only archaic but also immoral.

The development of the West destroyed the idea that the destinies of the country rested in the hands of an elite of either birth or breeding and helped to create a new synthesis which would be recognized as middle-class liberalism on both sides of the Atlantic. This great, diffuse tide of opinion, sentiment, idealism, and materialism never achieved the coherence of a philosophy but was nevertheless the greatest of all the forces concerned with the making of the modern world. Its characteristics were a passionate belief in freedom combined with a conviction that the protection of life and property was the primary function of the law. Western experience emphasized equal opportunity, but also respect for unequal achievement; it brought out the importance of the community, but awarded the highest prestige to triumphant individualism. It accepted toleration of diversity in religion and politics, but was fiercely intolerant of any who strayed beyond the limits fixed by dominant opinion. Mormons were persecuted; Utopian communities were barely tolerated; Roman Catholics were viewed with suspicion and hostility; but any variant form of Protestantism was readily accepted and won willing converts. This new synthesis of liberal values never included a clear definition of the role of government. Initially folk memories of the parson and the squire dictated a suspicion of any authority that was not controlled by popular vote, but this could easily be transmuted into a demand that government should actively promote development. This positive attitude toward political functions was, however, seen more in small projects than in the adoption of Hamiltonian precepts. Laissez faire as a code of economic behavior was largely the discovery of theorists; the natural evolution was rather toward a pragmatic attitude that placed development first and adopted any means at hand. There was, however, a significant shift away from the Jeffersonian belief that the best government was that which governed least, to the assumption that government under democratic control could be beneficial. There was a change—a shift rather than a transformation—from seeing the democratic process as a defense against power to accepting power as the agent of democratic aspiration. Another Jeffersonian precept lived on with increased vigor: the pursuit of happiness had become more than just a right; it now summarized the purpose of society.

For many Americans "happiness" was an ethical concept, and material achievement was the complement not the converse of moral blessedness. Many of the best minds were concerned with religion; so was much popular endeavor. The evangelical revival moved on both sides of the Atlantic; the American experience both imitated and stimulated the British revival of religion, and in both countries religion became a dominant force in nineteenth-century civilization. The focus of attention upon the enthusiasm and bizarre character of early nineteenth-century revivals has obscured the more solid achievements of the further revivals between 1850 and 1858. The first period of revival was vigorous but often sporadic in its effect: The second made Christian ethics the concern of the great mass of churchgoers in the Northern states. An increased participation of pious laymen in church leadership tended to emphasize the secular consequences of Christian belief, and the old debate on the duty of Christians to save souls or to improve society was renewed with more and more ministers stressing the duty of organizing society on Christian principles. Individual salvation could not be separated from the duty of bearing witness against evil, and to an increasing extent evil was seen in social as well as in individual manifestations.

The old Calvinist doctrine of predestination, which made men powerless over their own destiny, was more and more diluted, while another strain in the Puritan heritage—the duty of men to create a society in which the Godly could live—came to the fore. The strict orthodoxy of Princeton was declining in influence, Harvard was largely under Unitarian control, and liberal theology emanated from the Union Theological Seminary of New York and from Oberlin College (to name only the most influential centers). The new revivals borrowed the highly emotional methods of Charles Grandison Finney (who had drawn conservative censure in an earlier generation), but they flourished not in thinly populated rural areas and small towns but in the cities and old settled areas of the East. The ferment worked from the core of Northern civilization toward the periphery, not as a frontier aberration, but as a powerful thrust in the centers of intellect and population.

On the political duty of Christian men the most active leaders of Protestantism were divided. Should they speak to the heart, and trust that the diffusion of true Christianity would destroy evil? Or should they identify the evils of which they spoke, condemn individuals and groups, and identify themselves with the cause of reform? Should they lead, or confine themselves to blessing those who did? The problem was perplexing, with American distrust of political churches on the one hand, and the impatience of men who recognized evil and believed lack of will prevented its defeat on the other. Stimulated by religious revival American effort and charity flowed in many channels, into home missions and foreign missions, Bible societies, temperance societies, societies for the reclamation of fallen women, and societies for the accomplishment of every kind of good work. Many of these benevolent societies were under lay leadership, but they expected aid from ministers and their congregations and drew the Churches into active participation in movements for social reform. Amid all these crusading efforts, could slavery escape condemnation? And what then would be the attitude of Church leaders to an attack upon an institution so stoutly defended by their Southern brethren?

The forces of change moving in American society imposed a growing strain upon the political system. The Federal Union had developed with two assumptions: that differences between the states existed and would continue to exist, but that common purposes could nevertheless be served by a single government. It supposed that the interests and loyalties of men could be divided, and that once the custom had been established men would make a separation in their minds that reflected the federal structure of the country. This dualism was the prerequisite of harmony, and most Americans continued to cling to it. The rights of states and the rights of the Union should not, they believed, be opposed but complementary. Just as an individual accepted a distinction between what he might want and what he was allowed to have by law, so could he distinguish between his rights as the citizen of a state and of the Union. The federal man was, in a sense, an artificial man, because he was required to live under and reconcile two sets of man-made laws separated by man-made boundaries; but so far the federal man had been a real man and the model of good citizenship.

The forces of change were accentuating differences and blurring distinctions. It was becoming increasingly difficult to honor the traditions and beliefs of the society to which one belonged, while respecting those of other societies, and recognizing their right to obstruct what one wanted to do in the Union. The limitations imposed by the Union on freedom of action became the more irksome as the differences assumed the character of moral convictions. Interests might recognize the need for adjustment and compromise, but moral precepts demanded judgment upon those who did not observe them, and sooner or later judgment would demand action. The revered Constitution continued to be regarded by most citizens as the arbiter of all disputes; but the Constitution could not decide moral questions, because it had not been designed to do so. The Constitution had been designed as a political mechanism to enable Americans to live in Union, not as a court of appeal on profound questions about the moral character of society. When statesmen, or even judges, used Constitutional logic for a purpose for which it was not intended, their decisions would have as little ultimate authority as those of policemen trying to settle theological disputes. Changes in American society were bringing to the surface questions that could not be decided by political authority.

The real question was, therefore, whether American democracy could evolve new processes to meet the new situation. It was not enough to make the best of what one had, because innovation was essential. In this situation American democracy suffered from the handicap of its own virtues. Just because it had been, and in most respects still was, the most advanced form of political society, change was difficult to contemplate. How could one improve upon the best? Other countries based on a revolutionary experience have experienced similar difficulties, and nothing is harder to alter than traditions which have been preserved as a nation's claim to greatness. This is not to repeat the facile argument that a rigid Constitution prevented political evolution; in practice the Constitution has proved to be very flexible whenever the consensus of opinion has wanted it to be so. The real difficulty was not institutional but intellectual rigidity. By the middle years of the century the American nation was in the dangerous condition of a country in which social change had outrun the capacity of its people to carry out political change. Old techniques were being used when nothing but rapid adaptation could have averted a breakdown.

Territorial expansion in the 1840's produced the first major challenge to established patterns of political behavior. The annexation of Texas was carried out against a vigorous opposition critical of the way in which it was done and opposed to the acquisition of new slave territory. What was involved was not merely the acquisition of a comparatively small area under Texan control but also the vast boundary claims of Texas which included vast areas that the Texans had never controlled and carried slavery into the heart of the undeveloped West. The division in the country went far deeper than arguments over tariffs, banks, or federal aid for internal improvements; what emerged was not debate over means and methods but fundamental questions of national identity and purpose.

Still more divisive was the war against Mexico in 1846. President Polk's attempt to present the war as one of self-defense deceived no one. Supporters of the war agreed with Polk that war was necessary to open the road for western expansion and to the Pacific coast; opponents saw it as an aggressive war engineered in defiance of American traditions. Deliberate war against a peaceful neighbor was the kind of policy pursued by old despotic nations but not by republican countries. Opposition to the war of 1812 had been confined to comparatively small groups and was frankly based upon economic grievances; opposition to the Mexican war raised disturbing questions about the whole direction and inspiration of American policy. For many the Mexican war was not inexpedient but disgraceful, because it seemed to be based on crude calculations of national advantage. The Americans became a divided people as they had never been before. It is true that a referendum on the war would probably have produced a majority in support of it, but the appeal to popular emotions in order to beat down reasoned opposition was as shocking to the older generation as the war itself. The spirit of the federal Constitution called for consensus through debate, not the enforcement of one set of opinions at the expense of others.

Argument over the war was necessarily entangled with the question of slavery. Some men opposed the war primarily because they saw it as the instrument of slave expansion. Others (Like John C. Calhoun) opposed it because they believed that acquisitions from Mexico would produce an eventual majority of states opposed to slavery. Others, again, supported the war, but demanded that the new West must be secured for small settlers, not for great planters using slave labor. The war was barely three months old when one of the latter, David Wilmot of Pennsylvania, proposed (in the famous Proviso which he sought to attach to an appropriation bill) that slavery should be prohibited in all lands acquired from Mexico. If popular support justified the war, the will of the majority might keep slavery within the bounds where it existed by state law. The Proviso was passed by the free state majority in the House several times; each time it was defeated in the Senate where a few Northern senators voted with the solid block of Southern votes. Once more what was at stake was the character of national existence. Should slavery follow the flag? Should the United States stand before the world as a nation which employed policy and force to establish the institution by the acquisition of new Territories? Should the lives and taxes of men who disliked slavery be expended in order to extend its realm? On the other hand, the South might ask whether slavery, recognized by law and regarded as the basis of Southern society, should be condemned by the mere accident that a majority of people happened to live in free states. For wealthy Southerners the theoretical aspect of the question had the deepest significance, for they were unlikely to risk their fortunes in the arid West and had already ample room for expansion into Texas; they resented the antislavery attack and feared the eventual implications of a growing number of free states carved out of the West. But the question also united rich and poor in the South, for the most likely Southern migrants to the West were poor men who hoped to repeat the success of self-made men in the cotton belt. Resentment of moral attacks, fears for future political security, and barriers to the aspirations of the poor drove Southerners together in self-conscious hostility to the North.

By 1850 the impact of these fundamental issues had brought the Union to the verge of dissolution. Calhoun, who had foreseen the divisions and sought to avert them, now insisted that the South must make new conditions for remaining in the Union. As the tide was setting towards an antislavery majority in both Houses of Congress—and the first step would be taken if California were admitted to give free states a majority of one—the South must seek new guarantees to restore the equilibrium. Calhoun believed that the political mechanism set up by the Constitution had already broken down, and further development along familiar lines would destroy the Union by dividing it irrevocably. To meet this danger Calhoun evolved the theory of the numerical majority and the concurrent majority: for him the essence of federalism was its rejection of simple majority rule and its acceptance of the idea that sovereign power could not be exercised without the consent of both national and local majorities. The mechanics of the concurrent majority were hardly made clear by the dying Calhoun in 1850, but his posthumous *Disquisition on Government* (combined with evidence of his earlier ideas) suggests that he envisaged nullification as one foundation of the federal arch and a dual executive as the other. There should be two Presidents, elected respectively by the free states and the slave states, each with a veto over Congressional bills and executive measures, and thus able to protect state nullification from federal force. It is idle to speculate upon how this constitution would have worked; the important fact is that Calhoun, somewhat ahead of his time, saw that the Constitution as it was could not work when the nation was divided upon fundamentals. The process of decision which had been good enough in the past was no longer effective; either the Union would dissolve or the process must be altered.

Meanwhile other men had been seeking for a solution within the accepted framework of American political life. In 1848 Lewis Cass, soon to be the Democratic candidate for President, suggested what was subsequently known as "popular sovereignty." Cass argued that Congress had no power to prohibit slavery in Territories of the United States because it was unconstitutional to deprive men of property recognized by the law of states; but what Congress could not do, the people of Territories could do for themselves (or refuse to do). The correct policy was to stop arguing over the rights of Congress, or the authority of national majorities, and think instead of the rights and powers of local majorities. No one denied the rights of people in their states to sustain or abolish slavery, and surely the same principle should be extended to citizens in Territories. This attempt to use the democratic principle of self-government as a solvent for the corrosive acid of slavery, had superficial attractions and disastrous consequences. The denial of the right of Congress to exercise sovereign rights over Territories destroyed whatever hope an antislavery majority might have of containing the institution within its existing boundaries. Theoretically slavery could be defeated by free settlers, but the stakes were too great to risk an early take-over by proslavery elements. From the northern boundary of Missouri to the Rio Grande the new West was bordered by slave states which were in the best position to occupy and settle the new Territories that would be formed. "Popular sovereignty" offended, at one end of the political spectrum, those who wanted to see the West as a white man's country, and at the other the strong antislavery men who wanted an explicit condemnation of human bondage. It was equally unsatisfactory to the strong proslavery men who sought a recognition that slavery was a national institution entitled to all the protection and support that the Federal Government would give to any other interest of any other citizens.

The immediate consequences of the attempt by Cass to use democratic principles to bridge the division in American society were a split in his party, the emergence of a Free Soil party, and the victory in 1848 of the Whigs under General Zachary Taylor. It was a curious election: Cass of Michigan was branded as the advance agent of slave expansion; Zachary Taylor of Louisiana was supported with equal enthusiasm by Southern planters and Northern antislavery Whigs; while ex-President Martin Van Buren of New York, once known as the Northern man with Southern principles, was the nominee of radical Democrats, abolitionists, and Whigs who could not support Taylor.

Much neglected by historians, Van Buren's Free Soil Party (or rather the party that was forced upon a somewhat reluctant candidate) was an important symbol of the new era.

Heterogeneous in social composition and political antecedents, the Free Soilers joined together with tremendous enthusiasm. Adopting a splendid slogan—"Free Soil, free speech, free labor, and free men"—they found common ground in opposing the extension of slavery and drew together elements of middle-class liberalism which had hitherto been separated by party barriers. In 1848 the Free Soil Party was organized without sufficient central direction and too late to do more than defeat Cass and hand victory to the Whigs. It failed to detach many antislavery men from the Whig party and won over only radical Easterners from the Democrats. Nevertheless, it rehearsed the events of 1854 when a new and dynamic Republican party would absorb Free Soil, gather in more allies, and move forward to win a national majority on a sectional base. Free Soil, and its Republican heir, were not, however, merely new versions of old-style party alliances; for both, the cement of party was an ideological commitment to change society and to bring evil—as they understood it—under control.

At this point it is appropriate to ask how and why the democratic machinery of American life was failing. Fundamental questions were being asked, but a political system should be able to draw upon reserves to meet such a challenge. If the American people were becoming divided, they still retained common political institutions and shared many beliefs about the nature of political society. Why did the comparatively few (though important) issues that divided them prevail over deeply felt loyalties and pride in national achievement?

The basic units of American democracy were rural constituencies, often isolated from each other, and populated by people whose views seldom extended beyond their township or county. This isolation was more marked in the South because in the North society was more mobile (both geographically and in economic achievement) and better educated; but in both sections a politician depended upon his success in satisfying constituents whose views were both strong and limited. There was an obvious temptation to choose the local view, which would win support, rather than a national view that was beyond the range of local comprehension. Local electors were often suspicious of a representative who spent too much time in debating national questions and hostile to anyone who seemed to be assimilating himself in to a national elite. Thus it has been argued that democracy magnified differences, undermined authoritative leadership, and discredited the kind of wisdom that could stand above local prejudice. In place of steady and accommodating leaders, the people preferred appeals to emotion and intransigent postures.*

Sophisticated explanations can be facile, and this analysis is supported by hypothesis rather than by evidence. Rural constituencies displayed a strong sense of order. In the South they often returned the same representatives election after election and did not desert them when they became absorbed into the Congressional elite. Northern constituencies showed a more rapid turnover of representatives, but no particular affection for extremists. What most of them wanted were adept men who could serve their local interests. If local conflicts were turbulent, the product was stable; there were frequent changes in the faces sent to Congress, but considerable consistency in the type of man elected. The idea that Northern politicians "exploited" antislavery emotions is absurd, for there were few districts in which abolitionism won votes. North and South, and in both parties, the leaders in the states had every incentive to play down the emotive issues that could complicate the game of politics. Finally, the regions where antislavery was popular were among the most stable in the Northern states and tended to produce the same kind of continuity in representation as was common in the South.

The Senate was more remote from constituency pressures than the House, and the longer tenure and the success of many senators from both sections in winning second, third, or more terms, did produce a national political elite. It was a smaller assembly, and even men who were opposed in politics established working agreements on the conduct of business. Indeed, if this had not been so, the unlimited opportunities for obstruction in a House which refused to curb debate would have brought legislation to a standstill. Yet in spite of this stability and mutual agreement on the rules of the game, the Senate was as sharply divided by slavery as the more volatile House. Even in the House the real control of affairs devolved upon a group of old hands, who survived election after election and organized the conduct of business. The majority party naturally guided affairs, but the minority leaders learned to accommodate and to oppose without disruption. In both houses the controlling party groups were drawn from North and South.

After 1846 this political elite was breaking up, but it is impossible to demonstrate that this was caused by democracy in the constituencies. The disruptive force was the emergence of questions that could not be settled by the normal rules of politics. It has already been shown that the annexation of Texas and the war with Mexico began this process

---

* The argument in this paragraph refers particularly to an essay by David Donald called "An Excess of Democracy," reprinted in his *Lincoln Reconsidered* (New York, 1956).

of disintegration because important issues were settled without waiting for a consensus to emerge, and rightly or wrongly, the initiative in forcing through these momentous questions was attributed to the slave interest. The fundamental problem was the character of the nation, and this was imposed upon the political system, not generated by it.

In 1850 the old leadership in Congress, and especially in the Senate, made a gallant effort to restore the spirit of accommodation and consensus. Henry Clay stepped into the breach to settle the disturbing questions that had been generated by territorial expansion; he was joined by his old Whig rival, Daniel Webster, and by Cass, the Democrat. Prominent also in the move for compromise was the rising star of western Democracy, Stephen A. Douglas. Insisting upon the admission of California with a free soil constitution, drawing upon "popular sovereignty" to evade the need for congressional legislation on slavery, and adjusting the Texas boundary in return for a cash payment, the compromisers claimed to have taken slavery out of politics. To disarm the abolitionists at one point of their attack, they abolished the slave trade in the District of Columbia. To win Southern support for a settlement that gave free states a majority in the Senate, they recognized a national obligation to protect slavery, where it existed under state law, by passing a stringent act for the recovery of fugitive slaves from free states. The Compromise was hailed as a national victory and accepted by majorities in both sections. In 1852 the Democrat, Franklin Pierce, who stood firmly on the compromise, won a resounding victory over Winfield Scott who equivocated. If 1848 had shown the dangers of politics based on ideas rather than interests, 1852 seemed to restore national harmony and to repair the damage done to the mechanism of politics.

These omens were deceptive. If the Democratic elite had united to forget free soil and ignore slavery, the Whig elite had been broken forever. The new leadership was faced with the task of governing the country without a stable opposition, and with a considerable body of opinion convinced that their policy was not only inexpedient but also immoral. In 1854 Douglas tried to push the principle of popular sovereignty still further by applying it north of the Missouri Compromise line, where slavery had been prohibited since 1820. The case for organizing civil government in Kansas and Nebraska was clear, and it was equally clear that Southern support was necessary to pass the necessary acts. The opening of the new Territories to slavery, if approved by the people, was the price paid for Southern support, and, using their bargaining power, Southerners went farther and obtained the repeal of the Missouri Compromise.

On this issue the Free Soil alliance of 1848 revived. Stimulated by spontaneous protest movements in the Mid-West, and now recruited by many Northern Whigs who had previously stuck to the old party, the new Republican party won immediate success. Here at last was a political movement that had shaken free of anchors in the slave system; here was the channel through which middle-class liberalism could flow unchecked. Long throttled by the need for sectional harmony, the idealists and entrepreneurs, wild abolitionist agitators and moderate free-soilers, intellectuals and politicians in search of a cause could now unite. The disruption, which had begun with Texas, was now complete; the national political elite was dissolved to be replaced by groups opposing and favoring the expansion of slavery and facing each other across an unbridgeable chasm. The dialogue that had taken place between two opposed but national parties was no longer possible, and leadership rested with men who had ceased to talk the same political language.

These were the forces that drove men on to 1861, but they still operated within the framework of a revered Constitution. This had a profound effect upon the development of the struggle, dictated the terms of the argument, and explained the hopes and fears of the age. In the long perspective one can see that the Constitution created a tension that is usually described as nationalism against sectionalism. A more instructive way of understanding is to see the tension existing between national and local democracy. The constitutional checks upon the states left the local majority with the ultimate decision on most matters concerning the states; but all the constitutional checks upon the national majority still left open the possibility that this majority must, in the long run, control both the Federal Government and the states. The formal recognition of this was in the right to amend the Constitution vested in two-thirds of each house of Congress and three-quarters of the states; in practice this raised long-term expectations and fears, while providing for infinite delays. The form of the Constitution stimulated both a horror of what Calhoun called "the numerical majority" and the impatience of that majority in the face of imponderable obstacles.

This analysis can explain the intensity of the forces concentrated upon points where the Constitution provided no immediate mandate for either the national or the local majority. The problem of the Territories could only be brought within the letter of the Constitution by deduction and tenuous argument. Nor could the conventions of the Constitution provide much guidance: if anything, they favored the idea that Congress had power to prohibit slavery in the Territories; but it was not difficult to argue in the opposite sense if one was already convinced, and in 1857 a majority of the Supreme Court did just this in the notorious case of *Dred Scott v. Sandford*, when that portion of the Missouri Compromise Act which prohibited slavery north of 36 degrees

30 minutes was declared unconstitutional. The Act itself had already been repealed as a part of the price demanded by Southerners for their support of the ill-fated Kansas Act in 1854; but it was one thing for Congress to repeal an Act which it had previously passed and quite another for the Supreme Court to declare that the Act had always been unconstitutional. The decision was technically unnecessary (because, in an earlier part of the decision, the Court had found reasons for refusing jurisdiction), and was based upon tenuous reasoning. Where the meaning of the Constitution was in doubt it might have been assumed that the majority in Congress had the right to decide. The claim of the Court to make what was, in essence, a political decision, constituted another attempt to curb the power of the national majority.

The Supreme Court's attempt to solve a great political controversy by the use of constitutional logic was, however, only the most striking example of a habit that had become endemic in American political discourse. Appeals to the Constitution were a staple element in political controversy and provided an escape from the real nature of the crisis. The heart of the dispute was the claim of a sectional minority to do what the national majority deemed to be wrong and to use the law and Constitution to that end. In 1858 Abraham Lincoln, still a comparatively obscure lawyer politician from Illinois, defined the nature of this crisis in the most famous speech of the epoch:

> We are now far into the fifth year since a policy was initiated with the avowed object and confident promise of putting an end to slavery agitation. Under the operation of that policy, that agitation has not only not ceased, but has constantly augmented. In my opinion, it will not cease until a crisis shall have been reached and passed. 'A house divided against itself cannot stand.' I believe this Government cannot endure permanently half slave and half free. I do not expect the Union to be dissolved—I do not expect the house to fall—but I do expect it will cease to be divided. It will become all one thing, or all the other.

The clarity of the analysis was ominous, and it was remembered in the South when Lincoln obtained the Republican presidential nomination in 1860.

Lincoln's victory in the Presidential election expressed in dramatic form the conflict that had developed. Lincoln won on a minority vote, but with a large majority in the Electoral College. None of his electoral votes, and very few of his popular votes, came from slave states. The opposition was divided between two rival Democrats and a constitutional Union candidate; but the large majority of votes from the Lower South had gone to Breckinridge, the states' rights Democrat. Lincoln was to be President, elected in full accordance with the Constitution;

yet it was an election which the Lower South could not accept. Southerners, who had gained so much by appealing to the protection of the Constitution, now found the machinery of the Constitution turned against them. Turning from the letter of the Constitution to its spirit, they claimed the right to secede from the Union. Yet there was much in the secessionist case that must command respect if not agreement.

Was the Union indissoluble? And if so, when had it become so? Even if the Union was indissoluble in law (which was doubtful) common sense might insist that no political association could claim an authority which could deny the validity of a decision, by millions of citizens, to withdraw themselves from its jurisdiction. Lincoln's argument that, as President, he had no option but to enforce the law flew in the face of reality just as much as the Supreme Court's attempt to settle political controversy by constitutional logic. The Lower South had ceased to be a part of the Union; thus, the law of the United States could not be enforced. While it might be argued (as it had been by Jackson in the Nullification crisis) that no one state had a legal right to refuse obedience to federal laws, the case was altered when seven states, forming a geographical and political unity, claimed independence. The issue remained confused so long as the Union Government faced the new Confederacy across the still uncertain states of the Upper South. It became clear when Lincoln called for arms to suppress rebellion, and Virginia (followed by North Carolina, Tennessee, and Arkansas) responded by joining the Confederacy. It was no longer the legal right to secede that was in debate, but the right to preserve the Union by force. Many Virginians had believed that secession in the Lower South was rash, unnecessary, and inexpedient; but it was a different matter to say that Americans had no right to make mistakes when they acted in their states as a political people. Union by consent had been the glory of the Americans, but Union by coercion was a danger which threatened self-government everywhere. Force was a greater violation of the spirit of the Constitution than secession and took one back to the assertion of the Declaration of Independence that when a people become convinced that their government is hostile to their interests, "it is their right, it is their duty, to throw off such Government, and to provide new Guards for their future security."

Yet the balance of judgment cannot rest there. The majority of Americans had rights as well as the minority; that majority had decided that slavery should not grow, and it was this decision that prompted secession. It had been the hope of earlier generations that slavery would wither away, but the forces of change of the nineteenth century, which had brought anti-slavery to birth, had also strengthened slavery in its home. By 1860 slavery showed no signs of withering away, and even in Kentucky—most open of the slave states to antislavery influences—a modest proposal for very gradual emancipation backed by Henry Clay, the great patriarch of Kentucky politics, had been ignominiously rejected in 1849. In retrospect it can be seen that the best hope for the South and for the nation would have been a frank recognition that slavery was doomed and an adjustment of habits of life accordingly; yet what happened—in defiance of the trend in every other part of the civilized world—was a growing conviction that slavery was permanent and beneficial.

By 1860 the ideas of the proslavery South and of Northern Republicanism were too far apart for reconciliation, and the real failure lay much further back in time. At some point the slow process of democratic debate had been halted, and discussion of slavery became impossible in the South. Once this stage was reached the logic of the situation compelled Southerners to resent its discussion anywhere in the Union. The American Republic had been constructed on the assumption that differences between the states did exist, and would continue to exist, but that the flow of debate at the center and throughout the Union would dispense with the need for conflict. The differences were compatible with universal acceptance of a common political philosophy and allegiance to a Union embodying that philosophy. If government derived its just powers from the consent of the governed, consent could only be found out by open debate. When the slave-owning South refused to debate a question of fundamental importance, a prerequisite of democratic government was destroyed. This breakdown of democracy produced the Civil War.

CHAPTER VIII

CONFLICT

The effect of the Civil War was incalculable; it extended to every aspect of American life, and it altered everything it touched. For many the outbreak of war was evidence of failure. The high hopes of the Great Experiment were at an end: the Constitution had failed, leadership had failed, democracy had failed. These conclusions were proclaimed publicly abroad and privately at home. Perhaps despair was most evident in the border states where, in spite of slavery, there had been a ready acceptance of the ideals of American progress and a deep attachment to the Union. Here too were the sharpest divisions of opinion; Unionists had defended their position successfully against the secessionist challenge until April 1861, and not only states and districts but even families were divided. Yet the outbreak of hostilities was a tremendously exciting event and in the moment of failure the most articulate Americans looked forward to a new and brighter prospect which would follow upon victory.

The most articulate and convinced were the avowed secessionists of the Lower South who saw the consummation of a dream they had long nourished. An independent South would be free to make its own way in the world, to retain slavery, to ride the crest of cotton prosperity, and perhaps to expand its influence if not its dominion over Central America and the Caribbean. Freed from the nationalizing tendencies of a political and economic system based on the North, freed, too, from the necessity of listening to Northern criticism of their domestic institutions, and able to deal directly with foreign friends instead of through Northern intermediaries, the independent South would take a proud and progressive place among the family of nations. The real prospects of a rural society, with great inequalities in the distribution of wealth, poor education, few industries, backward communications, and an obsolete labor system, were hardly reckoned. Secessionist ardor saw the future through the eyes of an established upper class with little concern for the hard facts of life in a competitive world. Nevertheless there was ardor and enthusiasm in the ideal of independence, and many Europeans equated the struggle of the South with that of Italians or Hungarians against foreign rule.

Yet even in the Lower South hope was not unclouded. There remained devoted Unionists—some among the wealthy and others in remote country regions—and a larger number who admitted the right to secede but questioned its expediency. Some of these reluctant secessionists reconciled allegiance to their states with doubts about the wisdom of secession by claiming that Southern independence was a temporary prelude to a restored Union in which the grievances of the South would be recognized and remedied. None of these variants upon the secessionist theme had any influence upon the course of events, and men who took the first step by accepting disunion were forced to support the cause until the bitter end four years later. If it is possible to discover evidence of this unhappy dilemma among a small number of the articulate upper class, the feelings of the mass of the Southern white population remain unrecorded. Accustomed to follow the lead of the gentry these people were unlikely to break with the habits of a lifetime, and loyalty to the new Confederacy seemed to be built upon rock. Only in a few isolated areas did Unionism persist, and nothing could conjure into life the old loyalty despite the hope of many Northerners that it still lay beneath the surface of society. Like other wars the conflict would demonstrate the power of a dedicated minority to persuade the mass of the people that their cause was just, that sacrifice was the path of nobility, and that the God of Battles would not fail to smile upon His people.

In the Upper South the majority decision for war was taken in a more sober spirit. The first statement of the case for Southern independence had failed, but the determination of the Union government to use force succeeded where secessionist rhetoric had failed. Deep-rooted convictions, tenaciously held since the beginning of national existence, forced thousands of Southerners who loved the Union to resist when it came, armed and demanding submission. Did not the rights of states include the right to secede? Men of the Upper South who had condemned secession as folly could not countenance the denial of a right which they held as fundamental to the idea of Union. A Union that no one was allowed to leave was incompatible with their notion of federalism; a government which would fight to prevent a sovereign state from seceding, when the political means of reconciliation had failed, was not the Union as they had understood it. In a world that has suffered so much from great states, the view of the Upper South may command much sympathy, but it was not one that could be expounded with the same exuberance as the unfettered enthusiasm for independence. The Upper South would contribute its full share—and perhaps more than its share—to the cause of Southern independence; but many of them continued to hope that Southern victory would lead to a reconstitution of the Union (perhaps with the exclusion of the trouble-making New England States).

In the North the initial response to the crisis was a simple re-iteration of Andrew Jackson's famous toast, "Our Federal Union—it must be preserved." Whatever the theoretical distribution of power between Washington and the states, most Northerners had come to see the Union as a whole which was greater than any of its parts. The theory expressed by Lincoln was echoed and endorsed a thousand times: the states had never been independent but colonies of Britain and then states of the Union, and even if state sovereignty held the shadow of reality for states of the Revolution, it had no existence for those of more recent creation. Not everyone agreed with every act of the Union Government at every time, but no political society could survive if minorities were allowed to destroy the government as soon as it displeased them. Once people had joined together in a political association they accepted an obligation to all the other people in it. Interests had grown up, ways of life had been formed, associations had been forged, mutual advantages had multiplied; no minority could claim the right to destroy this web of benefits when a turn of fortune's wheel had given them temporary ascendancy in their states, or given their rivals a constitutional victory at Washington.

This line of argument assumed that secession was the result of a conspiracy formed by a comparatively small number of the ruling slave owners. Before the outbreak of fighting, Northern calculations (even perhaps the calculations of Lincoln) were influenced by the belief that if only the conspiracy could be broken, the mass of the Southern people would gladly resume their loyalty to the Union. After the fighting began it was logically necessary to continue and to reinforce this belief, because a war to preserve the Union could hardly be carried on if victory would be followed by the continued coercion of unwilling citizens. It had to be assumed that defeat of what was called the slaveholders' rebellion would be welcomed by the mass of the Southern people.

This logic hardened Northern resolution but also engendered a curiously limited view of the war. It must change nothing so that when loyal Southerners returned from the wilderness they would find again the Union which they had loved. Both houses of Congress had already approved, by the necessary two-thirds, an amendment to the Constitution declaring that Congress had no power over slavery where it existed by state law; and but for the war this might well have been ratified by a constitutional majority (three-quarters) of the states. The Crittenden-Johnson Resolution of 1861 (accepted almost unanimously in Congress) asserted that the sole purpose of the war was to preserve the Union.* "The Constitution as it is, the Union as it was," became the rallying cry of the very large number of people who feared the storms raised by war as much as they deplored the secession that had precipitated it.

Lincoln had great sympathy with this view and endorsed it with emphasis when the occasion arose. Yet Lincoln himself introduced into

---

* Some conservative Democrats in the House abstained on the first part of the resolution, which blamed the war on the secessionists; some Radical Republicans abstained on the second part which declared that the sole war aim was the restoration of the Union.

the debate new concepts that altered the balance of the argument. In his message to Congress on July 4, 1861, he argued at length against the case that secession was a legal remedy, and for viewing it as a rebellion by individuals and a blow against principles of democracy. It was a basic assumption of any democratic society that disagreements must be settled by majority vote within a constitutional system. "There could be no appeal from ballots to bullets," but it followed also that those who had won on the ballot had a right to use bullets if their decision was opposed. A majority could not do anything it liked, but it could insist that a constitutional decision must be respected. If this right were denied then democracy was at an end; any minority, any individuals, could claim the power to know what was best, irrespective of what the majority might think. Democracy was in peril, and this did not seem fanciful in 1861. Democracy had suffered a major reverse in France and had only a tenuous footing in the German states, the known will of the people was ignored throughout great parts of the Austro-Hungarian Empire, Turkish despotism ruled much of Eastern Europe, and even in England a majority of the adult male population were still denied the vote. The United States was the only true democracy in the world, and there its efficacy was under trial.

Democracy was, in Lincoln's view, an improving government "whose leading object is to elevate the condition of men—to lift artificial weights from all shoulders—to clear the paths of laudable pursuit for all—to afford all an unfettered start, and a fair chance, in the race of life." If this was the character of democratic government, could improvement be halted for the duration of a war? Indeed the voluntary absence from Washington of so many Southerners, who had been regarded as the principal foes of improvement, increased the possibilities of reform. Slavery had stood like a lion in the path, and many concluded that war was a God-given opportunity to destroy the menace once and for all. For what better purpose could victory be used? For antislavery men the need to maintain "the Constitution as it is" was a very inadequate argument against action, and for the first time since the Revolution a demanding reform movement possessed the means for attaining its objectives.

From the outset some Northerners saw the purpose of the conflict in this light. War was a scourge, but a scourge of God humbling iniquity and laying open the road to the Kingdom of Heaven. He was a jealous God, yet also a God whose merciful Providence would save His people through chosen agents and prophets.

He has sounded forth the trumpet that shall never call retreat;
He is sifting out the hearts of men before His judgement seat;

Oh! be swift my soul to answer Him, be jubilant my feet!
Our God is marching on.*

In a hundred ways this Messianic vision colored popular views
of the war, but the men called to the task of redemption were not
cloistered saints but hard-headed politicians, generals who had to find
the secret of victory, and old abolitionists who bore the scars of many
an antislavery battle. Not everyone was moved by biblical rhetoric, but
all could draw upon funds of emotion and belief that had been stored
up through the years.

The determination to make war the occasion for moral regenera-
tion blended with the secular drive for a humane and rational society.
The rationalist reformers, attacking privilege and condemning incom-
petence, had never had so strong a hold in America as they had had in
England, but their influence was abroad. Stanton, Lincoln's Secretary
of War, was not popular in America, but in England he would have
been readily recognized as a Utilitarian reformer, determined to impose
efficiency upon an untidy society. Charles Sumner often seemed
absurdly self-righteous to Americans, but in England he was readily
accepted as a moralist in public life. At one end of the reform
spectrum were businessmen, who might be little moved by antislavery
idealism but who were anxious to get things done and to establish
sensible policies now that Congress was no longer encumbered with
slow-moving Southern agriculturalists. At the other end were old abolitionists, who saw the war as a crusade against slavery and all its
resulting evils.

The winning of the war had to take priority, but the war itself
became an argument for a drastic change. Lincoln's attitude toward
slavery illustrated the point. It is probable that Lincoln hoped from the
start that the war would bring about the end of slavery; but he could
not say so. There were slave states in the Union with secessionist
minorities that made their allegiance doubtful. There was the deep-
seated conviction among Northern Democrats that the war should not
alter the Constitution, which had always protected slavery in the states.
Also, there was the unpopularity of Negroes among the white masses
of the North who had no intention either of fighting a "niggers' war"
or of accepting racial equality in their own neighborhoods. These
factors made it politically impossible for Lincoln to move quickly
against slavery and forced him to subscribe to the thesis that the only
purpose of the war was to preserve the Union. So indeed it was; but
the restored Union would not be the Union as it was. Throughout 1862

---

* From "The Battle Hymn of the Republic," written in 1862 by Julia Ward Howe to
the tune of "John Brown's Body."

Lincoln was pondering whether war needs justified an attack upon slavery; he issued a preliminary emancipation proclamation as soon as the military situation allowed a glimmer of hope, and a definitive Proclamation abolishing slavery in the Confederacy on January 1, 1863. Emancipation rested upon the questionable legality of an Executive Proclamation under the war power and did not affect slaves in loyal states or even in Confederate areas already occupied by Federal troops, and doubts about its permanency explain later doubts among antislavery Republicans about Lincoln's intentions. But with all its limitations, the Proclamation made abolition a war aim of the North in the eyes of most Northern people.

After some hesitation and setbacks Congress passed the Thirteenth Amendment, making slavery unconstitutional, in the early months of 1865. Thus the exigencies of war were used to justify a great social revolution, an unprecedented exercise of executive authority, and an enlargement of federal power. The Federal Government accepted a new responsibility and, for the first time, national government had intervened to regulate the condition of people in their states.

Men who looked for an early end to slavery realized that this made urgent the problem of Negro status in a free society. Abolitionists had been accused of ignoring this question in the past, and of offering no solution to the vexed problem of race relations. The point has often been echoed by historians. Abolitionists had replied that there was no point in trying to elevate Negroes anywhere so long as slavery degraded them everywhere. The approaching end of slavery made this argument obsolete, and many old Abolitionists turned their attention to the new problems of equality in a biracial society. On the national stage they pressed successfully for the employment of Negro troops and kept a watchful eye over the interests of the Negro soldier. Locally they campaigned, with varying success, against segregation in public places and vehicles. They even touched, with rather less success, upon segregation in education, and pressed with practically no success, for Negro suffrage. Indeed there was hardly an item in the twentieth-century struggle for civil rights that was not already rehearsed during the war years.

Intellectuals, particularly those who had learned their antislavery from William Lloyd Garrison, were sometimes disturbed by the way in which slavery was abolished. Garrison's language against slaveholders had been violent, but he had always worked for the conversion of minds, not for reform under coercion. Though his antislavery propaganda passed the bounds of decency (and almost of sanity), a sound instinct told him that voluntary abolition was the safe method and that reform achieved by force would leave behind it a sea of troubles. Emerson had made the same point in more Olympian language. John Brown's raid had put antislavery men of this school in a dilemma. Should they condone the use of force, and welcome the possibility of a slave rebellion that would, in the South, inevitably be a savage war against the whites? It was not John Brown's action but his failure and subsequent execution which solved this dilemma. Defeated, condemned, and executed, John Brown was no longer a man who had brought the sword, but a martyr who had given his life for the oppressed children of God. Abolitionists everywhere rushed to celebrate his heroism while avoiding the necessity of justifying the means he employed. John Brown was seen as a Christian prophet. Emerson delivered a notable oration in his honor, and his soul went marching on with the Union armies.

From this it was a short step to see force as the instrument of reform and this conclusion was aided by the belief that secessionists had invited retribution by their rebellion. It was no longer a question of using force to achieve reform but one of resisting those whose avowed intention was to establish evil. Even so, some example of voluntary emancipation would have been widely welcomed and commended everywhere to those true Southerners who were supposed to be laboring unwillingly under the Secessionist yoke. Lincoln hoped manfully for some action in the loyal slave states and would have been ready to press Congress for compensation schemes that would have made the pill of abolition easier to swallow. In the event only one slave state, Maryland, voted to end slavery and that by a tiny majority. In all the other Union slave states abolition had to await the ratification of the Thirteenth Amendment and came as an unwelcome measure that had been resisted and condemned in advance. War had brought with it an increase of national power which would be used against friend and foe alike, but for the first time many reflective and humane men saw authority as the friend, not the enemy, of freedom.

In the more mundane matters of economic policy and administrative improvisation the same trend was evident. The old Whig advocacy of national policies bore fruit in a protective tariff and a national banking act. Unwillingly, but under the financial strain of war, the Federal Government became responsible for a paper currency that derived its value from national authority, not gold. Wartime exigencies forced the adoption of more and more administrative agencies and federal responsibilities; Lincoln has the reputation of a careless administrator, but his Presidency saw the real beginning of "big government" in the United States. The handful of clerks and the easygoing departmental routine, which had sufficed before the war, were no longer adequate, and by 1865 the Federal Government displayed the power, the efficiency, and also the drawbacks of modern bureaucracy.

Even in the South the same tendencies were present. Everyone in the South, including even the old Southern Whigs, entered the war with the conviction that government ought to be decentralized, that governmental activity was itself a symptom of danger, and that if positive action had to be taken in any social field it was the exclusive responsibility of the states. Some Southerners, especially in Georgia and including her most eminent son, Vice-President Alexander Stephens, continued to act upon these premises to the great embarrassment of the Confederate Government. In spite of this, Jefferson Davis's administration was forced to accept and to implement wide responsibilities. The difference was that in the South this growth in the authority of the central government was accepted as an evil consequence of war which would cease with peace; in the North powerful interests, both ideological and economic, learned from the experience that the world might be changed.

Apart from the quarrel over states' rights, and a good deal of niggling criticism of Jefferson Davis, the South was free of dissension and displayed remarkable unity in defense of independence. Former Unionists either remained impotent or made their peace with the Secessionists, accepted the decision of their states as binding, and stressed the duty of resisting federal aggression. This was the attitude of the two most eminent prewar Unionists, Alexander Stephens and Robert E. Lee. Others who could not honestly accept secession retired into obscurity and hoped to ride out the storm. If some active supporters of secession hoped privately that the result would not be independence but a Union restored on Southern terms, they kept their counsel to themselves. In any case, the bulk of Southern Unionists were poor men in remote districts, who had neither the education nor the opportunity for articulate opposition. Thus the South fought as a unit and began to develop the characteristics of a nation, until defeat, poor equipment, and the loss of hope cooled down the initial enthusiasm. Even then the dissenters made no public case but simply deserted from the armies or quietly withdrew civilian aid. The public face of the Confederacy remained unclouded by doubt or self-criticism and gave no evidence of the drastic decline of morale away from the fighting front.

Things were very different in the Union states. Maryland was in a condition of secessionist rebellion in 1861 and was held to the Union only by some high-handed federal actions. Kentucky was uncertain, Missouri was divided by civil war. In the great Eastern cities the war was always unpopular with large numbers of vocal people. There was a continuous undertone of protest in Philadelphia, and the city was virtually paralyzed by internal dissension in 1863 when Southern victory at Gettysburg might have brought Lee's troops into the Quaker city. New York was torn in the same year by terrible riots against the draft. Southern sympathizers, or "copperheads," were particularly strong in the Southern parts of Ohio, Indiana, and Illinois, and there was always the danger of local rebellions that would disrupt federal communications or even take states out of the war. There was a fairly close correlation between Southern sympathies and anti-Negro feeling. The New York draft riots produced despicable mob violence against Negroes; popular hostility to the war in Philadelphia was coupled with opposition to all efforts aimed at improving the status of the free Negroes in the city; throughout the Mid-West the most popular theme of antiwar orators was that of "the white man's country." Emancipation raised to a new height of endeavor the campaign against the war and against the "usurpations" of the national government. Thus the experience of war strengthened both nationalism and suspicion of nationalism; but whereas the former claimed to embody the humane and reforming spirit of the age, the latter played upon the old yearning for local self-government and exploited fears of Negro equality.

It is necessary to stress these dissensions to dispel the myth of a united people or the abolitionist hope of a nation moving steadily forward to accept the ideals of racial equality; yet it is also necessary to record that a large majority of the Northern people did support the war, did accept conscription as essential, and did welcome the end of slavery. During the war opinion in the North had to travel a vast distance from the limited aims of 1861 to the exigencies of total war, acceptance of a great social revolution, and new views of national responsibility. What was done was far more remarkable than dissent and protest, which never achieved more than local significance. Moreover the changes were accomplished in a truly democratic fashion: the North was, of course, deluged by pro-Union and anti-Southern propaganda, but the people had every opportunity to say what they thought, the democratic processes were not suspended, and twice during the course of the war, in 1862 and 1864, the purposes and policies of the war were put to the test in national elections and the issues were argued in numerous state elections. Thus the record vindicates Lincoln's claim that, on the part of the Union, it was a people's war.

Critics of the war, the "copperheads," were not all disloyal, and few of them wished for Southern independence. They were Peace Democrats who believed in the Union, but maintained that an honorable peace could be had by negotiation. If the Peace Democrats had been able to establish contact with Southern Unionists (with whom they had much in common), they might have had something to show for their efforts, but their hopes were dashed by Southern solidarity and they were strongest in the first half of 1863 when the South had the best chance of outright victory and was least likely to settle for anything short of independence. Even so, Democrats fought the election of 1864 on the platform that the war had failed and should be ended by negotiation, though General McLellan, their candidate, repudiated disunion. A favorable turn in Northern military fortunes brought Lincoln and his party a landslide victory, but the Democrats still collected a great many votes. Internal dissension came uncomfortably close to ruining the cause of the Union, and the Negro would have been the sacrificial victim in any ritual of white reconciliation.

Southern solidarity seemed an enormous advantage, while Northern divisions came near to destroying the will to fight. Yet in the event it was Southern morale that cracked and Northern morale that held firm. This may cause one to look beneath the surface and to ask whether controversy is necessarily a weakness or whether the assurance of the South was really a symptom of strength.

Southerners entered the war with an enthusiasm for independence; but was independence alone an adequate war aim? The white people of the South were offered no promise of a better life; an independent South would still be a society in which wealth was concentrated in a few hands, economic opportunities severely limited, education wretched compared with the North and West, living standards low, disease endemic, and malnutrition a way of life. The absence of public debate in the South meant that no one was forced to translate the vague promises of progress after independence into concrete proposals. Indeed an examination of these promises will quickly reveal that they were concerned with the romantic ambitions of a restless upper class rather than with anything so material as living standards or wider distribution of wealth. At the same time the experience had taken many of them out of rural isolation and had weakened some of the conventions of traditional society; war made no revolutionaries, but it raised many questions. Before the end many Southerners had come to believe that they were fighting a rich man's war, but the effect was to weaken morale and induce apathy rather than to encourage constructive political action. The South, which had once been so fertile in political thought, emerged from war without a single new idea about the organization of society.

Things were different in the North, where open debate and continued argument forced men to define their aims and to demonstrate that Union victory would bring a better society. For the most part the argument was conducted in moral terms, but it was a morality which happened to fit well with the material aspirations of the age. Indeed it was often difficult to separate the two, particularly in a society that assumed a close connection between moral probity and practical success. Was the tariff, which would enable the manufacturer to sell more and so to increase the wealth of his community, to be condemned for making profits or praised as a social benefaction? Individual ambitions were not incompatible with the interests of the community in which they lived, and the spokesmen for emerging society offered land for the settler, profits for the manufacturer, high wages for skilled men, high prices for farmers, improved communications for remote regions, splendid opportunities for small entrepreneurs, and a stable banking system for established businessmen. The picture was not without shadows—some of which were seen at the time—but the composite picture was that of a new society, coming into being, sustained by and sustaining the progressive forces of the age.

Most Republicans identified themselves with these progressive forces, just as the Gladstonian liberals (combining very similar social and intellectual ingredients) saw themselves riding in the vanguard of progress against privilege, inefficiency, and the unenlightened past. Within the Republican party a group of Radicals epitomized this spirit and carried its precepts to logical conclusions and, so far as lay in their power, into action. They gained great influence in Congress, but their power derived neither from numbers nor from organization, but from their position (on most questions connected with the war) slightly in advance of more moderate Republicans but separated from them by no political or emotional chasm. The Radicals were not isolated men, but representative men.

The Radicals formed an interesting, much abused, and unusual group in American history. Most of them came from good antislavery backgrounds, though a few came from the border states and were primarily inspired by hatred of the old slave-owning ruling class. They had no formal organization apart from their position in the Republican party; yet they acted together with great political consistency. They maintained this coherence for about seven years, and during that time had the unusual experience—for an American party or faction—of seeing all their major policies carried into effect. They were able to do this so long as the Southern Democrats were excluded from Congress, first by secession and then, during Reconstruction, by a policy of exclusion. In other words their success showed what could happen when the sectional balance was destroyed and when a group of determined and politically inspired men were able to break through the conventional barriers of the political system. Only the impact of the New Dealers in and after 1933 can be compared to that of the Radicals. Among their major achievements was the abolition of slavery, the Fourteenth Amendment giving national protection to civil rights, and the Fifteenth Amendment giving the suffrage to Negroes. Through their agency the Constitution was fundamentally changed, the balance of responsibility between nation and states was permanently altered, and the legal foundations of a biracial society were laid. Yet these things could never have been achieved if the Radical case had not been put in such a way that it had compelling force for moderate, cautious, or confused men.

The Radicals played an essential role in the war; from the start they were committed to total victory and prepared to work at the hard drudgery of politics. Often regarded outside Congress as rash and irresponsible, inside they were the workhorses who applied themselves to committees, were always on the watch, and were not above the political arts of intrigue. Their attacks upon generals, and upon members of the Government who were suspected of something less than whole-hearted commitment to victory and abolition, frequently irritated and embarrassed Lincoln. But Lincoln never parted company with them, and to the day of his death he trod along the path laid down by the Radicals. Whether he would have followed them into the thickets of Reconstruction policy has always been a moot question.

In retrospect Lincoln has every attribute required of a war leader, except perhaps a liking for war. He was politically sensitive without ever losing sight of major objectives. He was slow to decide but adhered to decisions once made. After some initial blunders with military men who were as unused as he to great responsibilities, Lincoln established a working relationship with his generals, and especially with Grant, which provides a case-book study of civilian leadership in war. This book must, however, be concerned less with Lincoln's personality and achievements than with his permanent effect upon the Presidency. Since Andrew Jackson left the White House in 1837 no President had touched the public imagination, and though Polk had been determined, his strength had been displayed behind the scenes and in a peculiarly narrow way. For four years Lincoln was a national personality and everyone knew where the decision lay. This did not mean that he was universally popular; he was attacked for executive tyranny and for political ineptitude; he was the target of attacks from Peace Democrats and the principal object of Radical impatience. He was more popular with soldiers in remote camps than he ever was with civilians in or out of his own party. Deification came only after his assassination. Yet even the most unfair attacks confirmed Lincoln's place at the center of the stage, and the key role of the President in giving expression and direction to national policies became explicit.

In a sense it was a strange outcome. The Republican party inherited the Whig tradition of Congressional rather than Presidential government, and Lincoln's inexperience with national politics seemed certain to relegate him to a subordinate role in a national capital dominated by men who had grown grey in the public service. If Lincoln had been granted peace he might have served out a relatively uneventful term, while history was made elsewhere. It was the war power—the authority of the commander-in-chief—which gave Lincoln his unique place as director of a nation's destiny. This was a power which, by its very nature, only one man could wield. It substituted the civilian concept of checks and balances for the military pattern of personal responsibility and a strictly observed chain of command. In administration also Lincoln presided over a growing and complex organization of which he was the acknowledged and exclusive head. In these two important ways the President escaped from the net which the Constitution had woven around his office. The accretion of Presidential power was greater and more durable than under Jackson. The authority of Andrew Jackson had been exercised with negative purpose; he added nothing to national power, and the federal administration was left as weak or perhaps weaker than at his accession to the White House. Lincoln by proclamation called men to arms, suspended habeas corpus, and emancipated slaves; under the war power he directed great armies; during his Presidency the federal service grew from a small, slow moving group of secretaries and clerks to the dimensions of modern government. His example was not followed by his successors, nor did the circumstances warrant such executive power, but the record remained and provided the model for a later generation of Presidential giants.

The force of war flowed into every part of American democracy. Following Lincoln many Union men had seen it as a war for democracy, but the democracy they won was different from that which they had known. Democracy now allied with nationalism where it had once allied with local autonomy. It proclaimed that a political union was indissoluble, where earlier generations had thought that the right of men to choose their own government was the bedrock of freedom. Democracy had accepted executive authority and big government where fear of all authority, and a belief that the best government was that which governed least, had been the guidelines of democratic action. Democracy had joined with the dynamic forces of industrial capitalism in a country where the independent farmer had been regarded as the natural defender of individual rights. The great surge forward, released by war, gathered up abolitionism and was prepared to agree that Negroes also had inalienable rights.

These great changes were clothed in the emotions of war. Constitutional doctrine had been settled on the battlefield, and the strongest of all arguments was that the dead must not be betrayed. For the survivors the war remained an experience that had changed their lives; it could not be eradicated, and the fact of sacrifice would remain long after the arguments that preceded the conflict were lost in oblivion. For years to come loyalty to the ideals of the Union would remain as the great touchstone of Northern politics. In the South the effects were as profound and more tragic. The cause was lost but not repudiated. Unlike the Germans after 1945 the Confederates were not prepared to turn their backs upon their leaders or their past. Renewed allegiance was necessary; a change of heart was not. Indeed, in the aftermath of defeat, it was the failing morale, the errors, and the frustrations that were forgotten. If many Southerners still believed that the original act of secession had been a grievous mistake, they held their peace; if some went still further back and condemned slavery, they were not prepared to give emancipation more than a sour welcome. The Old South became purer gold as the years passed, and her leaders were all uniquely heroic. Conversely the postwar generation came to the simple belief that all the evil in the world was made by the Yankee.*

The paralysis of thought which had permeated the South during the war, continued after it had ended. Obsessed by the tragic destruction of a happy past, Southerners had no taste for formulating ideas about the future. Only one thing stood out: the need to preserve as much as possible despite defeat and the Northerners' laws. Other peoples have been stirred by defeat to great efforts of recovery and have profited by the destruction of the old to build a new society. The tragedy of the South was that no new impulse was generated, and even when economic recovery came it was clothed in the half-defensive, half-arrogant imagery of the Old South. A century after the war was over, the war still lived in the Southern mind as a terrible wrong that must be revenged but never could be revenged.

At the heart of the social problem was the status of the freed Negro. He had not made the war, though many regarded him as its principal cause. In the South, few Negroes had ever been anything but servants and menial laborers (the craftsmen, preachers, and free men of property were too few to make much difference), and they came to freedom without land or education. In the North they lived under a heavy load of discrimination and were everywhere regarded as inferior beings, but their service in the Union army added moral obligation to the abolitionist plea that they should be allowed to better themselves. In the South, freed Negroes were expected to perform the same functions as they had when slaves; their presence in towns was deplored (except as domestic servants), their hope for education was derided, and attempts to choose work or bargain for wages were treated as gross

---

* It has been argued, correctly I believe, that the Southern leaders of the Reconstruction period were not original secessionists but former Whigs who had opposed secession. But these men had rallied to the cause of Southern independence, and had led the Confederacy after taking over control of the movement from the original secessionists.

insubordination. Southern democracy was hedged round with notices that read "For white men only," and if Negroes were free, Southerners expected them to accept their "natural" place as working men whose rights and comforts depended upon the goodwill of their superiors. Southerners proclaimed that they knew the Negroes (which was true), and that they intended to act fairly by them (which was also true, though only for Negroes who kept in the place which white society designed for them). Negro aspirations were not recognized, and every obstacle would be placed in the way of their recognition. Yet within two years after the end of the war white Southerners were compelled to accept Negroes as voters, legislators, and equal citizens. The shock was one from which white Southern society would not recover.

The war had begun in a predominantly rural, loosely organized society; it was conducted at the outset from offices which looked like the premises of small country lawyers. It began with Union leaders promising to guarantee slavery where it existed under state law; it had been initiated by buoyant enthusiasts of the Lower South and by Northerners who expected little more than a police action. No one had wanted the war; all had hoped to achieve their objectives without war, but the war came, and when it ended the world was changed.

CHAPTER IX

NATIONALISM AND RACE

In the aftermath of war the word "nation" sprang to life. In earlier years it had been little used, but now made frequent appearance in political discourse. If friends of the Confederacy had equated its struggle with that of subject nationalities in Europe, supporters of the Union had compared their fight to the contemporary drive for German unification and to earlier victories in other European countries over the forces of separatism. In the argument which became most familiar the United States had always formed a nation, but many aspects of nationalism had been smothered by slavery and lain dormant until released by Southern defeat. The government of a nation must be able to speak and act for the nation, but this had been impossible so long as every wish of the majority was obstructed by a minority. The way was now clear for the American nation to become what it ought to be.

The nation was one and indivisible. It had a government capable of acting on its behalf; it need no longer hesitate once the will of the majority had been declared. Nationalism was conceived in moral rather than material terms; in the antislavery analysis the power to do right had been prevented in earlier days, and this power was now unencumbered. Yet moral idealism did not make it easier to define loyalty to this invigorated nation, for how could one demand universal loyalty to moral precepts which were not universally accepted? The abstract question became of immediate relevance when one had to ask whether men in the defeated South were "loyal" to the Union. Was loyalty a formal act of submission to the United States, or did it imply a change of heart and new concepts of social justice?

In a sense this dilemma had always existed. The United States had no focus for loyalty beyond the Revolutionary tradition and the ideas it inspired; but revolutionary ideas made a disturbing nucleus for national sentiment. There had been conflict between the universality of rights proclaimed by the Revolution and the protection of minority interests, and this tension had been a root of conflict; but now Union victory seemed to have ended the dilemma by removing all obstacles to the ideals of the Revolution. Inalienable rights, consent as the basis for authority, and the equality of all men could shine forth as the controlling principles of national destiny. Allegiance to these principles would be the characteristic of American loyalty.

Even in the North these elevated concepts of nationalism were challenged. Appeals to national power could be readily interpreted as a mandate for Republicans to reconstruct the Union as they saw fit and for old abolitionists to assume the mantle of authority. Yet the war for the Union had been fought by Democrats as well as by Republicans, by supporters of states' rights as well as by strong nationalists, by men who believed in white supremacy as well as by abolitionists. The vote of confidence given by the electorate to Lincoln in 1864 endorsed emancipation and the pursuit of victory without conditions, but many who voted the Union ticket did not mean that the balance between states and Federal Government should be permanently altered, that the national government should assume new moral purposes, or that new concepts of loyalty should be introduced.

In 1865 these difficulties were temporarily submerged; secession had been defeated and this was the key to future harmony. Imagination could hardly grasp that the difficulties of the Union preserved might be as formidable as those of the Union dissolved. The rhetoric of nationalism was carried forward on the euphoria of victory, and dissenting voices were stilled; but the testing time was near. It was easy to talk of national power in elevated terms, but, in the period following the war, national power had a specific and incredibly difficult task to perform: it had to decide the future of the South.

In 1865 the Northern triumph was complete. No Southern armies remained, no civil governments existed in the Southern states except with the consent of the Federal victors. The theoretical consequence of war was to deny that secession could ever be used with impunity; secession was revolution and would be treated as such by any American government. With secession went the ultimate sanction against the National Government and the national majority. Constitutional restraints upon authority still existed, but in the long run the national majority would decide how authority should be used. This political result of war was dramatically illustrated in the defeated South: here the Federal Government and Federal troops provided the only authority capable of carrying on the basic functions of government; and behind this authority lay the elected representatives in a Congress from which Southerners had excluded themselves by secession. Defeat had turned the Confederate States into dependencies, and their future lay entirely in the hands of the Federal Government. It was to be the apparent good fortune of the South to find the component parts of this Government divided among themselves but perhaps, in the long run, this would prove to be a misfortune for all Americans.

No one can ever know what Lincoln planned, for his assassination came before he had shown his hand. It is known that during the war he had tried to form local governments, in states occupied by Federal troops, as soon as ten per cent of the adult male population were prepared to take oaths of allegiance to the Union. But governments based on a collaborating minority were unlikely to have much future when Federal troops were withdrawn. Lincoln may have hoped that enough secret Unionists would emerge to make the ten-per-cent governments viable, but if this might possibly happen in Louisiana (and had happened in sadly-divided Tennessee under the iron governorship of Andrew Johnson), it was unlikely to provide a solution in the Lower

South or in proud Virginia. It is known that Lincoln resisted the congressional plan of reconstruction (the Wade-Davis Bill of 1864) which would have required a majority of loyal voters before a government could be formed; but it is not known how he would have acted when the end of war brought a flood of former Confederates ready to take a formal oath of allegiance. It is known that he urged the government he had recognized in Louisiana to give the vote to Negroes, who were qualified by property, education, or service in the Union armies; but his real thoughts when this advice was rejected can never be known. In the last speech before his assassination he clung to the idea that it was possible to build upon the loyalist governments in Louisiana, Tennessee, and Arkansas, but he made some comments that could be read as pressure on these states to act quickly on the question of Negro civil rights. In any case these states were only a small part of the South, which lay broken and unreconciled under military rule.

The responsibility of power could not be abdicated, it could only be exercised. The question was not whether the victorious North would order affairs in the South, but how. The Union was restored, but decisions of the victorious authority would determine what kind of Union it would be.

Acceptance of emancipation was a necessary condition of settlement. In the North even those who had opposed abolition now accepted the fact that slavery could not and should not be restored. Northern Democrats had attacked Lincoln's proclamation as an unwarranted exercise of executive authority; they had opposed the Thirteenth Amendment because it ruptured the spirit of the Constitution by overriding the rights of states to regulate their domestic institutions; but a fact accomplished was different from an act contemplated. Some resistance remained to ratifying the Thirteenth Amendment, but it was doomed to be ineffective, and it was almost taken for granted that Southern acceptance of abolition would be a prime condition of their restoration of the Union. But antislavery opinion in the North was not likely to be content with emancipation as a mere formality. It was necessary to recognize and to treat Negroes as free men with the rights of citizens. If the South failed to do this, only a further exercise of federal authority could secure the desired result. A great social revolution had been implemented by Northern arms, and there was a moral commitment to see that the revolution was not betrayed.

There was more than this in the situation. For four years Northern opinion had been educated to believe that the Southern ruling class had been not only the architects of secession but also the enemies of democratic society. The restoration of this class to power in the South would resurrect a force that had imperiled democracy and the Union, and would do so again. Even Lincoln, bent on reconciliation, had assumed that the Confederate leaders must be excluded, for a time at least, from public office. The Radicals thought of excluding more and for a longer period. The awkward question was who, under these conditions, would govern the South: Unionists who were in a small minority; the army; or former Confederates ready to accept the situation by taking an oath of allegiance? The first could not govern without the support of federal troops, the second was undisguised military rule, while the third would mean the restoration of the old ruling class whose overthrow had been acclaimed as one of the fruits of victory. A Radical minority within the Republican party looked at the logic of the situation and concluded that the only solution was to keep the Southern states in territorial status until such time as Northern influence and the changes wrought by war had changed the character of the South. The Radical leader, Thaddeus Stevens—an unattractive personality and a great congressional tactician—was an uncompromising enemy of the Southern ruling class and his vindictiveness condemned him in the eyes of many subsequent historians; it is only in recent years that he has won respect for his uncompromising advocacy of racial equality. Charles Sumner, whose name is often coupled with that of Stevens as the leader of congressional radicalism, was in some ways a more typical representative of antislavery idealism, but he lacked Stevens's mastery of the art of politics or his practical capacity for extracting the most out of any situation. The Radical phalanx in Congress was a strangely mixed group, comprising New Englanders who had grown old in the antislavery cause, Pennsylvanians who combined radicalism with the interests of small industrial entrepreneurs, a few mid-Westerners (especially from the Western Reserve which had been a great antislavery stronghold of prewar days), border state radicals who were more interested in eliminating the power of the old planter class than in Negro rights, and a contingent from the Western states (including Ignatius Donnelly the later Populist leader) for whom the issue was a clear cut need to impose democracy upon the South and to defend the Union against its enemies. On Negro suffrage, which was to become a vital issue, they were not at first united; Sumner would admit no delay, Stevens was prepared to play a waiting game, many in the rank and file had serious doubts. More moderate Republicans were confused and cautious, and many came ultimately to support Negro suffrage less as a measure of racial justice than as the only means of ensuring a core of reliable Unionists in Southern politics and voters devoted to their party in marginal Northern constituencies.

Moderate Republicans did not accept the Stevens plan of treating the Southern states as territories for an indefinite period, and they sought for ways of restoring the former Confederate States to the

Union without sacrificing the gains of the war. It was largely through the skill of Thaddeus Stevens that they came to believe their objectives could not be achieved without drastic measures. If the Southern states were to be readmitted to the Union, and if one could look forward to the day when restored Southerners and former Peace Democrats would renew their prewar alliance and acquire an ascendancy in Congress, it was necessary to amend the Constitution so that the fruits of victory would be placed beyond the reach of ordinary legislative action. The Thirteenth Amendment abolishing slavery was well on the way to ratification, but further amendments would be necessary to guarantee Negro citizenship and legal rights, prevent the leaders of secession from recovering power, safeguard the national debt against repudiation, and prevent payment of the Confederate debt. In 1865 the most effective argument for new amendments however, was the realization that the Constitution as it stood would give the South increased congressional representation as the former slaves would count as full members of the population for the legislative apportionment. As slaves they had counted for three-fifths of a man, and it was calculated that emancipation would give the South about twenty additional members on account of Negroes to whom they would give no voting rights. Here then were clear arguments for doing something, but no one had a clear idea of what form the action should take.

The situation was vastly complicated by the assassination of Lincoln and the succession to the Presidency of Andrew Johnson. It is quite probable that Lincoln would have moved towards the kind of settlement that came to be embodied in the Fourteenth Amendment. It is difficult to believe that he would have left the status of former slaves to be settled by their former masters, or have allowed the South to receive increased representation on account of nonvoting slaves, or accepted with equanimity the wholesale restoration of the Southern ruling class to power. If Lincoln saw reconciliation as the major task of peace, he was not insensitive to the views of the Republicans who had elected him; his successor was a somewhat old-fashioned, and exceedingly obstinate, Jacksonian Democrat from a border state who had little in common with Northern Republicans.

Johnson was identified with the small white farmers of the South, and it was to them, not to the planter gentry, that he intended to commit power. Possibly he was misled by his own success in building up a Union strength on this basis in Tennessee; but Tennessee was exceptional in possessing a large and politically conscious small-farmer class. He accepted emancipation, but as a means of undermining the economic ascendancy of the upper class rather than as a step towards racial equality. Indeed, Johnson was fully representative of his class and region in believing that America was a white man's country;

unlike some he was ready to give Negroes a fair deal, but only as inferior beings whose best hope lay in white goodwill. Johnson intended to hand over the South to the white majority and free Negroes would have to accept the place to which the white majority assigned them.

President Johnson's plan of Reconstruction was straightforward on paper. In the summer and fall of 1865 he permitted states in which a majority of voters were prepared to take an oath of allegiance to elect conventions, set up constitutions, choose assemblies and provisional governments, and offer themselves for readmission to the Union. His wish to deprive the old ruling class of their former monopoly of public office was clearly indicated when he added, to the list of persons not covered by the general amnesty, all with property in excess of $20,000 who had supported the rebellion. Unfortunately the plan was betrayed by events. The old ruling class captured the conventions and were elected to the new legislatures, executive office, and Congress. What emerged was not a new South with a new social and political structure, but the Old South restored. In many cases Johnson was driven to choose between rejecting the electors' choice and giving personal pardons to the disqualified persons who were elected. At the same time the provisional governments showed their intention of setting up a legal framework that would recognize the Negroes' freedom while confirming their inferiority. Johnson's Reconstruction produced precisely the result that most Republicans feared: a confirmation of the political ascendancy of the old ruling class and (for them) an evident intent to deprive the former slaves of the benefits of freedom.

This is not the place to recount the tangled politics of the Reconstruction era; it is enough to emphasize those aspects which had decided consequences for the evolution of democracy. The first thing to note is that in one important aspect Reconstruction proved to be a constitutional dead end. Thanks to the absence from Congress of the Southern states and to the very large Republican majority returned in the election of 1864, Congress was able to approach the Parliamentary style of government. The familiar tactics by which organized minorities can block majority decisions could not operate because the Northern Democrats were so few and so uncertain of themselves, and a broad measure of agreement among Republicans (with the exception of a handful of conservatives and Administration supporters) provided a most unusual party solidarity. With President and Congress at loggerheads it was necessary to pass all the important Reconstruction measures over the Presidential veto, and there has been no other occasion on which it has been possible to pass measure after measure, by a two-thirds majority in both houses of Congress, over a period of four years.

A logical development from this situation might have been the subordination of the executive to the legislature, and the Republican majority moved some way along this road. Early in 1867 they passed the Tenure of Office Act which prevented the President from removing federal appointees (including members of the Cabinet) without the consent of the Senate, and in 1868 when Johnson dismissed Stanton, the Secretary of War, a large majority in the House of Representatives decided to impeach him. The President had a technical defense, for the law could be read so that it did not apply to Stanton, who had been appointed by Lincoln, but the real issue was whether Congress could remove a President who had become politically unacceptable to a majority and had used his authority to execute the letter but not the spirit of laws passed by Congress. The trial in an impeachment takes place before the Senate and requires a vote of two-thirds for conviction; seven moderate Republican senators decided that they could not vote "guilty" and the President was saved by one vote. This single vote may have had a decided influence upon the later course of constitutional development; at least it decided that a President could not be removed on political grounds, and that the independent authority of the executive to veto bills passed by Congress and to execute the laws in his own fashion remained inviolate.

In other respects the politics of Reconstruction left a permanent imprint on American democracy. In earlier days it had been assumed that the states were the natural guardians of freedom against attack by federal authority, but the new situation meant that in several instances the National Government would interpose between states and their citizens to guarantee individual rights. The principle was evolved to guarantee the status of former slaves as free men, but it had universal significance; it recognized the right of the National Government to impose standards of justice accepted by a majority. The old Constitution remained, but in spirit it became a new Constitution.

The cardinal document of the "new" Constitution was the Fourteenth Amendment (passed by Congress in the summer of 1866, ratified in 1868). Its first clause declared that all persons born or naturalized in the United States were citizens of the United States (thus reversing the objectionable judgment of the Supreme Court in the *Dred Scott* case), and went on to provide that "no State shall make or enforce any law which shall abridge the privileges or immunities of citizens of the United States." The "privileges or immunities" were not defined, but they clearly pointed to the first eight Amendments (the Bill of Rights) in which citizens were given defined rights which could not be invaded by the Federal Government. The first clause of the Amendment went on to declare "nor shall any State deprive any person of life, liberty, or property, without due process of law." This repeated a phrase already found in Amendment V and was taken to mean that every person could avail himself, against his state, of all the common-law safeguards for life, liberty, and property, and that where there was just cause to believe that due process had been denied a case could be carried to the federal courts. Ultimately the Supreme Court would have oversight over the legislative acts and judicial processes of the states, not only (as heretofore) when these conflicted with the Constitution, but also when they conflicted with the common-law standards recognized by the Court. Finally, the first clause provided that no state should "deny to any person within its jurisdiction the equal protection of the laws." Here the restraint upon the states applied not only to their own citizens but to any "persons" within their borders (for example, to immigrants or fugitives). Though sadly abused by judicial interpretation and official evasion, this "equal protection" clause was to prove the bedrock of the whole legal movement for equal rights in a biracial society.

The Fourteenth Amendment was, however, less forthright than it might have been. Some Republicans would have liked to have given Congress full and explicit authority to guarantee rights by positive action, but their timidity and respect for states rights left power to act in the hands of the states and gave federal courts the power to remedy breaches of the amendment only when proved in court. Prosecutions could be initiated by the Attorney General, but if the administration was unsympathetic the only procedure was for injured parties to initiate legal proceedings themselves. It was too much to expect that ingrained habits of racial discrimination would be eradicated when the initiative must lie with illiterate Negroes, living in hostile white communities and inheriting the traditions of servility. This applied with even greater force to the Fifteenth Amendment, which stated that the right to vote should not "be denied or abridged . . . on account of race, color, or previous condition of servitude." Here again the denial of suffrage had to be proved before the courts could act, and the way was left open for states to impose other qualifications for suffrage, provided that they were not specifically based on "race, creed, color, or previous condition of servitude." After a brief period of political participation the vast majority of Southern Negroes were denied the vote by rigged qualifications or simple terrorism. On the other hand, in Northern states, where there was no threat to white supremacy, and where there was always one party anxious to get out the Negro vote, the Fifteenth Amendment was effective.

Both of the great amendments added a clause giving Congress the power to enforce their provisions by appropriate legislation. The great question was whether this new authority would be used to give

the National Government direct responsibility for law, order, and civil
rights. Would it open the door for positive and effective social legislation? Congress did intervene in 1870 and 1872 to stop terrorism
in the South and to protect Negroes from intimidation at the polls.
Charles Sumner proposed a sweeping civil rights measure that
would outlaw racial segregation in public transport, hotels, parks,
cemeteries, and schools; after his death Congress enacted a Civil
Rights Act in 1875 but without the important educational provision.
In 1883 the Supreme Court invalidated those provisions of the 1872
voting act which were likely to be most effective, and struck down the
whole of the Civil Rights Act on the ground that it extended the power
of Congress beyond the intention of the Fourteenth Amendment. In
practice the Act had already failed because the Federal Government
had no enforcement agency and was not willing to stir up trouble,
and because discrimination on racial grounds was difficult to prove
even when a Negro could be found with the courage to start court
proceedings.

The fact was that in the North the heat was going out of Radical
enthusiasm for equal rights, and opinion was moving towards a compromise under which Southern states would give formal adherence to
the law while federal authority would not look behind the scenes to
investigate or to correct what actually happened. In some parts of
the South, where it suited the dominant upper class to avail themselves
of the support of a docile Negro population, Negroes continued to vote;
in other areas Negroes who attempted to vote were likely to feel white
displeasure in many ways, of which economic reprisals were the least
painful. In 1877 the disputed election betwen Hayes and Tilden gave
Southern leaders the opportunity to strike a bargain under which the
remaining Federal Troops were withdrawn and the South was implicitly left to settle the racial problem in its own way.

Between the first commitment to legal equality with the Fourteenth Amendment and its abandonment came an attempt to force
color-blind democracy on the South. In the fall of 1866 the Southern
states rejected the Amendment while the Northern electorate implied
approval by large Republican majorities in the Congressional elections.
Southern intransigence and Northern support placed the Radicals in a
favorable position to advance their plans for a drastic reconstruction
of Southern society. They were unable to carry the Stevens proposition
for keeping the Southern states in territorial status until this reconstruction was complete, but they were able to make the temporary
disenfranchisement of the ruling class and Negro suffrage the condition for readmission. The Fourteenth Amendment had proposed to
exclude from public office all men who had formerly taken an oath

of allegiance to the United States and had subsequently supported the Confederacy until pardoned by a two-thirds majority in both houses of Congress. This would have made ineligible for office all active Confederates who had held civil or military office before 1860. The first Reconstruction Act of March 1867 dissolved the provisional governments, temporarily restored military rule, and instructed the military commanders to call constitutional conventions elected by adult male suffrage but excluding those whom the Amendment would disqualify from office. These same people would also be disfranchised until the new Constitutions had been approved by Congress and the states readmitted to the Union, and before readmission the Southern states must enact adult male suffrage and accept the Fourteenth Amendment. In effect the older leaders were excluded from the process of political reconstruction, allowed to vote when the process was complete, but disqualified from office under the Fourteenth Amendment until pardoned by Congress. The new constitutions were made with the participation of Negroes, and the subsequent Fifteenth Amendment ensured that they would not be disfranchised when the States reentered the Union.

Under the provisions of the Reconstruction Act many Negroes were elected to the conventions, and to the legislatures set up under the new constitutions. At the same time the old upper-class leaders, who still possessed much economic and social influence, and whose prestige was increased by the congressional attack upon them, were prevented from reentering public life. A political revolution had been implemented, but the customs of the white South, and the influence of the most respected citizens, were inevitably thrown on the scales against the experiment. Few new leaders, either white or black, emerged and the new governments displayed much goodwill and many sound instincts but also ignorance, inexperience, and susceptibility to the corrupt practices which were becoming common in every part of the United States. There could hardly have been less favorable conditions under which to inaugurate a great experiment in biracial democracy. In judging the record of these new governments it is necessary to recall that the story that survived was that which the white South wished to believe; but after making all allowances it is still a record of failure. The Reconstruction Governments did more good than Southern memories allow: they set up public schools systems, they presided over a large measure of economic recovery, and they attracted capital to the South. But they failed to gain the confidence of a majority of the people, and without that any government in a democratic society is doomed.

Even without the racial factor Southern democracy faced difficult decisions. The white majority had always voted for planter gentry and their lawyer allies. The defeat of the South left the ascendancy of this class in jeopardy, and if there had been a rival white leadership prepared to offer a challenge the future of the South might have been very different. Johnson undoubtedly hoped that such leadership would emerge, and his disqualification of wealthy Confederates indicated the class basis of his politics. The state conventions that he ordered in the summer of 1865 were therefore crucial. Some members of these conventions were truly representative of the "plain people," but the upper-class members who escaped disqualification had little difficulty in turning their experience and habitual leadership to good advantage and were easily able to control the situation. Faced with the dual challenge of political disabilities and economic ruin the Southern upper class proved remarkably resilient, and the sociopolitical structure of the new South was not greatly different from that of the old South in appearance and manners.

Within the upper class there were subtle changes. The ardent secessionists of 1860 had been discredited (and few of them had ever achieved wide popularity); but there were plenty of old Whigs and moderate Democrats to step into the breach. The forced diversification of economic interests, as many planters looked for other outlets for their energies, introduced a stronger element of commercial and industrial interests into the upper class, and the new leaders who emerged in the 1870's might act like representatives of the old Southern gentry, but they were often deeply interested in banking, commercial ventures, railways, and manufactures. Indeed their economic base became stronger and wider than it had been in prewar days, and they were in an even better position to retain their former ascendancy. As in earlier days they had to operate in a democratic society, but the racial question proved to be the cement that bound together the new structure of politics. The Old South had never been solid, but the New South achieved solidarity on the common determination of all whites to exclude Negroes from political participation, and Southern leaders, who were often paternalistic and well-disposed towards Negroes "of the right type," were led to adopt a more specifically racist tone.

Thus the era of Reconstruction brought American democracy face to face with the problem of race. The Republicans had attempted to deal with the problem on the traditional assumptions of American society: legal equality, the right to vote, and an open door to advancement. Many of them believed that given this basis, and relieved from the burden of chattel slavery, the Negroes would take their rightful place in American society. Most of them believed that ignorance and the attitudes inherited from slavery would make the achievement of real equality a slow process, and some believed that the inherent inferiority of the Negro would mean that his ceiling of achievement would always be low, but many of the old-stock Anglo-Saxon Americans had much the same feelings about the Catholic Irish and about immigrants from Latin and Slav countries. They were therefore involved in the apparent contradiction that men ought to be treated as though they were equal even though race and heritage made them unequal. How far should the National Government intervene to ensure that the unequal should become equal? And would special protection for one class infringe the principle of equality itself? For many the solution to this dilemma lay in placing upon Negroes themselves the onus of winning equality once they had been given the legal and political basis for advancement. It was not expected that more than a small minority would avail themselves of opportunities to rise to positions of economic or professional excellence; men of whatever color could enjoy the advantages of American citizenship, but from that point onward their advancement must depend upon their own efforts. Few in the North thought that Negroes should be given positive aid to offset their weakness. Proposals to reward freedmen with land taken from confiscated Confederate estates received scant consideration, and there was great hesitation in supplying them with positive aid.

The racial theory of Reconstruction rested heavily upon the idea of protected rights. Men in society had rights which ought to be protected by law and authority; these were the rights defined in general terms as those of life, liberty, and property. Could the phrase of the Declaration of Independence—"life, liberty, and the pursuit of happiness"—be interpreted more widely as an obligation to remove the barriers to happiness? In practice American lawyers had never given any precise meaning to "the pursuit of happiness," but the political traditions associated with Jacksonian Democracy had added a gloss to the lawyers' brief by holding that government must confer no privilege by law that might hinder others in their pursuit of happiness. Once privilege conferred by law was removed, freely acting individuals could pursue their own happiness and find their own level in society.

In the prewar South, American democracy had encountered the phenomenon of an upper class that had no privileges given by law but which was nevertheless privileged. Within the South white democracy had hammered at property qualifications for suffrage and at unequal apportionment of representation in the legislatures. By 1860 all white males in most parts of the South could vote, provided that they fulfilled residential qualifications, and though the old tidewater counties still had more than their fair share of representation, much had been done to provide a fairer distribution of legislative seats. Yet these constitutional reforms had been regarded mainly as providing the means by which the rights of the poorer whites and the interests of internal areas could be protected. The upper class retained social privileges and a virtual monopoly of all the superior public offices.

The privileges of the upper class had been seen in the North as a major discrepancy in the democratic pattern but had been attributed to slavery with the inference that when slavery was ended Southern society would take on the equalitarian structure of the rest of America. It seemed necessary only to give Negroes their rights as citizens to remedy these ancient inequalities. A few Radicals, and especially Thaddeus Stevens, had seen a further need to transfer land to former slaves and thus, at one blow, to undermine the economic ascendancy of the upper class and provide a secure basis for Negro citizenship. Most Republicans were unwilling to move against property in so drastic a way and their timidity has sometimes been interpreted as a major cause for the failure of Reconstruction. It is, however, doubtful whether the effects of land grants to Negroes would have had magical effects: a division of the best land among former slaves, while the white majority subsisted on poor land, would not have fostered racial harmony, and Negro landowners without capital would have quickly sunk into debt and economic dependency.

State governments dependent upon Negro votes suffered obvious handicaps in the South, but their difficulties were compounded by traditional attitudes to all government. Suffrage was conceived in the traditional American way as the means by which men protected their rights, but not as a means by which the more positive concept of "the pursuit of happiness" could be translated into legislative action. One root cause of the failure of Reconstruction in the South was that inexperienced and unpopular governments were forced by events to undertake more positive roles than any previous governments: they had to tax, borrow, and spend; provide relief and education; foster economic recovery. In some instances white political movements in the South tried to adopt a more positive attitude toward the tasks of government, but their effort was soured by its association with Negro suffrage, and the Southern tradition that government should do no more than was absolutely necessary remained dominant. The social task of government was complete when it had provided for the security of life, liberty, and property; its economic tasks were complete when it had prevented monopoly and rooted out economic privilege conferred by law.

Faced with a situation in which all that was necessary — on traditional democratic principles—had been done, and yet equality was plainly denied, the Republicans in Congress fumbled for new concepts. So far as they found them, their conclusions were invalidated by the Supreme Court. Many Republicans attempted to draw lines between natural rights that must be protected, political rights that were within the discretion of the political sovereign, and social rights that could not be touched by any legislative authority. The distinctions were often unreal, and attempts to reconcile these concepts with the real situation in the South led to interminable debate and inconclusive results. Was education a natural right? Hardly so; but surely ignorance deprived men of the ability to make the best of their natural rights. Was education a political right? Perhaps it was; but the responsibility for education had always lain with states, counties, and cities. Or was it a social right that was the exclusive concern of individuals and local communities? Faced with these abstractions many supporters of a national education system were forced to fall back upon the right of the Union to protect itself against the consequences of ignorance. In the South education also raised the important question of racial segregation. If the National Government supplied the funds for a public education system, could it make school integration a condition for educational grants? Faced with these awkward questions Congress failed to legislate on education.

Charles Sumner took the line that anything touched by law could be regulated by law. This abandoned the distinction between different kinds of rights and brought forward the idea of equal protection which had been written into the Fourteenth Amendment. If the states failed to provide equal protection, then Congress had the duty to intervene, and this applied not only to occasions on which they had passed discriminatory laws but also to occasions on which they ought to have legislated against discrimination. Thus inns were licensed by law; it was the duty of the state to make the equal treatment of both races a condition for a license. Public transportation was regulated by law; therefore, all public transport must be forced by law to provide equal treatment to all users. Congress finally accepted this argument, but the Supreme Court thought otherwise.

The failure to evolve any clear doctrine of equal rights was to plague the United States to the present day. At the same time neither Northerners nor Southerners, Republicans nor Democrats, would contemplate separate development. At one extreme old abolitionists insisted that society was one and all men its citizens irrespective of race; at the other extreme economic realists knew that Southern economy would collapse without Negro labor. The United States was left with a society in which men were said to be equal, were treated unequally, and were commanded to live together in amity. It is small wonder that as antislavery ardor cooled, the Northern majority fell back upon the hope that the South would somehow discover its own solution. As whites were in a majority almost everywhere, and could easily intimidate in those few areas where the Negroes were more numerous, the effect was to entrust the intricate question of race relations to the care of those who had the clearest motive for asserting inequality. The first major attempt to construct a biracial society of free men deteriorated into a dismal condition in which violence stopped up the few breaches in the segregational barrier and evasion of the law became a way of life.

Despite the melancholy conclusions, Reconstruction marked a great watershed in the evolution of American democracy: equal protection was embedded in the Constitution; political discrimination against races was unconstitutional; national responsibility had modified the tyranny of the state majority. If the letter of the law was often ignored in practice and under the pressure of events, it still remained the letter. Lawyers who wished to avoid its meaning had to employ tortuous arguments which hardly stood up to later scrutiny. The precedents of the years after 1875 were weak in logic, and a later generation could dispose of the theory with comparative ease, however difficult the practical implications of the law might prove. The Constitution had got ahead of democratic practice, but the balance could be redressed.

What would have happened if the Republican majority after the Civil War had simply decided to abandon the Negro? The hypothetical question is worth asking in a race-conscious age. Suppose that slave-owners had been allowed to restore slavery or impose peonage? Suppose that the Civil Rights movement of the twentieth century had not been able to appeal to the Constitution? Suppose the Negroes had not been assured by the law that time and justice were on their side? It is possible that white Southerners could have found an equitable solution to the racial problem, but the failure in this respect of most of the white races is so apparent that a Southern solution seems improbable. It is very possible that wiser, more patient, and less acrimonious handling of the racial question by Republicans would have produced happier results. But what happened could not be undone, and the great failure of the future was to imagine that the specter of racial equality could be exorcised by pouring abuse upon Radicals. The heritage was an uneasy one and would reveal some damaging flaws in American democracy.

CHAPTER X

THE QUEST FOR STABILITY

In July, 1876, the Americans celebrated one hundred years of national existence, and though the natural exuberance of the people produced the expected quota of gratitude for the past and hopes for the future, heavy clouds lay upon the horizon. The Union had been preserved but sectional animosities remained. There was a feeling abroad that the politicians had betrayed the idealism fostered by war and that public spirit and public morality were at a low ebb. The great and growing cities of the country were disfigured by slums, crime, and civic scandals, while party bosses exploited ignorant voters and cynically displayed the ease with which they could rob the public purse. The concentration of economic power in the hands of railroads and large industrial combinations created alarm and brought weak state and municipal governments face to face with new men of power. Since 1865 doubts about the character of American life had been growing, and in 1873 the country had plunged into the deepest and longest depression yet experienced, all the more alarming because, despite attempts to blame the folly of individuals or institutional scapegoats, it demonstrated that the hopeful dynamism of American economic life was at the mercy of impersonal, international, and irresistible forces. Depression brought its train of labor troubles and 1877 would see a series of great strikes that shattered for ever the belief that America had avoided the class conflicts of the old world. It is not surprising that the best minds of the nation mixed the rejoicing of the centenary with doubts about the future and sought for principles of stability which would restore harmony and harness profitably the energies of the people.

Lincoln had taught the people that the cause of the Union was the cause of democracy, but democracy was a very different thing in a predominantly rural society, dominated by homespun legislators and the close-knit community of small towns, than it was in a new era of industrial growth, urban concentration, racial problems, and large-scale immigration. Unscrupulous industrial magnates, unprincipled professional politicians, ignorant voters untrained in American traditions, and disruptive foreign agitators seemed to typify the new America, and heirs of the old Puritan tradition—educated and well-to-do merchants, ministers, and professional men—found that times were out of joint. Politicians were the principal targets of their criticism, but the Liberal Republican episode of 1872, which attracted so much support from the intellectuals and the "good citizens," had proved to be a political disaster which demonstrated only the strength of an unattractive political establishment.

The political discontents (whatever they were) flourished in a democratic society. It had become axiomatic that every adult male citizen of the United States had the right to vote so long as he ful-

filled simple residential qualifications, and outside the South all qualified voters used this right freely. Democratic suffrage reelected Grant
in 1872, supported the infamous Tweed ring in New York, and chose
state legislators who seemed ready to betray the public interest for
their own gain. By 1876 it was clear that the experiment of color-
blind democracy had failed in the South, and disillusionment with the
equalitarian impulse of Radical Reconstruction spread to other parts of
the political spectrum. The right of the Negroes to vote had been defended because there were white voters who were as ignorant and
shiftless as ex-slaves; but the apparent failure of Negro suffrage in
the South suggested that discrimination against ignorance ought to be
applied to other new citizens. It had been a basic precept of Jeffersonian
democracy that the people could be trusted to make a better choice
than their rulers who could not escape the influence of their own
selfish interests; now it was suspected that the educated elite had a
duty to guard civilization against the violence and ignorance of the
people and against the criminality of their chosen leaders.

These disquiets did not fuse together into one great movement of
protest. Rather, there were a number of separate streams which occasionally ran together without losing their separate identities. The
intellectuals, growing in influence but weak in numbers, could be more
effective as insiders than as outsiders. Businessmen had no wish to
become involved in the regular routine of political activity; their
complaints were typical of the tension that has existed in most
advanced societies between democratic government and the business
community, and provided no base for a party of reform. Farmers
spoke with regional and divided voices. Organized labor, with remarkably few exceptions, avoided political commitments. None of the
critics raised issues which were likely to be popular, though they might
sometimes be important in marginal contests, and the late nineteenth century was not a period in which great ideas were brought
into political conflict. Foreign observers noticed the lack of coherent
programs in party platforms and gave further currency to the idea
that politics in general and the parties in particular were failing in
their proper function.* Too often these laments for the condition of
American politics failed to diagnose what their function really was.

---

* Lord Bryce, *American Commonwealth.* (New Edition, 1910, Vol. II, p. 21.) "Tenets
and policies, points of political doctrine and points of political practice, have all but
vanished. They have not been thrown away, but have been stripped away by Time and
the progress of events, fulfilling some policies, blotting out others. All has been lost,
except office or the hope of it." Bryce did not minimize the importance of parties
(describing them as "the great moving forces") but attributed their influence to
organization, not to principles. "The less of nature the more of art; the less spontaneity
the more mechanism." (*Ibid.*, p. 5.)

An American party has seldom been the means by which policy is created; it is rather the means by which diverse groups are organized to support government. Policy-making comes when elections have been won, and is most often formulated by dialogue within the party and between President and Congress. The processes which win an election may be more relevant to the local structure of power than to national policy, and even positive commitments to national policies are not legislative promises but undertakings that mean the majority leaders will allow a fair hearing and congressional time for the favored cause. In other words, the party commitments, when made, are procedural not ideological. The inner group of leaders in the majority party would be acting dishonestly if they failed to arrange congressional business so that policies which had persuaded men to support them were not discussed, but no members of the party (including the leaders) are blamed if personal opinion or constituency interests persuade them to oppose those policies in debate. This explains the phenomenon that party solidarity is more often demonstrated on procedural votes than on substantive votes.*

This does not mean that party contests in the later nineteenth century were unimportant or that their outcome was of no significance, because the real issues were not specific policies but what kind of men should hold the reins of power. The various groups aspiring to local leadership were familiar to voters, and so were the kind of alliances they were likely to make across the nation, so that the local choice blended into the national choice. The weight given at any one time to local or national reputation might vary. A dramatic national issue might persuade a majority to accept a local leadership which was not their first choice; conversely, a very popular and respected local leader might win support for a national ticket that would otherwise have been denied to it; but from the decline of Radicalism to the rise of Populism the major preoccupation of national party leaders was to combine together a large number of strong and sometimes temperamental local parties. The ideal Presidential candidate was Ulysses S. Grant, who had a nationally known name and recognized the paramount need for organization, while the least acceptable President was Rutherford B. Hayes, who tried to pursue his own policy without seeking a party consensus. Between the two came James G. Blaine, whose long congressional career left few records of legislative achievement but who had the personality to break through the dullness of politics, inspire the party regulars, and convince rank-and-file voters that their

---

* The most important procedural vote was the election of the Speaker, and on this, party solidarity was usually complete.

local aspirations could best be achieved by supporting the national party.

At one end of the political road was the Presidency at the head of a centralized Federal administration; at the other end were local concerns and groups with all their centrifugal tendencies. The national party was the bridge between the two, and to be strong it had to make local success dependent upon national favor. This reciprocal relationship was sustained by patronage, "spoils," and a network of obligations linking politicians and their supporters. Patronage could not win large numbers of new recruits to an old party organization; it might win support for particular issues from the indifferent or doubtful but was unlikely to change a man's actions on matters which he or his constituents regarded as vital. A great part of patronage consisted in filling posts with candidates whom the President did not know and could not investigate, and the names were more often submitted from below than imposed from above. Patronage was a means of playing with forces which already existed, and Presidents who tried to give it a more constructive role speedily found its limitations.

Patronage operated at various levels within this framework. Major interests and different regions had to be assured of representation in the cabinet, the Federal judiciary, and important noncabinet positions. Diplomatic appointments might be influenced by regional considerations but were also a way of paying political debts to individuals. In the state organizations political leaders had to be assured that their services would be recognized in due course, and though the supply of posts might not meet the demand, party regulars had to be rewarded in turn. For local political leaders it was important that their nominations should be respected in the lesser federal appointments, because their own power depended on the extent to which they could make or mar careers in these humble but desirable offices when their party was in power in Washington. Finally, although the days of big government were still far in the future, the Federal Government was already a large spender with profitable contracts to negotiate, rivers and harbors to be improved, dockyards and military installations to be maintained. Nineteenth-century government had nothing so massive as modern defense contracts, but there were already profitable activities that could be directed to individuals or districts. It was usually the task of the United States senator—in most cases a leading man in his party in his state—to keep an eye on all this, and senatorial mail was filled with every conceivable appeal for help in obtaining office or favor as well as with advice from political friends at home about the men and matters that required special attention.

The patronage system contained some internal regulators which prevented it from debasing the public service to the extent that some of its critics supposed. A leader and a party were judged in part by the kind of men whom they put in office. A bad cabinet member could be a disaster for a party, and an incompetent or unpopular postmaster (the only federal official with whom most Americans ever had any dealings) might lead to serious local repercussions. Scandals or errors were always liabilities, and no President liked to have his reputation tarnished by scoundrels whom he had appointed to office. The worst episodes of the age did not arise from the normal operation of the patronage system but from men who tried to act for themselves outside the system: Congressmen who accepted direct or indirect bribes from private interests, officials who feathered their own nests, and revenue officers who absconded with public funds were parasites upon the system not the system itself. Indeed these abuses came about because political men followed the ethics of unregulated business rather than the well-understood and open conventions of patronage.

If the primary task of politicians was organization they had still to organize for a purpose. A conventional view holds that the inner circle of political leaders were interested only in power and that their occasional espousal of policies was a sham intended to create the illusion that something useful was being done. This supposes that American voters turned out in considerable numbers at election time in order to vote upon "unreal" issues and fails to comprehend how deeply the shadow of the Civil War hung over succeeding years. The Union had been preserved but the problem of national existence remained. Should it be solved by the alliance of forces that had triumphed in the war, or by an alliance between former Confederates and "copperheads" who had been convinced of neither the necessity nor the justice of war? The alliance for the Union had drawn many different men into its orbit but basically it had been composed of Northern and Western Protestants of North European descent. They were farmers and businessmen, intellectuals and skilled workers, old men who remembered Henry Clay with veneration, young men who were impatient with the old fogeys, men who had been tempered in the fierce blast of evangelical revival, and entrepreneurs on the make. Their heartlands were Massachusetts, Vermont, western New York, central Pennsylvania, the Western Reserve of Ohio, and the arteries of commerce spreading out in the Midwest and on to the great plains. Their ideas came mainly from New England but the focal point of their political life was found in the hundreds of small towns where politicians and people could meet face to face. In the nature of things Republicans drawn from this soil came to occupy positions of influence as businessmen, ministers, newspaper editors, and college teachers. They regarded themselves as the keepers of the nation's conscience and believed that Divine Providence had shown special care for their material well-being. But what was at stake was much more than the status of an elite; it was the nature and purpose of national existence.

The opponents of Republicanism clustered together in the Democratic party, and its remarkable revival after the electoral disaster of 1864 was a testimony to the need for an alternative to Republican leadership. Shortly after the centenary, the Presidential election would show the two parties almost at dead heat, and Rutherford B. Hayes won for the Republicans only after the disputed returns in three Southern states had been resolved in his favor. Between 1870 and 1896 the Democrats had a majority in the House in eight of thirteen Congresses and twice in the Senate, and twice won won the Presidency, in 1884 and 1892, with Grover Cleveland. During this period the Democrats assumed the pattern of alliance that they were to retain until 1928. The South became solid Democratic country with prewar party differences forgotten and only vestigial remains of the Southern Republican party in evidence. The Democrats also recovered ground in their traditional rural strongholds in the southern part of the Midwest, and in most of the larger cities except Philadelphia their political machines throve on the support of low-paid workers, recent immigrants, racial minorities other than Negroes, and a growing body of urban Roman Catholics. Industrial workers in good employment tended to be Republican but might turn to the Democrats in time of depression.

With their voting strength drawn from groups who, for one reason or another, were deprived of a fair share of economic rewards or of full participation in American life, the Democrats were a permanent opposition and when they led in Congress behaved more like an opposition than a majority party. The Democrats in Congress did not differ greatly in social status from their Republican opponents, but they served different constituencies and observed different traditions. They continued to deplore the dangers of "centralism" and to defend Southern "home rule" in the name of states' rights. They attacked federal expenditure, but normally to ensure that rural Democratic districts got their fair share of government spending. From time to time they attracted dissident Republicans and independents, and their victory in the Presidential election of 1884 was probably due to the support of the so-called "Mugwump" Republicans who refused to support Blaine in the belief that he was corrupt and preferred Cleveland, a small-town politician of limited accomplishments with a reputation for honesty and parsimony. But neither Cleveland nor his party could provide constructive ideas to meet the challenge of the times; tied to the past and dependent upon the South, they could do no more than organize resentment against the assumed superiority of the Republicans.

Practical politicians shunned theory and sought for the pragmatic solution to problems as they arose, but the era as a whole showed an increased concern with social theory. Disillusioned with politics, and alarmed by the tendencies of democracy, intellectuals sought for the solution in a self-regulating society. Because businessmen were impressed with their own ability to organize affairs as they wanted them, and because of the ingrained traditions of limited government, the notion of a society that could dispense with political regulation found ready support and spread its influence into every corner of American life. Businessmen who claimed only experience and common sense as their guide repeated precepts formulated by economists and philosophers, ministers of religion found the same principles sanctified by Holy Writ, and educators taught that the laws of society could be comprehended as exactly as those of the physical world. The theory has been tagged as "laissez faire" and is often represented as a purely negative attitude to government and as a blanket endorsement for all private business activity, but this concept does scant justice to its range or cohesion. Rational enquiry, combined with a belief in progress, drew support from the latest deductions of science and produced a vision of a society that would move forward, impelled by its own inner forces. Competition and evolution were the keys to a world view that taught that one must learn to live with temporary hardship in order to promote the betterment of man. Special cases made bad policy, and one must look at the overall and eventual results rather than legislate to protect failure.

The British philosopher, Herbert Spencer, achieved an American reputation far greater than that which he enjoyed in his own country. His *Social Statics* formed only a small part of his application of evolutionary principles to the whole field of knowledge, but it was the work most easily comprehended by unphilosophic minds. In society, as in all other fields, the struggle for survival led to the survival of the fittest, and the principle applied to economic progress, social adaptation, and moral improvement. The civilized world of the later nineteenth century was demonstrably more humane, more skilled, more rational, better informed, more efficient, and morally superior to any preceding age; but Spencer's view of history suggested that civilization owed none of these benefits to government save the preservation of order and the protection of property. Enlightened government should confine itself to these functions, abdicate other responsibilities and allow men to seek betterment in their own way. Government intervention could be justified only when the public interest was clearly affected (as, for instance, by the introduction of dangerous diseases from abroad); in debatable cases there was no reason to assume that governments would decide more wisely than individuals or to suppose that authority could improve upon the continuous operation of competitive forces. Intervention that hampered the fittest ensured the survival of the unfit.

This social theory borrowed heavily from Charles Darwin's theory of biological evolution—and has sometimes been known as Social Darwinism—but other influences were equally strong. The theories of classical economics explained economic behavior by immutable laws, which could not be resisted without distorting the economic process and producing a drop in the quantity or quality of goods and services. A healthy economy was one in which economic laws operated freely; an unhealthy economy was one in which their operation was impeded by the restraints of law, custom, or religious opinion. This proposition assumed that the free play of economic forces would lead to individual improvement and collective benefits, and translated into secular theory older concepts of Divine Providence. Men were subject to God's will and must accept the rational laws of society which were a part of His purpose; Providence, the unseen hand, and natural harmony on earth—reflecting Divine harmony in heaven—remained the guiding principles of social theory even when expressed by known agnostics; but this proved to be an element of strength in reconciling dangerous new science with principles of religion which still dominated the American mind, while faith in human destiny explained the hold of laissez faire upon humane and intelligent men. It was not merely a reflection of economic acquisitiveness but also of confidence in progress and man's intellectual growth.

Evolution (which educated Americans learned as a social theory from Herbert Spencer rather than as a biological theory from Charles Darwin) had radical implications for traditional beliefs. The marvelous biblical allegory of creation and the origins of life was accepted by many Americans as a literal, exact, and incontestable statement. Darwin's picture of the evolution of the species over millions of years from simple to complex forms was regarded as a shattering blow to Christian belief, and it remains technically illegal to teach evolution in the public schools of some states. Yet the theory of evolution could reinforce conservative conclusions. It could, for instance, provide material to support the argument that some races were superior to others (having adapted more successfully and evolved a higher form of intelligence), and this could be used to justify not only the superiority of whites over blacks but also of Anglo-Saxons and North Europeans over the Mediterranean and Slav immigrants who were arriving in large numbers. A majority of Americans were prepared to demand fair play for these "inferior" races, but evolutionary theory encouraged them to rationalize their instinctive belief that the superiority of the older American stock should be maintained. Before the end of the century it was remarked that many Northern Americans had come to accept Southern views of race; this was manifested in an unwritten agreement to leave Southerners to settle their race problem for themselves, in more open assertions of the American right to govern newly acquired Pacific possessions, and in demands for immigration restriction. If the majority of Americans did not go to these lengths they did come to assume that once Negroes and new immigrants had been given basic legal rights they must make their own way in the world without any special aid or protection from government. To help the weak against the strong went against the teachings of science; civilization depended upon the survival of the fittest and would be debased by preserving the less fit.

Laissez faire demanded limited government but it could hardly have flourished under a government that was not already limited. It rationalized existing conditions and resisted innovation, and in this way a progressive ideal became entwined with political conservatism. In England laissez faire was a liberal creed battling against privilege and antique regulations; in America this battle had been won in earlier generations and the theory provided the intellectual defense of existing economic power against political control and labor organization. At this point inconsistency set in, and a theory which claimed inspiration from a scientific analysis of nature became exhortation to prevent men from doing what their interests and instincts suggested. If competition was "natural" so was the capacity and desire of men to act collectively; if the struggle of man against man was "natural" so was the success of some men in defeating competitors and establishing monopoly. Even if trade unions were antisocial and consolidation harmful, how could either be prevented or controlled except by law? Thus the premises of laissez faire laid the foundations for government intervention while its exponents treated political authority as the enemy of progress.

Although laissez faire claimed to be a philosophy of freedom it was uncomfortable with democratic freedom. Majorities and their representatives were commanded to abstain from intervention in social and economic affairs, but all too often they seemed to ignore or defy correct principles. It followed that the people must be prevented from acting against their own best interests. This was partly consistent with older themes in American political traditions, for all constitutions acted to greater or lesser extents as restraints upon majorities. Divided sovereignty prevented federal majorities from acting in wide fields of society, while the federal Constitution contained explicit restraints upon the states whatever their own majorities might wish; but there had been loopholes through which both federal and state governments could advance to wider social responsibilities. The Fourteenth Amendment had opened the wide field of civil liberty to federal action, and the states had always had reserved powers to regulate economic activity within their boundaries. Thus there were inadequate safeguards in the political system against intervention in economic affairs.

Faced with the danger that the elected representatives of the people might intervene in ways which were deemed harmful, the exponents of laissez faire had to appeal to a higher law; to say, in effect, that some actions allowed by the Constitution were, nevertheless, prohibited by reason and justice. This position would have been untenable had not a majority of the federal judges been ready to read laissez faire into the Constitution and to use the power of judicial review to check the legislative activities that they deemed to be theoretically undesirable. In this development the Fourteenth Amendment proved to be of decisive importance, though had it not existed, other means might have been found of achieving the same objective. The Amendment guaranteed the "privileges and immunities" of United States citizens against abridgement by state legislatures; if economic freedom was among these "privileges and immunities," protected by the Constitution and the first ten amendments, then the Fourteenth Amendment provided the same guarantee against state action and made the federal courts the watchdogs over state social and economic legislation. "Due process" and equal protection could also be interpreted to render unconstitutional any legislation that discriminated against particular kinds of property or imposed conditions upon some individuals which were not imposed upon all. When the Supreme Court accepted the argument that the "persons" guaranteed equal protection included corporations, as persons in law, the safeguards of the Constitution for business activity were complete, and formidable legal barriers could be placed in the way of any state legislature wishing to regulate corporations, fix railroad rates, enact minimum wage laws, or determine the hours and conditions of work. If the right of states to protect the health and welfare of their citizens remained, the Supreme Court came to require that the burden of proof rested with those who wished to regulate; it was not enough to support action with reference to hypothetical or indirect dangers to health or property, they must be demonstrably real and direct.

If the doctrine adopted by the Supreme Court allowed great freedom to private business it imposed drastic restrictions upon the organization of labor. Free enterprise could be threatened by the private action of workers as well as by the public action of legislative majorities, and without denying the right to associate, the judges went as far as possible in making association ineffective. The right of individuals to refuse to work could not be removed, but the traditional hostility of the law to conspiracy could be invoked to make this right as innocuous as possible. A union could order a strike, but action against strikebreakers was an illegal interference with economic freedom; workers had the freedom to starve themselves by refusing to work, but interference with property could be stopped by law. Moreover, evidence that property might be endangered by strike action, even though property had not yet suffered, could lead to judicial injunctions ordering strikers to desist from all actions held to be dangerous. Thus in considering industrial action the judges adopted different criteria from that applied to state economic regulation: private employers had only to demonstrate a hypothetical danger to property, but public authorities had to prove conclusively that health or morals were in danger before the courts would recognize their right to intervene.

In pursuing this course the Supreme Court was supported by the most articulate and respected opinion in the country. The "higher law" of economic freedom commended itself to most property owners, and the Court was applauded for the skill with which it threaded its way through the apparent conflict between freedom and social order. Was there, however, a contradiction between the idea of a self-regulating society and a society in which economic freedom could be secured only by restricting the rights of majorities and voluntary associations? Could free enterprise be assured only by denying the freedom of the people, through their representatives, to lay down rules for the conduct of business? The problem was made more complex by the belief that while competition was beneficial as a general principle some kinds of competition were "unfair" and ought to be regulated by law. The question became urgent as the size and influence of business corporations increased, small business was overwhelmed by the giants and whole regions complained of the arbitrary way in which railroad corporations fixed rates and discriminated between favored users and the general public. Dissatisfaction bred numerous attempts in the states to place business under public regulation, but most of these experiments (originating in popular movements of protest) sought to establish independent and quasijudicial commissions rather than to entrust more power to elected majorities.

The movement for the regulation of railroads was carried from the states into Congress and led, in 1887, to the Interstate Commerce Act. This act accepted at the national level the idea that the right way to regulate was not through legislative action but through an independent commission with members appointed for long terms by the President with the consent of the Senate. The authority of the Commission was derived from an act of Congress and rested upon the constitutional right to regulate commerce among the states, but the men who executed the law would be removed from legislative pressure. Significantly the first chairman of the Interstate Commerce Commission was Thomas M. Cooley, whose book, *Constitutional Limitations*, was regarded as the authoritative statement of legal and theoretical restraints upon legislative functions.

The threat posed by monopolistic combinations (called "trusts" after a short-lived legal device to evade the restrictions imposed by most states on the right of corporations to hold stock in other corporations) was met in a different way. The celebrated Anti-Trust Act on 1890 declared that "every contract, combination in the form of trust or otherwise, or conspiracy in restraint of trade or commerce among the several states, or with foreign nations" was illegal. This made a new law but set up no special machinery to execute it. As the law of the land it would be interpreted by the courts, and the main responsibility for prosecution would rest with the executive under the general constitutional duty to execute the law. The Act did provide the means by which private individuals could initiate suits, but the expense of engaging in a legal battle with great corporations, able to afford the most expensive aid and advice, was a major deterrent, and in practice the effectiveness of the Act would depend upon the President and the Attorney General, and upon their understanding of when the somewhat vaguely worded act had been infringed. In effect the Act armed the Department of Justice with the power to inquire into the structure of companies and to decide whether a combination of interests warranted prosecution as "a conspiracy in restraint of trade." It would then be up to the federal courts to decide whether the case had been proved.

Neither law fared well at the hands of the Supreme Court. There was natural suspicion of a new tribunal that combined executive, judicial, and legislative functions, and judicial interpretation reduced the Interstate Commerce Commission to little more than a fact-finding body without power to compel the production of evidence. The Court was more sympathetic to the objectives of the Anti-Trust Law—which embodied the old Common Law principle that contracts in restraint of trade were void—but found itself confronted with a vaguely drafted law under which substantial penalties could be imposed upon those convicted; under these circumstances the Court had no alternative but to allow defendants whatever advantages the most generous construction of the law might permit. In fact, the decade after the passage of the law saw an acceleration in the process of industrial consolidation, and its principal beneficiaries were probably the corporation lawyers who found lucrative employment in helping their clients to evade the law without ostensibly defying it. The failure of cases instituted by the Federal Government, the difficulty and expense of instituting prosecutions by private action, and lack of enthusiasm on the part of Presidents Cleveland and McKinley for the principles of the Act, meant that only the most arrogant and indiscreet abuses of power were likely to find their way into the courts.

Despite the disappointing early history of the Acts of 1887 and 1890, they provide landmarks in the development of modern

American society. They established the principle of federal responsibility for economic ethics, and they remained on the statute book as the basis for further action. The Interstate Commerce Commission became the model for several subsequent commissions—of which the Federal Communications Commission and the Securities and Exchange Commission are the most notable—while from the Anti-Trust Law and its subsequent amendments have flown a vast and complex code which governs the conduct of large-scale business. The Acts and their later manifestations may well be regarded as the principle means by which order and fair play have been imposed upon the system of free enterprise without sacrificing individual initiative and decision. It is equally true that they not only impose discipline upon private economic behavior but also abridge legislative responsibility: they implement the public consensus that special rules should apply to conduct of business, but they remove these rules from direct response to majority decisions. The paradox is that free enterprise does not survive by trusting the people but trusting judges, administrators, and independent commissions.

One aspect of the ideal of a self-regulating society was the devotion of its adherents to the gold standard. It might seem that to adopt an artificial metallic standard, and to base the currencies of expanding nations upon a limited supply of gold, was the negation of laissez faire and a serious qualification to the idea of nonintervention. Economic development demanded a free flow of investment capital into areas and occupations that had not yet become productive, yet currency tied to gold was likely to be short when and where it was most needed. "Easy money" had always had supporters in America, and late nineteenth-century expansion provided an armory of arguments. Profiting by war experience, Greenbackers proposed a national inconvertible currency which could be regulated in quantity in accord with the needs of the country, but the suggestion was anathema to exponents of laissez faire. Government money gave dangerous power to the politicians who would control it and to the people who elected them, but it was only a shade less dangerous to give this sovereign power to private bankers. Moral argument as much as economics turned the scale in favor of gold; a monetary standard which always preserved its value meant that assets could never be depreciated by popular delusion, private manipulation, or political whim. Gold was honest money, and this was its appeal to men whose moral probity was not matched by economic knowledge. Bankers and merchants engaged in overseas trade had obvious reasons for preferring a currency that commanded the confidence of foreign lenders, but for moralists the hand of Providence could be traced in offering gold for the use of men. Gold became one of the pivots of self-regulating society and ministers of religion and economists united to see the specie standard endorsed by divine and scientific law.

The traditional friends of paper currency and inflation had been small industrial and agricultural entrepreneurs. Much has been made of debtor support for easy money, but its most influential advocates were not men in debt but men who wanted to get into debt: in other words, the men who wanted to finance enterprise by borrowing. Their views could be widely reinforced in regions where development seemed to lag for want of money, and supporters of the gold standard rightly suspected that democratic pressures would break through the barriers of sound money if allowed their head. Popular dissatisfaction could become frantic when depression caused not only tight money but demands for the repayment of the loans and mortgages that were already out. Until 1879 opponents of gold managed to stave off the resumption of specie payments, but the gold standard was then adopted and became a part of the higher law of a self-regulating society. In practice the gold standard proved more flexible than its enemies had suggested because of the great increase in supply following discoveries in California, the Yukon, Australia, and South Africa, and because increasing facility in the use of paper instruments of payment economized in the use of currency. But the enthusiasm of its advocates failed to allay the criticism of those who found gold an unwelcome curb upon individual activity and a great handicap to those regions which were short of capital and least likely to enlist the support of international bankers.

The idea of progress demanded that "sound" business should be protected against the politicians and the people. Constitutional restraints, which had been regarded as checks upon the democratic impulse, became absolute barriers between majority rule and economic enterprise. The Constitution itself was not enough, but became sufficient when judges read into it the higher law of social philosophy. The stability desired by the wise, the rich, and the good was contrasted with the turbulence of emotional and ignorant electorates. In this way, and in the eyes of the educated and intelligent, the American political system fulfilled the Madisonian purpose of protecting "the permanent and aggregate interests of the community" against the violence of a "faction" whether composed of a minority or a majority.

This attitude can be presented in unattractive guise, and modern commentators may hold that the ignorant people showed a truer perception of economic and social reality than their guides and pastors. In a more profound sense the late nineteenth century touched upon one of the basic dilemmas of democratic society. Once government had been very simple—though never quite as simple as a Jefferson or Jackson claimed—and many electors had had first-hand knowledge of the few problems it tackled. Moreover, the democratic process was viewed as a way of protecting rights and legitimizing rule, and, since the areas in which government impinged upon the lives of the people were few and small, it had required no great expertise to prevent their enlargement. It has already been seen how disastrous were the consequences when Reconstruction governments of the South had to suddenly reverse traditional attitudes and accept responsibility for action in numerous fields; but the problem, though less obvious outside the South, was nationwide. Governments of the late nineteenth century, limited though they were, did far more than any earlier governments; the problems remote from common experience multiplied, and immediate problems became vastly more complicated. The electorate could not understand, and was likely to decide for wrong reasons. The basic premise of American political life—that governments derived their just powers from the consent of the governed—was not denied, but it became increasingly important to avoid the danger that the wrong people should be given the wrong mandate.

Men who led this retreat from democracy were, however, reluctant to accept the proposition that government should be entrusted to experts. It is true that civil service reform, and the creation of a professional administrative class on the British model, became a favorite cause with the middle-class intelligentsia; but a permanent civil service was seen as a protective device against politicians, rather than as an elite of administrators. Then as now bureaucrats were as much feared as demagogues, though for different reasons.

Evidence for the truth of this generalization can be found in the abortive experience of municipal reform. From time to time the good citizens gathered their forces and elected a reform mayor and administration, but as the momentum slackened, institutional reform was abandoned (if it had ever been contemplated) and the same socio-political logic that had brought the old boss to power led to electoral victory for a new boss over the weary reformers. The truth was that the business and professional men, who provided the mainstay of reform movements, were themselves unwilling to undertake the time-consuming duties of local government, and were inhibited by their laissez-faire philosophy from installing (and paying for) the experts who could alone have given continuous supervision to the badly needed tasks of social and administrative change. Despite the intermittent enthusiasm of reformers, American cities remained the worst governed in the civilized world. In fields where popular government might be expected to have the most beneficial effects—because the problems were local and most easily comprehended—the efficacy of democracy failed to meet the challenge of modern society.

If late nineteenth-century America failed in some respects, it was not a barren age. The material achievements produced unattractive consequences, but they were achievements none the less: America was growing richer, and if the wealth was very badly distributed, at least many people lived fuller and more comfortable lives than ever before. It was a period of educational achievement, and new idealism combined with new wealth to reinvigorate old universities and colleges and to promote the founding of hundreds of new institutions. Experience has shown that it is difficult for democracy to survive poverty or economic stagnation, and the enlarging benefits of industrialization provided new material foundations for government that would remain popular and become modernized. In economic development, in technology, in science, and in education the late nineteenth century was the formative period of modern America; the growing pains were sometimes acute but so were the symptoms of vitality.

Nor was the late nineteenth century so complacent as is sometimes imagined, and confidence in the future often bred impatience with the present. Criticism was often directed against the wrong objects— and the preceding pages have shown how Negroes, immigrants, Catholics, professional politicians, and even big businessmen were made the scapegoats for ills which were endemic in society—but the period also saw the forging of ideas which were to take on constructive roles in the next century. Socialism made little headway, but Lester Ward made telling criticisms of the misuse of evolutionary theory and provided a theoretical justification for greater governmental responsibility. Ward pointed out that man's ability to control and organize his environment was as "natural" as competition, and that there was no logical reason why doctrinaire limitations should be placed upon projects for amelioration. The effects of control might be debated, but the principle of control was unassailable, and since businessmen imposed order and discipline upon the economic processes they controlled, there was no reason why the representatives of the people should be denied the same discretion.

Of more immediate influence was Henry George, who attacked the basic propositions of classical economics. There was ample evidence that economic progress produced wealth, but wealth tended to concentrate in too few hands while poverty actually increased. The vision of a self-regulating society that would yield the greatest possible benefit for all its members was challenged at its root; the "unseen hand" was at work but not as men had supposed. George's own diagnosis focused upon the private ownership of land as the cause of these inequalities, and he proposed to finance social improvement through a single tax on land values. As society acquired wealth the value of land would rise, so that the public income for social use would keep pace with economic improvement. His ideas achieved great popularity, and his attack upon economic orthodoxy inspired many would-be social reformers who did not accept his remedies.

Movements for municipal reforms seldom achieved the expected results but fostered a continuous stream of criticism, which ranged from members of the newly formed American Economic Association to journalists who found good copy in the exposure of social evils. America had always lacked a party committed to reform, and the new critics did not form one; but their streams of thought were flowing together and would soon work a ferment within the existing parties. Moral impulses which had always been felt so strongly had once fused together in the antislavery movement; they were now coalescing again in strong though diffused pressure for social improvement. The Churches were influenced by what came to be known as the "social gospel." Several universities, and particularly the University of Wisconsin, became centers for new economic and social theories. In a somewhat different vein, Andrew Carnegie, head of the world's greatest steel company, preached the duty of rich men to feed back their wealth into society through institutionalized charity, while, with less theoretical inspiration, John D. Rockefeller followed the biblical precept of giving a tithe of his wealth to charity. Carnegie gave huge sums for education, research, and culture; Rockefeller founded the University of Chicago and gave away millions with a special preference for medical projects. The efforts of these, and many other men of great wealth, added a new and unexpected dimension to the fabric of American civilization.

The late nineteenth century was the first era of modern America; if it was not an age of reform, it was certainly an age of change. American democracy had gone through a time of troubles, but it emerged not wholly unequipped to tackle the problems of the unknown. Somehow the political system survived the terrible failure of civil war and endured the tensions of rapid growth and dislocation. In political history the period has been characterized by corruption and the betrayal of ideals, but there was also solid achievement in a system that could build a bridge between the rural but divided past and the complexities of modern society. It was not in politics an age of greatness, but it was one of great significance in the history of American democracy.

CHAPTER XI

MODERNIZATION

From the later years of the nineteenth century American society has undergone successive changes which have transformed institutions and attitudes. The statistical evidence for these changes can be measured in population growth, the increasing proportion of people living in towns and among them the growing preponderance in very large towns; in industrial production, consumer purchases, and in all the accessories and luxuries of a highly developed society; in the size of private corporations, trade unions, and public administration. Against recurrent but ineffective protests, government has assumed greater and greater responsibilities, and to an ever increasing extent is blamed if things go wrong. Since 1933 the Federal Government has assumed responsibility for the inner mechanism of American capitalism, and is expected to regulate and direct in order to avoid depression. The shifting internal balance of power and responsibility has dominated the domestic scene, but a whole new dimension of policy and action was opened when the United States intervened in the European War in 1917; from that time it has been less and less easy to think of American problems in isolation from those of the rest of the world.

An early generation could see a pendulum swinging between laissez faire and intervention, but from the contemporary perspective one sees a continuous trend with a few variations and interruptions. What has been constant has been the growth in the size and power of the institutions—both public and private—that dominate American society, though the pace has not always been the same in the different sectors. From 1900 to 1914 there was a rapid increase in public functions while business was held in check; from 1920 to 1928 there was a formidable increase of power in the hands of corporations, while government seemed to be abdicating many of the functions of public responsibility ("seemed" because the number of federal employees actually increased); from 1933 to 1941 there was a very rapid accumulation of public responsibilities and much administrative experiment; since 1945 the federal and state governments have brought an ever-widening circle of private activities under public control. During both World Wars the Federal Government assumed numerous responsibilities and concentrated power on a vast scale. Viewed at the time, even by advocates of government intervention, as temporary and dangerous, these wartime experiments became merely the pioneers and precursors of peacetime administration.

Bred in the assumption that there was a universal conflict between authority and individual freedom, and convinced that what the one gained must necessarily be at the expense of the other, Americans were profoundly disturbed by these developments. Fears were not allayed by evidence that all other advanced nations were moving in the same direction, and the belief that America was adopting foreign ideas added notes of hysteria to the debate. At every stage during the past century there have been vocal Americans who seriously believed that other Americans, occupying positions of authority, were engaged in international conspiracies to subvert American life. First socialism and then communism were targets for this kind of attack; but conspiracies were not found solely by the Right on the Left—international bankers, the gold ring, "big business," were all pictured in the same conspiratorial way. Recently the Left has discovered a "Power Elite" composed of influential politicians, the top executives of great corporations, and the military establishment which is supposed to run the country. No other nation has been so prone to discover secret and sinister designs to account for the size and complexity of modern life.

There is no need to fall into this trap. There are general problems which have occurred in every society going through the process of modernization, and if some have been seen most clearly in America they were not uniquely American. Indeed, a feature of this contemporary world was that the forces that had made America distinct were ceasing to operate exclusively in America. The United States was no longer alone in having universal male suffrage, and everywhere hereditary ruling classes were in retreat, if not already relegated to picturesque ineffectiveness. Quick access to abundant land, and the exploitation of virgin resources were no longer forces in American development. The great streams of science and technology which altered the character of the civilized world flowed in all advanced countries, and if, since the Revolution, American civilization had diverged from Europe, convergence would come to be the rule in the twentieth century. The knowledge that America was no longer unique was difficult to accept, and the frantic quest for subversive conspiracies was one way of refusing to face it.

In the great political and social changes Americans were handicapped by the heritage of past ideas. More than other peoples the Americans had seen authority and power as the enemy of freedom; and the increase in government responsibility led inevitably to the conclusion that freedom was being whittled away. A more realistic view would suggest that men have usually seen government in the right hands as an ally in the struggle against class rule, private economic power, privilege, exploitation, poverty, disease and hunger. The constant aim of democratic societies to wrest power out of the wrong hands, and to divert it from the wrong purposes, has not produced a diminution of public authority but its continuous augmentation.

Conditioned by their history to believe that the purpose of democracy was to limit the exercise of governmental power, Americans have been slow to accept these concepts, and many Americans regard the multiplication of governmental responsibilities as an aberration and as a betrayal of the true American tradition. Conversely some American liberals are so impressed by the value of what has been done that every critic of centralization is treated as the foe of social justice and the spokesman of special interests and prejudice. In this chapter the transformation of American political society since 1890 is described as "modernization," but no value judgment is implied. The process has produced society as we know it today; but this does not mean that other lines of development could not have been pursued, or that the best possible outcome has been achieved. "Modernization" is a neutral word and merely describes how society changed from what it was into what it is; but one should not infer from this that modernization has been the product of chance or random choice; rather the similarity between the process in so many advanced countries implies the existence of general and underlying causes in the transformation of rural, hierarchical, and predominantly agricultural societies into urban, democratic, and largely industrial societies. The various aspects of change have not coincided or moved at the same rate in different countries, and it is impossible to establish a uniform pattern of modernization or to lay down a precise timetable for its achievement; but it is possible to see experiences and expedients that cut right across the separate national histories. In some aspects of political evolution America was the pioneer; in some aspects of social legislation she came late into the field. The United States was among the first nations to accept a public responsibility for free education and one of the last (among advanced nations) to accept public responsibility for medical care; it had an antimonopoly law on the statute book when the existence of the problem was hardly recognized in Europe but remained unalterably opposed to public ownership when several other countries moved in that direction; it possesses the best museums and national parks (run by public authorities), an excellent telephone service (privately owned under public regulation), and a television service (run by private enterprise) which rouses little enthusiasm. If it is impossible to lay down a precise timetable, it may be equally difficult to make valid generalizations about the role of public and private enterprise in modernization.

In the political history of the United States between 1890 and 1940 the process of modernization can be illustrated by five landmarks of modern times. The first was the Populist upheaval, and the second was the Progressive ferment. The third was the shock of involvement in World War, and the necessary expansion of governmental power to mobilize and direct national resources. The fourth was the depression which laid bare certain weaknesses in unregulated capitalism and delivered over a large portion of an affluent people to poverty, and the fifth was the massive improvization of the New Deal, which provided governmental institutions for regulation and control while giving a majority of the people a vested interest in their success and perpetuation. It would, however, be wrong to think only of these five formative episodes and forget the long-term transformation of American industry which went on throughout the period, for all the other episodes would have appeared in a quite different light if the economy had not proved itself capable of maintaining more people at a higher standard of life than ever before in the history of the world.

The first major attempt to attack the central problems of responsibility and power in America came from Populism, which reached its peak in the Western and Southern states between 1890 and 1896. Angry and confused, unable to decide between a leap back into the Jeffersonian past and a look forward to new concepts of public responsibility, and too closely related to the immediate difficulties of distressed farming regions to become a permanent national party, Populism nevertheless tackled real problems and asked questions which would provide the stuff of politics for the next half-century and more. The Populist platform of 1892 included a general statement that the power of government, "that is of the people," ought to be increased and used as an instrument of social justice. In specific terms it asked for a reform of the currency, the public ownership of railroads, and for more processes through which democratic pressures could be brought to bear upon politics. Behind their preoccupation with the currency was the difficulty of financing an underdeveloped rural economy in a world ruled by orthodox finance, and their proposal to use abundant silver as well as scarce gold as the basis for currency, though crudely expressed, touched upon truths that all modern societies have had to recognize. They raised also the whole question of public responsibilities for the economic activities providing essential services for the community. To rescue legislative activity from domination by pressure groups and over-mighty corporations they sought such democratic devices as the referendum, the initiative, and the direct election of United States senators. Associated with these new approaches to the problems of the day (and of the future) were proposals for a graduated income tax, a postal savings bank, and a shorter working day in industry. A demand for the restriction of immigration illustrated both their ethnic base among farmers of Anglo-Saxon and North European stock and their attempt to appeal to the skilled "aristocracy" of urban labor.

In its immediate outcome the failure of Populism was complete. In 1896 the Populists sacrificed their wider ranging proposals for reform in order to fuse with the Democrats and to concentrate upon the single issue of silver under William Jennings Bryan. Of all their proposals this was the least attractive to urban labor and the most alarming to intellectuals of orthodox economic faith; the result was a campaign which brought together business, skilled labor, and the educated middle class under the Republican banner, and so far from laying the foundations for Populist and Democratic power, the election of 1896 established Republican ascendancy for many years to come. In the long run most of the Populist proposals would find their way into the legislative achievements of other parties. The initiative and the referendum would be adopted in many states, the Seventeenth Amendment passed in 1913 secured the direct election of United States senators, a federal income tax would become legal under the Sixteenth Amendment and today provides the Government's major source of income. Railroads were taken over during the First World War, and though returned to private ownership after its end, the Federal Government came to exercise a firm control over national communications of all kinds through regulatory commissions. Beginning in 1920 drastic limitations were imposed upon the number of immigrants allowed into the country. Finally, during the New Deal, the Federal Government would come to accept responsibility for the economic health of agriculture. This list of measures proposed by the Populists is impressive and places them among the architects of the twentieth century. In one field only was the legacy less impressive: in the South the Populists made cautious advances into the field of biracial politics, but in 1896 this experiment was sacrificed to the Democratic alliance and never revived.

Populism had raised some of the questions; Progressivism supplied some of the answers. Populism had expressed the grievances of farmers who felt themselves left outside; Progressivism flourished among the classes who had been the principal beneficiaries of nineteenth-century civilization. In origins Progressivism was a movement within the Republican party though some Democrats later identified themselves as Progressives. It was middle class, Protestant, and drawn predominantly from families of old American stock. With a movement that was diffuse and characterized by attitudes rather than by theories of government, there were many exceptions to any generalizations that could be made but most Progressive leaders were drawn from the kind of men who had been accustomed to run the churches, the professions, the universities, and the older forms of business. The rise of progressivism was therefore the symptom of a split within a dominant class rather than the emergence of new men or new classes. For most Progressives Populism had looked like the threat of barbarism, but it also stirred a great deal of questioning and criticism directed especially to the conditions of the poor, slums, corrupt politics, and business, which seemed to have influence without a sense of social responsibility. In its first phase, before 1900 and before anyone coined the name, progressivism consisted of a large number of local movements with varying objectives, from social work to attacks on political bosses in the larger cities and campaigns against the power of corporations in Western states. In Wisconsin, Robert LaFollette mobilized rural support for a campaign against big business and their political tools in the old parties and engineered a significant alliance with intellectuals from the University of Wisconsin whom he brought into the political arena as idea men and publicists. The second and longest phase of progressivism began when a madman's bullet ended President McKinley's life and put Vice-President Theodore Roosevelt into the White House.

In 1901 Roosevelt was the youngest man ever to have become President. He came from a wealthy and patrician New York family and was one of the few men of this type to engage in politics. He was also a writer, historian, amateur cow boy, leader of rough riders in the Spanish-American war, and a dominant personality who constantly dramatized his own ideas and actions. Men who disliked him thought him emotional, erratic, and unreliable; to his friends he seemed to personify the need for America to escape from the materialism of the late nineteenth century and to rediscover a sense of grandeur and mission. As President, Theodore Roosevelt did not so much initiate progressive measures as provide a focus for all the men and movements conscious of a need to improve society. As a politician, he was much shrewder than appeared on the surface and was more interested in keeping together a broad-based Republican alliance than in sponsoring reform crusades; but he also realized that if the party was to have a future it must find room within its ranks for the Progressives. This conviction was not merely the result of political calculation, for Roosevelt grasped and approved the heart of the Progressive idea that social evolution had been possible because men, unlike other animals, had the power to control their environment. From this it followed that one must ask which men had most power to control and for what purposes, and if the answer showed that society was being controlled in the wrong way by the wrong men, then good citizens had a duty to do something about it. The impulse was not purely humanitarian for there was also the question of efficiency; Roosevelt disliked corrupt politicians and selfish businessmen largely because of the human and material resources they wasted or misused.

Bosses distorted democracy in their own interests, and ended by turning great cities into political jungles. The private owners of urban property defended indignantly their right to administer their own affairs, and produced in slums the most inefficient social institution one could imagine. Railroad magnates grasped at political power but did not seem to be very good at running railroads. Criticisms on these lines were not new. There had been periodic movements (often successful) against political bosses, particularly since the notorious rule of

Boss Tweed in New York and his overthrow by a reform movement in 1870. Disquiet at bad conditions in the cities went back a long way, and each new influx of immigrants into the lowest strata of city population had increased anxiety about the alien and depressed condition of urban life. Railroads had been a frequent target for criticism and an incentive for political action, while the intention of controlling monopoly had been declared in the Sherman Anti-Trust Act of 1890. Progressivism, therefore, was the result less of novelty than of a convergence of many older strains of criticism together with an awareness that all the efforts of past years had produced remarkably few permanent results. Faced with this situation some Progressives looked back to a world of free competition and others forward to social regulation; some pursued limited local objectives while others considered major programs of reform. Some were pacifists who had been shocked by the imperialist sentiment at the close of the nineteenth century while others (including Roosevelt) enthusiastically supported a vigorous expansion of American power. Nevertheless, the Progressives did talk a common language and shared some basic assumptions; they all assumed that laissez faire was an inadequate social philosophy, and most of them believed that the channels of communication between politicians and people should be opened. Unlike their nineteenth-century predecessors they wanted more and not less political participation. They demanded, and ended by getting, direct primaries so that voters could have an immediate responsibility for choosing party nominees. They demanded the direct election of United States senators (to replace choice by state legislatures) and this was achieved when the Seventeenth Amendment became a part of the Constitution in 1913. A majority of the states adopted the referendum under which certain measures (usually specified in the state constitutions) had to be referred to the people, and some, especially in the West, also adopted the initiative under which a proposition securing minimum public support, had to be placed before the people and considered by the legislature in the event of a favorable vote. Finally some states adopted the recall (under which officials could be dismissed after an adverse popular vote), the direct election of judges, and the review of judicial decisions by popular vote.

Though the Progressive democratic reforms were uneven in their application and often disappointing in their results, the cumulative effect was profoundly important. They provided a major exception to the principle of convergence and accentuated the distinctive political characteristics of the United States. In economics, social structure, the responsibilities of government, administration, and urban culture the United States has grown more and more like other advanced nations;

yet the political base of the country remains different, and twentieth-century developments have accentuated the differences. A striking characteristic of American democracy had always been the frequency of elections and the number of officials and legislators to be elected; twentieth-century reforms increased the number of persons to be elected, provided for direct participation in the nomination of candidates and in the legislative process, and even opened some judicial proceedings to public scrutiny and pressure. No other democratic country followed this American path. British democracy became crystallized with infrequent elections, participation limited to the choice of single legislative representatives, and the exclusion of most voters from the nomination of candidates for office. The French voter was offered slightly greater opportunities for participation in his own country, but far less than in the United States. In other countries the democratic forms were abandoned altogether, while only the Scandinavian countries offered anything like the profusion of democratic choice provided in America.

Though the trend was set toward greater activity on the part of the national Government, much freedom of action remained with the states, and the way in which this freedom was used depended largely upon the effectiveness of popular participation. While some states lagged in every social field, others experimented in the adoption of social legislation. There were considerable variations in the structure of politics from state to state, with business dominating some, the trade unions becoming influential in others, and intellectuals affecting policy in some areas while their voices were ignored elsewhere. Ethnic minorities could become politically significant in some districts, even though their numbers in the nation were small. These variations would have existed in any event, but Progressive reforms gave greater opportunities to organized and articulate groups, so that the political features of states and regions were more and more likely to reflect the social conformation of the locality. While a metropolitan economy and culture stretched across the nation, the principle of local political autonomy was reinforced, and while all countries increased power at the center, the United States did more than any other to retain regional differences.

This could produce tension at various levels. It was most obvious in the South where local autonomy allowed a whole section to contract out of many functions which were elsewhere accepted as public responsibilities. The reverse happened in some industrial areas which moved quickly into the field of economic and social regulation only to find themselves out of step with the rest of the country. These local variations had always been present, but the speed of change, in both material achievement and social philosophy, meant that the gap widened between the areas which were resistant to new ideas and those which responded quickly to them.

The third and final phase of progressivism came when, under Roosevelt's successor William Howard Taft, a decisive breach developed between the progressive and conservative Republicans. In 1912 Roosevelt returned to politics, after a short absence, to campaign for the Republican nomination, and, when this failed, to launch his own Progressive party. Released from the conservative brake, progressivism emerged as a more radical, more constructive, and more positive movement. Their program anticipated many of the ideas which would inspire the later New Deal and presented the ideal of a national government undertaking wide responsibilities in the social field. Yet Roosevelt was never opposed to capitalism in principle and he fully sympathised with the need for large-scale economic organization condemned by others as "big business." What he envisaged was a partnership in which the National Government represented the public interest and laid down the the rules for business behavior while encouraging and fostering the dynamic and productive role of big business. In this way, therefore, Roosevelt looked forward to the present situation under which American capitalism flourishes alongside and in harness with the massive machinery of a regulatory state. In 1912 these ideas were premature, and though Roosevelt captured the larger part of the Republican vote, the party split let in Woodrow Wilson as the first Democrat to win the Presidency in twenty years. Thereafter, the independent Progressive movement languished; they had ideas and enthusiasm but lacked organization. The Democrats were doing well and this argued for a restoration of Republican harmony; and in the fall of 1914 the tragedy of European war drove undramatic domestic reform from the center of the stage.

The democratization of the Progressive Era was not intended to be revolutionary. The most influential leaders were professional men, intelligent business men, and intellectuals; moral reform, the amelioration of social abuses and a corrective to overly large economic power were their objectives. They did not contemplate fundamental changes and had little in common with European socialists; they wished to bring popular pressures to bear more directly on politics but not to produce revolutionary consequences. The purpose was to allow more scope for active, humane, and intelligent voters, and the consequence was to be a further installment of middle-class liberalism on the nineteenth-century model, not mass democracy or a totalitarian state. Yet the ferment of ideas and readiness to experiment were moving America into a new era. In politics the elections of 1888 and earlier years had, by modern standards, an old-fashioned flavor, but the issues and arguments of 1912 seem fully contemporary. In economics the second industrial revolution associated with electricity and oil was well under way, and manufactures were about to go over to mass production on an extensive scale. In religion and morals the old certainties no longer commanded universal assent. In intellectual life it had become possible to discuss the functions of government without assuming that it was "natural" for government to do as little as possible.

In a way that could hardly have been anticipated, the Presidency was the first great institution of government to benefit from the new mood. Roosevelt had a barely concealed contempt for the second-rate men who had dominated politics; he believed in leadership, he believed in government, and he believed that America was faced with the choice of seizing greatness or falling into moral decline. He and his friends looked to Hamilton rather than to Jefferson and believed that the drive and initiative in government must come from the executive. Though an "accidental" President, no man had thought more about the problems of leadership than Roosevelt, and he was determined to make the office the dynamic instrument of national aspirations. Woodrow Wilson, apparently mild and academic in manner compared with the "rough rider," concealed a will of iron and a clear conviction of his own intellectual superiority over his fellow politicians. Indeed one often finds Wilson driving and dictating in situations which Roosevelt would have met with maneuver and conciliation. These characteristics would finally bring Wilson to disaster in his attempt to force acceptance of the Versailles Treaty in 1919, but they made him an extremely effective President in domestic affairs. In addition, where Roosevelt had declared general principles, Wilson had usually mastered the detail so that he was never compelled to defer to his departmental heads. Thus Wilson not only impressed his personality upon the nation but was also the first President since Lincoln to be truly the master of his administration; and he was a much more orderly and consistent administrator than Lincoln had been.

Personality alone does not account for the rise of the strong Presidency and its survival. In earlier years the latent power of the office had been obscured by the assumption that the initiation of policy would rest largely with Congress, but the cumulative growth of the federal administration had steadily increased the authority of the President. Civil service reform, which could be interpreted as a curb on Presidential patronage, had actually increased his administrative authority and relieved him from political pressure. The Anti-Trust Act had given him new responsibilities; the war with Spain in 1898, the increasing importance of foreign affairs, and the government of new overseas territories all imposed fresh responsibilities upon him.

The greatest single factor in the growth of the President's power was, however, his representative character. If Congress seemed to be dominated by local and special interests, if lobbyists seemed to be more powerful than legislators, and if the social balance was deranged by plutocracy, the President represented the whole people and had the authority to promote the public good. Soon Presidents would be expected to act as masters in the federal house and be blamed for weakness if they failed to do so.

When one compares the experience of political modernization in the United States with that of other countries, one striking omission appears. In every other advanced country working-class political movements (and especially movements based on organized labor in industry) became active and influential in all spheres of social reform; moreover, in most of them, working-class activism led to a rejection of capitalism and a welcome for various brands of socialism. In America, organized labor adopted a deliberately noncommittal attitude to politics, renounced socialism, and fought on a limited front for a larger share of the economic cake. In 1912, and again in 1932, socialism seemed to be politically significant but picked up no momentum for further advance. Under the masterful leadership of Samuel Gompers the American Federation of Labor refused to support independent political action or to throw its weight behind either main political party. The few occasions on which organized labor has definitely endorsed the Presidential candidate of one party have not provided happy precedents, though the antiunion attitude of many Republican employers has tended to push the majority of labor leaders toward the Democrats.

The comparative unimportance of working-class politics can be explained in various ways. American society already provided many of the things for which European labor fought: in the Northern and Western states there was free elementary schooling and an educational ladder considerably wider than that in the Old World; in an expanding economy there was not only opportunity for promotion but also great demand for skilled labor; the open structure of politics already gave scope for working-class participation. At the same time the federal system made it easier to obtain limited local objectives and much harder to put together national alliances. Finally, the gap between skilled and semiskilled, which was everywhere an obstacle to organization, was emphasized in America by the frequency with which the line between them ran along ethnic or religious differences.

There is a paradox in the rejection of socialism because the rhetoric, used by the Populists and other protest movements to attack big business, passed into the language of European radicalism. From them derived the image of "Wall Street" as the malign, controlling interest behind politics, the idea of an international conspiracy of wealth against the people, and denunciations of the sham battle between supposedly democratic parties. Contemporary spokesmen of the European Left use terminology that was formulated by angry farmers of the American West, though the heirs of Populism have adopted a conservative pride in capitalist institutions. The truth is that the Populist attack on capitalism (and that of some Progressives) was always discriminating; it was never "capitalists" but always "some capitalists" who were at fault; the enemy was not the hard-working small businessman of the West, whose prospects were identified with his region, but remote capitalists who manipulated without being aware of local needs. John Pierpont Morgan was the villain, not the Babbitts of Main Street. The attack was ethical, concentrated upon the immorality of individuals, and did not assume that men were made immoral by the economic system they served.

European socialists were able to supplement their attacks upon capitalist ethics by demonstrating the supposed inefficiency of capitalism. In their analysis capitalism was not only immoral but also failed to live up to its own precepts of amelioration through competition. American socialists lacked similar evidence; indeed the evidence pointed the other way with increasing efficiency, lowered costs, better rewards for skill, more even distribution of wealth, and a genuine anxiety to employ talent whatever its social origin. As industry converted to mass production and consciously sought the big consumer market for standardized products, the relationship between free enterprise and rising living standards became clear. Consequently American socialists have usually found themselves arguing that men should abandon material rewards in favor of hypothetical moral gains. Their position can be compared to that of the abolitionists; but where the abolitionists could win a response from people who were deeply indoctrinated by evangelical religion, Socialists battle in a world in which all the conditioned responses favor capitalism.

The place of the debate elsewhere over socialism was taken in America by controversy over capitalist monopoly, trusts and corporations with a significant refusal to go on from an attack upon monopoly to an attack upon capitalism. For many the purpose of legislation, and of prosecutions under the Sherman Anti-Trust Act, was to make the magnates of industrial and finance capitalism behave according to the ethical rules of small enterprise. While big business came increasingly under criticism, small business was idealized and shared in the virtues that had once been attributed to the cultivators of the soil. Only a few adopted socialist criticisms of private enterprise as a whole, and there was no movement akin to the British Fabians. On the other hand European critics have too readily assumed that the failure of American socialism revealed an American weakness, and it may be that the Progressives made more significant contributions to the problem of private power in a democratic society than their British contemporaries.

Progressives inherited the Act of 1890, which made combinations in restraint of trade illegal; but it was not clear whether the Act condemned economic consolidation unequivocally or only when the consequences were demonstrably harmful to the public interest. The wording seemed to permit no argument, but literal interpretation was clearly impossible if simple partnerships or trade unions were not to be brought under the axe. In fact, the Supreme Court did extend the Act to trade unions, while some great combinations were not even prosecuted. Theodore Roosevelt adopted a rough and ready distinction between "good trusts" and "bad trusts," which allowed the President and the federal Attorney-General to discriminate in their prosecutions and to proceed only against those combinations which promised harmful consequences. In 1911 the Supreme Court followed the same line when the majority found the Standard Oil Company guilty of an infringement of the Anti-Trust Act but also announced that they would adopt a "rule of reason" in future decisions; the implication was that the judges would look not at the fact of monopoly but at the consequences of monopoly. In other words, the letter of the law was left behind, while the Supreme Court concerned itself with economic and social evidence.

Woodrow Wilson was not satisfied with the "rule of reason," and warned that Roosevelt's approach held out the promise of a Hamiltonian alliance between big government and "good" business at the expense of individual freedom. Wilson preferred to weight judgment against bigness and to put upon corporations the onus of proving that their operations were not harmful. In practice Wilson initiated fewer prosecutions than Roosevelt, and neither of them was so active in this field as the conservative Taft. The Clayton Act of 1914 did, however, try to spell out what was "unreasonable" and also exempted unions from the operation of the Act.

What was evolving as a result of prosecutions, judicial decisions, and the Clayton Act was a code of behavior. Faced with the menace of overwhelming economic power in a few hands, the American consensus avoided a direct confrontation between democratic authority and monopoly power, but worked toward the establishment of rules, partly written and partly resting upon convention, under which the wielders of economic authority could be required by the political authority to defend themselves in the courts. And partly by judicial decisions, partly by *obiter dicta*, partly by the arguments heard in court, the judges worked out "rules of reason." The situation was not wholly satisfying, either logically or in practice, but the problem was common to all developing societies. No one found a fully satisfactory answer, and the American solution was as acceptable as most. It recognized that private power was accountable to public authority but did so without placing economic growth in a doctrinaire straight jacket.

If Progressives were puzzled by the relationship betwen democracy and economic power, they experienced equal difficulties in reconciling democratic power with constitutional limitations. The late nineteenth century had been an age of judicial veto, and the most striking examples had been designed to protect private enterprise from political interference. The Progressives therefore inherited a situation in which the scales of justice were weighted against the kind of legislation many of them supported. States might find the courts standing as a barrier between the political authority and the regulation of corporations, the enforcement of health standards, the regulation of hours of work, the compulsory improvement of slum property, and the prohibition of child labor. Like the Abolitionists before them the Progressives were inclined to assume that the Constitution, just in itself, had been subverted by the power which they disliked; stripped of its laissez faire accretions and relieved from judicial obsession with property rights, the Constitution, they believed, would once more emerge as the guardian of social rights.

This attitude was undermined and eventually overthrown when Charles A. Beard published his *Economic Interpretation of the Constitution* in 1913. The Constitution, argued Beard, had not been subverted; from the first it had been expressly designed to protect commercial and financial property from political interference, and modern judges merely followed the "founding fathers" when delivering "anti-democratic" decisions. He concluded that the Constitution had endured because it had been made by practical men to meet practical needs, but his book was greeted as a wicked attack upon fundamental institutions by conservative men and as a gospel of freedom by many Progressives. The claim of the Supreme Court to review the social legislation of the states and to protect property against "unwise" legislation had been justified by the belief that the Constitution embodied universal laws; now Beard demonstrated that it had originally been the product of circumstances and deserved no more respect than any other reasonably successful law. If the Constitution had been a successful remedy in 1787 there was no reason to assume that it contained absolute rules for 1913. The road was open for a new era in which the judges would cease to be the Olympian administrators of universal law and become the agents of public policy. Indeed the judges themselves had already moved a little way along this road by admitting evidence of social need when considering the validity of a law, and thus accepting by implication the argument that law was to be judged by its results.

Charles Beard disclaimed Marxist inspiration, but his analysis of the making of the Constitution rested heavily upon the thesis that institutions and ideas were most readily explained by the interplay of fundamental economic forces. His ideas gained an almost unchallengeable supremacy over American intellectuals for the next forty years and found their way into most college texts. There was some confusion in a theory that claimed fundamental forces as the determinants and yet found it necessary to rely upon evidence of superficial economic motivation, and it was not always clear whether Beard was explaining the Constitution as the product of imponderable forces that could not be denied or as the result of a conspiracy of merchants and public creditors that could easily have been defeated if anyone had had the political skill to do so. It was an unsubtle economic interpretation, but it carried the day and left American intellectuals and their students with an uncomfortable paradox: in a nation with a public philosophy of free enterprise and natural law they suggested that the fundamental institutions could be explained in pseudo-Marxist terms.

Into this arena of anxious but not unprofitable controversy came the agonizing fact of war. Progressivism as a separate movement was already dying down, but its influence had percolated widely. Woodrow Wilson, at first somewhat hostile to the theory of social legislation, had begun to move much closer to the positive attitude of Theodore Roosevelt. Indeed the closing year of his first administration saw a number of measures which set up a bridge between the states' rights, limited government, the Democratic creed of the past and the nationalist and interventionist party of the future. But these latter day movements of Wilsonian progressivism took place under the enormous shadow of war in Europe, and six months after Woodrow Wilson had been reelected (largely as a vote of confidence in the way in which he had kept America neutral), the country was at war with Germany.

Hitherto the majority of Americans had assumed that it was their destiny to stand apart from the Old World and to work out their democratic destiny without reference to foreign blunders. They were deeply and instinctively isolationist, but in 1917 they were brought suddenly face to face with the fact that American interests might demand intervention in European quarrels. In the evolution of American democratic ideas Woodrow Wilson's justification for war played a special part, for he was not content to plead German threats, the danger to American shipping, or the possibility of Germany controlling the Atlantic. Rather, he rested the main burden of the case upon the duty of the United States to impose a just peace upon the world.

Democracy and self-determination were American gifts to civilization, and it had become the duty of Americans to ensure that they not be placed in jeopardy. In practical terms no other appeal could have rallied Americans in quite the same way, and it would be unwise to denigrate the real force of idealism behind American intervention. In the long view one can see more and can stress the enormous importance for the future of the idea that the United States had a duty to defend threatened democracy. Historians usually trace the story of America's involvement in international affairs at least to 1898; but to contemporaries the great break with the past came in 1917—and came because their President insisted that democracy in a single country was not enough. The interests of America and the interests of authoritarian, aggressive states were so opposed they could not exist peacefully together.

It is true that a majority of Americans would not follow this logic through when the war was over and support American membership of the League of Nations. The idea of the League charter as an international version of the Constitution did not convince them, and the possibility that the United States might contract treaty obligations that would make them dependent upon the decisions of others was alarming. It was one thing to intervene in a conflict at the right moment for chosen objectives; it would be quite another matter to be bound by decisions of a League Assembly. The immediate consequence of the debate occasioned by Woodrow Wilson's concept of the League was therefore a sharp reversion to isolation, but later events would prove that 1917 was a watershed and that the relationship of American democracy to the rest of the world had been fundamentally altered.

In domestic affairs the impact of war ran a parallel course. As soon as America entered the war it was assumed that victory depended upon the most efficient deployment of economic resources and production, with the added complication that the American economy was geared to deliver goods to the home market, not for a massive trans-Atlantic exportation. Industry came under the most minute direction, railroads were placed temporarily under the absolute control of the Federal Government, shipping came under strict government direction, and within a few weeks the United States was converted from a free enterprise society into one in which every economic activity was directly or indirectly controlled by authority. But, as in international affairs, war pushed events prematurely in the direction they would eventually take, and the massive experiment in a directed economy was too great a departure from the past to be accepted as a precedent for the peacetime function of government. The machinery for regulation was quickly dismantled, and wartime habits of government direction were replaced by extravagant confidence in the capacity for free enterprise capitalism to deliver the goods and inaugurate a glorious new era of plenty.

The experience of war accentuated divisions that had already existed in the Progressive period. A growing number of Progressives had seen an intellectual and emotional gulf fixed between themselves and the "old guard" in politics and economics; but even so the dialogue had been preserved and leaders such as Roosevelt and Wilson insisted that they served a unified America and not a divided society. Progressives and their conservative opponents came out of the same school of nineteenth-century thought; if they disliked each other, they continued to talk the same language; but after 1920 it became apparent that this continuum of debate had collapsed. Intellectuals who regarded the Constitution through Beardian eyes believed in a conspiracy of armament kings and saw hypocrisy behind Wilson's idealistic explanations. They had no stock of ideas or rhetoric to counter the business reaction against wartime controls, the postwar "red scare," or phobias about foreign influence. Along with Wilson the whole Progressive movement went into eclipse, and men who had looked forward to an era of rational betterment found themselves in an era when the myopic aphorisms of small-town businessmen were accepted as expressions of profound truth. Meanwhile the apostles of corporate business proclaimed that, thanks to the wisdom and foresight of the great enterprisers, America was launched upon a "New Era" of unimagined plenty.

American society had been divided in this way before, but the precedents were not happy. The gulf, between the political and business establishment on the one hand and the intellectuals on the other, could be compared to the divisions over slavery, and everyone knew the outcome. Intellectuals themselves were not, however, anxious to identify themselves with the Abolitionists—who represented a puritanism from which they were trying to escape and a philosophy of free enterprise that was interpreted as the parent of the New Era—and instead adopted a curious blend of parochial agrarianism, international sophistication, and economic determinism. The 1920's were stimulating and frustrating, creative and abortive, lively and lost. For the first time American intellectuals could feel that they were making a world of their own; but it was a world without traditional roots, and, confronted with a generation of feverish bad taste they gloried in their alienation.

The nation was also divided in other ways. The decision to prohibit the manufacture and sale of alcohol was one of the most extraordinary ever made in a democratic society. Passed by two-thirds of both houses of Congress and quickly ratified by three-quarters of the states, the Eighteenth Amendment was certainly the will of the majority. In was the fruit of long-sustained Prohibitionist propaganda and of disquiet about the effects of heavy drinking in cities, and was imposed by the rural, religious, and middle-class vote upon people who repudiated the morality that inspired it and bitterly resented its enforcement. The "wet" minority would not respect the law and had ample means for evading it. Prohibition crushed the old-time saloon, fostered organized crime, and made hosts of otherwise law-abiding citizens the accomplices of criminals.

To men who lived through the decade without accepting its manners or assumption, it seemed a bizarre period of moralism and organized crime; of small-town Republicanism in power and big-city finance building monstrous pyramids of power; of people crazy and callous with good living. The hopes of progressivism had produced a farce, yet it was comedy with raw, crude, ugly scenes. The white world first became conscious of Negro culture in the sudden upsurge of jazz, but millions of Negroes—tucked away on forgotten share cropping farms or herding together in city slums—gained little from prosperity. Nor, for that matter, did millions of white farmers.

The truth was that, for the first time, American democracy had to face life in a new-style capitalist society, and if liquor was forbidden there were other things to intoxicate the mind. For a century Americans had prided themselves on their standards of comfort compared with low-paid Europeans; now luxury was brought down from the sky and conferred upon the man in the street. There were automobiles, radios, labor-saving devices, and apparently unlimited credit for anyone in a good job. This life could reconcile one to Italian gangsters, arrogant millionaires, coarseness in high places, corrupt politicians, and the abandonment of ideals. There is little wonder that American democracy refused the responsibilities that progressivism had demanded, and decided to be content with the flesh pots of an incredibly productive economic system.

The oddities, errors, and exuberance of the 1920's capture attention; but it is worth remembering that most public men remained honest, that most businessmen worked hard, and that unless one lived in certain areas in a few large cities one never met a gangster. Beneath the surface men were tackling seriously the problem of how to deal with the economic giant who had sprung suddenly into such vigorous life, and there were few precepts to work upon. Progressive aims had been formulated to deal with economic power which could be isolated and brought under the law; now high power business had become a torrent flooding into every home and fed from innumerable streams. Should one blunder about and call for public action when the evils were not defined and might even be nonexistent? In fact a good deal of work was done to diagnose the problems of the age, but most of it was of the quiet administrative and academic kind, which leaves few traces in textbook histories. The methods of collecting statistical information improved and spread into hitherto neglected fields, and whether government was active or inactive, it had a great deal more accurate knowledge of society than ever before. Administrators were becoming more experienced, more efficient, and more numerous. There was still an enormous gap to be bridged before the modern era of big government, but a man of 1890 would have been amazed to observe the silent revolution that had taken place. Without anyone realizing what was happening, American democratic government was being equipped for the incredible tasks that lay ahead.

The depression which began with the financial crash of November 1929 and developed with increasing severity during the next three years was the testing time of modern American democracy. It was more inexplicable than the War, and more far-reaching in its social consequences. There had been no major depression since 1893, and confident business publicity of the New Era assumed that the economy was too flexible and too efficient to suffer more than temporary setbacks. Even after the Wall Street crash of 1929 the best-informed public men were able to say (and believe) that the economy would emerge in a healthier condition after rash speculation had been suitably penalized. There was, indeed, no possible precedent for sudden catastrophe in a giant, heavily industrialized economy, and neither bankers nor industrialists nor politicians nor academic economists had the faintest idea of what ought to be done. Politically the beneficiaries were the Democrats who overthrew the Republicans in the congressional elections of 1930, and advanced toward certain Presidential victory in 1932. But what could the Democrats do? In spite of Woodrow Wilson, it was hard to see them as the party with a key to the future. Heavily manned by Southern Democrats, whose major interest was white supremacy and the defense of an agricultural economy, with support in large cities and the more backward rural areas, but clinging to states' rights and Jeffersonian ideals, the Democrats seemed more conservative and less constructive than their rivals. The Republicans at least had their feet in the twentieth century, even if they clung to concepts that lay under a cloud.

There was little in Franklin Roosevelt's record to indicate that he was the man to deal with the crisis. An affable product of Groton and Harvard, paralyzed from the waist downward, and apparently conventional in his ideas, he had been a successful but hardly outstanding Governor of New York. He had acquired a reputation for flexibility and a readiness to listen; as a politician he depended mainly upon his gifts as a phrase-maker and an ability to get on with the bosses and politicos who controlled the Democratic party. He was elected by a handsome majority in 1932 in a year when any Democrat could have won, but the significant outcome was his interpretation of victory. Roosevelt believed that he had a mandate for action; not for specific policies (like other successful campaigners, he had made as few commitments as possible), but to take the initiative, sell his ideas to Congress, and to provide positive leadership. In other words Roosevelt saw his election as a vote of confidence comparable to that with which the democracies of Italy and Germany handed over their destinies to single leaders. His enemies were not slow to make the comparison.

Precedents for this kind of relationship between American democracy and its elected leaders existed, but they were neither firm nor satisfactory. The nearest parallel was Wilson's second election in 1916; but his margin had been so slender that the vote could hardly be interpreted as a popular mandate. Just as there never had been a depression of so disastrous a character, so there had never been a comparable election; whether or not the electorate had given Roosevelt a blank check, he acted as though they had. The effect was to confirm the barely established trend toward a strong executive and Presidential leadership. Nothing could, of course, be done without the acquiescence of Congress, but Congress had clearly relinquished its claim to initiate policy.

On the day of Roosevelt's inauguration the banking system came to a halt; there were some ten million completely unemployed and many more underemployed; many were faced with actual starvation or at least with serious malnutrition as private and municipal charities sank beneath the weight placed upon them; among those suffering from acute distress were many white collar workers and even former employers. Two years of consoling statements that recovery was just ahead had ended with the economy in a deeper trough than ever before. The tasks of the new government were numerous and bewildering. The pressing demand was for relief, and after that, for recovery; but the situation also called for long-term measures to prevent the recurrence of depression and avoid the infliction of mass suffering from future malfunctioning of the economic system.

The stock of ideas to be drawn upon was meager. Direct federal participation in relief had previously been limited to single grants for the victims of disaster. The traditional government action to promote recovery was to cut expenditure and balance the budget; though President, Hoover had cautiously moved toward federal loans to large productive enterprises. Policies to avoid future depression would depend very largely upon the diagnosis of its causes, on which there was no agreement among academic economists. The only certainty was that all the old and tried remedies had failed: the protective tariff had made matters worse by increasing the difficulties of foreign economies; sound money had apparently made no difference, and the United States possessed the largest gold reserves in history; a businessman's government had failed to understand business. The only agreement was that some speculative business had acted irresponsibly and that the extremes of economic freedom ought to be curbed. Apart from this there was no real agreement between adherents of the old antimonopoly tradition and of Theodore Roosevelt's argument that economic consolidation ought to be encouraged, though regulated. For possibilities in the sphere of social security the only source of ideas lay in the experiences of Germany, Great Britain and Scandinavia; with the European economic and political systems tottering, the examples were not likely to commend themselves. Nor had clear directives emerged from democratic debate during the 1932 campaign, which had been rich in old rhetoric and largely barren of new ideas. Whatever was needed would have to be decided by the President and the circle of advisers he drew around him.

This is not the place to examine New Deal remedies; what is relevant is their effect upon the democratic system. Was freedom increased or diminished? Was democracy made more or less effective? Should the enormous increase in the number and responsibilities of government agencies be seen as crushing individualism or as providing new instruments for democratic policies? None of these questions can be answered precisely, and it has already been argued that they may be the wrong questions to ask. The men who clamored most about restrictions upon freedom were those whose wealth or security still allowed them freedom of action; the men who gave the warmest welcome to new regulations were those for whom freedom had meant unemployment, slums, and unprofitable farms. Democracy can be more effective if the instruments of government are more efficient, but what really matters is deciding how they should be used. The increase of officials and of public responsibilities means that the authority of government is to be used to reward or curb certain individuals, institutions, or practices, but size without wisdom may be purposeless; the heart of the matter is whether the tasks have been well chosen.

Many Americans felt this instinctively. Roosevelt got a landslide vote of confidence in 1936 because large segments of the American people knew that his opponents were not talking their language. Democracy voted for "big government," but did so not on theoretical grounds but because government activity had restored hope to the poor and dispossessed. The particular issues were less important than this general verdict. People sensed that the real conflict in society was between various interest groups, and democratic government gave one the right to opt for the power that helped most people. Rhetoric that worked out in the interests of the rich had no appeal to the poor who concluded that they could only prevail by increasing the power of elected governments. The enemy of freedom was not government but private interests and a free-wheeling economic system.

What emerged was a total transformation in the attitude to government. This can be expressed briefly by saying that before 1933 the burden of proof lay with those who argued that the government should act in any given circumstances; after 1933 the burden of proof lay with those who objected to action. If argument continued over the relief of distress, plans for backward areas, or help for the old and injured, the case for the large-scale regulation of the economy was tacitly accepted. Treasury controls over the economy to prevent depression became essential for the business community, even though the language of laissez faire remained fashionable in smart residential areas. Another aspect of the transformation was the way in which ideas became institutionalized; the Progressive era had talked about government responsibilities in the abstract, the New Deal turned them into agencies with expert staff. In the past it had been plausibly argued that individuals could judge their own interests better than any civil servant; with unregulated enterprise discredited by depression, and with government agencies possessed of far more information than individuals, this was demonstrably untrue.

The real alternative to government direction was not individualism but organization by the great corporations. Here were institutions which could buy the same techniques and expertise as the government, and take long views which transcended individual judgment. As private business rallied from the shock of depression, the greater corporations found their feet, and their attitudes were more responsible than they had been in the 1920's; at least they were more interested in the long-term problems of production and marketing and less in the techniques of quick profits and financial control. The economic empires of the 1920's had been hierarchies of holding companies in which ultimate control rested with manipulators of capital; but many of them had been struck down in the crash of 1929 and others had foundered under their own weight. In an economic system that depended upon profits, control would inevitably gravitate toward those who could make profits and away from those whose only function was to hold stock. The men who were assuming control might own very little, but they were expert managers who knew how to organize for production and sales.

A third new factor was the rise of trade unions. They had suffered badly during the depression and from the consequences of American Federation of Labor conservatism, but in 1933 they were given a specific role in the economy under the National Industrial Recovery

Act, and when this act was rejected (on other grounds) by the Supreme Court, the official blessing for organized labor was ratified in the Labor Relations Act of 1935. Collective bargaining was recognized as a normal part of the industrial scene, and encouragement was given to unionization of the unskilled. If the effect was to broaden the horizons of the skilled unions in the American Federation of Labor, it was also a recognition of the "business unionism" which they had championed. The union organizer was recognized as the rightful representative of labor at the same time as he became useful as the manager of labor.

Thus big government, big business, and big labor moved on parallel lines toward an administrative society. It was not government alone that became more complex and more professional but all the controlling forces. The unanswered question was not whether democracy could control government but whether it could control all the complex institutions of modern society with political processes that adhered to traditional forms modified by progressive measures. But if the form of politics remained unchanged, there was a new governing elite, a realignment of sociopolitical forces, and an alteration in the rhetoric.

Roosevelt gathered around him an inner circle of advisers that included a high proportion of academic intellectuals. This association of the intelligentsia with government had a tonic effect upon intellectuals generally; turning away from the mood of conscious alienation, they became deeply involved in the processes of government, and the effect spread outward like ripples to persuade the intelligentsia that the New Deal Government belonged to them as no other government had ever done. In the intoxication of discovery some intellectuals overrated their influence, some believed that they played a dual role as servants of the government and as reformers responsible to a higher law, and most of them expected too much from the application of academic intelligence to politics and administration; but in spite of misconceptions, the bridges built between the world of government and the intellectuals formed an important new element in American politics.

From 1896 to 1928 the Democrats had been the minority party in urban and industrial America. They were the party of ethnic minorities (except Negroes), but this meant control of only limited areas in the metropolitan centers. The Roosevelt party became something quite different: without losing traditional rural support, especially in the South, it became the party of industrial labor and low-paid urban workers, and because Negroes were numerous in this category the Democrats won the black vote as well. The alliance of intellectuals, organized labor, and city masses was something new in American life, strangely like the alliance that had made the Labour Party a major force in British politics.

The Democrats had been the party of states' rights and limited government; the Republicans, even when most affected by laissez faire, had been the party of national power. The New Deal brought about an exchange in rhetoric. The Democrats became the party of intervention and national responsibility, while the Republicans stressed individualism and states' rights. The changeover was not complete and party attitudes continued to be very confused. Southern Democrats continued to talk in the traditional way, even though they supported New Deal measures from which their region benefited enormously, while some Republicans continued the nationalist traditions of Theodore Roosevelt and found themselves in alliance with the New Dealers. Indeed, by the end of the New Deal period, these "liberal" Republicans had acquired much influence in their party, and they were able to bring it to the point of accepting much that had been done in the New Deal while arguing that it ought to have been done better. The opposition would continue to oppose what had been done but would not undo it.

Though the New Deal alliance had similarities with the British alliance of the Left, it was not socialist. The position of orthodox New Dealers was that capitalism was basically sound; it had got on to the wrong track but could be made to work justly. There is considerable force in the argument that the New Deal saved American capitalism; a further installment of passive government would have intensified criticism of the economic system, while the New Deal pointed the way to a solution of an old democratic dilemma: if economic health depended upon the enterprise of a few, how could it be reconciled with rule by the many? The New Deal answer was to develop expert government and entrust it with the dual task of promoting economic efficiency and social justice while leaving decisions about economic detail in the hands of individuals; direction was concentrated, decision was diffused. Whether this solution was right or wrong, it proved the one toward which most advanced societies have moved, and in the history of American democracy it can be said that the New Deal fulfills and completes the first stage of modernization.

From 1920 to 1939 the United States had gone through a long period of introspective crisis. Reaction against participation in war, and against Wilson's sponsorship of the League of Nations, led to a period in which Americans proclaimed that both their triumphs and their difficulties belonged to themselves alone, and that explanations were to be sought solely in American conditions. Though Herbert Hoover had attempted to excuse American responsibility for depression by stressing its international character, the New Dealers had deliberately turned their backs upon prospects of international cooperation and sought internal remedies for domestic weaknesses. Secure on the continent and preoccupied with their own problems, Americans watched from a distance the difficulties of Great Britain and France, the rise of dictatorships in Italy and Germany, the development of totalitarian communism in Russia, and the expansionist aims of Japan in Asia. They did not like much of what they saw but, for the most part, resisted suggestions that the United States could or should influence events. This was the prelude to a war fought on a worldwide front, to the organization of American power on an unprecedented scale, and to permanent postwar international commitments. If 1917 had been a watershed, the trends then set in motion were magnified and given abiding force between 1941 and 1945.

The experience had some superficial resemblance to that of the earlier war. Once again the European war had unfolded its drama before American intervention, and once again the decisive factor that precipitated United States entry into the war was not sympathy for the Western European powers but enemy action. The Japanese attack on Pearl Harbor served the same purpose as the earlier German declaration of unrestricted submarine warfare in convincing Americans that they could not stand aside and that their particular dangers could not be divorced from a worldwide conflict. A dramatic and unnerving event demonstrated the obsolescence of the isolationist assumption of American immunity from external attack. It was not a new philosophy but science, bombs, and long-range aircraft that reversed the teaching of Washington's Farewell Address. The similarities must however be set beside some marked differences. Involvement in the Second World War was longer and much more extensive; American forces fought on two major fronts and on several minor fronts, Franklin D. Roosevelt had a much greater influence than Wilson on the planning of war strategy, and American generals and admirals assumed much more important responsibilities in the Allied chain of command (in the final phase of the war Americans were in supreme command of the Allied forces in two of the major theaters of war). Even more significant was the acceptance of responsibilities for postwar reconstruction, participation in the United Nations, and long-term commitments to foreign military and economic aid. For good or ill the decisions of the war made future isolation impossible, and twenty-five years after its conclusion American troops are still in Europe, two large-scale wars have been fought in Asia, and the United States continues to give economic aid to less prosperous nations.

In institutional terms the most important consequence of the war was to enlarge and continue Presidential leadership and to increase still further the commanding influence of federal administration. As Chief Executive of the nation, the President remained subject to the familiar checks and balances, but as Commander-in-Chief and even more as the representative of America in the Allied discussions, he was under no constitutional limitations. Even before America's entry into the war Roosevelt had gone very far in committing the United States to the support of Great Britain, and during the war his meetings with Churchill and Stalin led to decisions that could not be reversed and for which he alone was responsible. Indeed the war gave the President responsibilities for the future of something which could be vaguely defined as "the free world" (so that millions of people in distant countries looked to him for leadership). This role as world leader continued after the war and has produced the ironical situation in which the President can be harried and thwarted on questions of comparatively minor domestic significance while freed from constitutional checks in reaching decisions in international affairs. At the same time, with no violent reaction against control and regulation after the war, the federal domestic administration grew stronger. This was partly because the wartime agencies built upon foundations already laid and accepted during the New Deal era, so that increased activity during the war years did not appear as an innovation but as an extension of existing modes of government. The war also brought out the tremendous economic role of the Federal Government; defense contracts, and other forms of federal spending, became the lifeblood of the private economy. Thus the war confirmed and enlarged tendencies that had already set in before 1941 and helped crystallize the idea that federal initiative was the normal way of getting things done and of solving social and economic problems.

The war greatly increased the amount of work required from Congress but at the same time proportionately reduced the power of Congress to decide upon fundamental questions of policy. In the long-term struggle for political initiative war gave a decided advantage to the executive at a time when the pendulum might well have swung back toward Congress. Congress, like the President, was compelled to take decisions which directly affected non-American countries, and Congressional debates had repercussions upon peoples who had no way of participating in its political process. In the postwar world Congressional decisions on appropriations for foreign aid directly affected the lives of millions throughout the world, and Congressional investigations become international events. Congressional discretion may seem to have less scope than that of a powerful executive, but its consequences are more significant than ever before. In handling these international responsibilities neither the federal departments nor Congress could rely upon established precepts or conventional wisdom, for no previous generation and no other nation had handled the same kind of problems. Did the role of Congress make it easier or more difficult to tackle these new problems? The question is, in a sense, unanswerable. On the one hand the controversy in Congress over international issues often gave an impression abroad of indecision, division, and reactionary strength; on the other hand policies which have been subjected to scrutiny and criticism have often proved more durable than those achieved with secrecy and dispatch.

A final consequence of the war for democratic processes was that society as a whole proved itself to be remarkably efficient. This was something apart from governmental competence (which was not always above reproach); it meant that soldiers, businessmen, scientists, and individual administrators proved themselves highly efficient, with teamwork and organization achieving striking results. This was a tribute to education, technical expertise, and free institutions. Totalitarian regimes had based their claims upon the need for direction in order to obtain national efficiency and upon the superiority of national purpose to democratic debate. The American experience of war demonstrated that while a democratic society might move more slowly at the outset, it ended by generating more power, while Americans themselves took efficiency so much for granted that they hardly bothered to comment upon it. Society was not only democratic but also capitalist. Throughout the whole process of modernization Populists, Wilsonian Progressives and liberal intellectuals had seen big business as the principal enemy of social justice; yet where would America have been in two world wars without the achievements of industry, and was not efficiency the product of business training and the universities rather than of government direction? Thus American business emerged from the war with increased prestige, and criticisms that had seemed valid in the shadow of depression looked hollow in the light of victory, there would be no return to the unregulated capitalism of earlier days, but neither would there be any temptation to move in the direction of socialism.

At the very moment when everything in the American past seemed to be justified by magnanimous victory, anti-Americanism became a force in the world. Roosevelt had certainly hoped for the opening of a cautious dialogue between the United States and Russia, but within a short space of time it became clear that Russia would treat her former ally as the major enemy in an undeclared war. Even in more friendly countries anti-Americanism became vocal and occasionally violent, and whatever American industry might achieve, it became apparent that American advertising and propaganda agencies had not discovered techniques for selling an attractive image of America to the rest of the world. The shock was greater than it would have been for a nation familiar with unpopularity, for Americans wanted very much to be liked and could see no rational reason why they should be hated. Throughout American history they had assumed that the virtues of their system were self-evident, that their great experiment showed the way to the rest of the world, and that Americanism was the obvious alternative to oppression and injustice. Yet, at the very moment when American civilization was vindicated, when Americans had most to offer, and were prepared to pour out technical, scientific, and economic aid, they were named by a large proportion of the world's population as the imperialist enemies of civilization and justice. The discovery of anti-Americanism was hard to bear and would produce, in the long run, profound consequences. Was it true that in becoming modern and successful Americans had sacrificed their earlier claim to universal right and justice? This question lies at the heart of the crisis of modern democracy which must now be explored.

CHAPTER XII

THE IMPLICATIONS OF POWER AND THE CRISIS OF MODERN DEMOCRACY

In 1945 the terrifying achievements of science and technology were dramatized by the atom bomb: Here was a power beyond imagination produced by an army of scientists and released by the decision of a single man. Gunpowder had made possible the destruction of fortresses, then cities and whole industrial areas had lain at the mercy of high-explosive bombs, and now a civilization could be completely destroyed. Once war had been the concern of professional soldiers, now whole peoples were involved. Nuclear energy highlighted the way in which technological innovation and political decision could be used; but it was only the most striking example of the fact that the modern government of America possesses power beyond the earlier dreams of man. Yet political control remained the product of systems designed for earlier and simpler times.

The power of "the bomb" was massive, but it was also concentrated and enormously expensive. The knowledge it required was so rarified that it was necessarily confined to a minority and only wealthy societies could afford to employ it. The minority of men who understood the problems of control were further removed than ever before from the mass of mankind, and the gap between rich countries and poor countries widened immeasurably. Power was concentrated but the few men able to wield it became servants of the great organizations to which they belonged, and the simple mechanism of democratic control was confronted with governments and private corporations so vast and so complex that ordinary men could neither understand their operation nor direct their energies. The power to destroy was the most striking example of this divorce between decision and the will of the people, but in every sphere the new capacity to control environment raised similar issues. There was little that science, technology, and organization could not do; but the means and objectives became more and more elusive and less and less amenable to the familiar process of discussion, election, and majority decision. The implication of massive power was a deep crisis in the character and conduct of democracy.

The control of power generated professional administration, and in both private and public organizations amateurism became a thing of the past. Civil servants, the managerial staffs of great corporations, military administrators, and scientific workers have increased prodigiously, and each group requires an expertise that cannot be practised by untrained men. Computors take on some of the routine tasks and calculations but both their management and the interpretation of their results require still more skill, so that the saving of labor gives yet greater ascendancy to the expert. Modern government and modern business cannot function without economists, statisticians, and consultants in every field of human relations, and the two organizations become more and more like each other as business becomes more bureaucratic and government agencies become more and more concerned with the task of selling policy to the people.

The democratic voter, who is supposed to exercise ultimate control, is the target for pressure and persuasion from every side. He cannot turn on a television set, open a newspaper, or travel on a highway without being told what he should eat, wear, use, or think. Private advertising accounts for most of the overt persuasion, but governments have their own methods of conditioning people to accept policies or to voice the required demands. The ordinary man is presented with a small number of preselected possibilities. Public opinion polls predict his choice and may, in course of time, replace the old-fashioned method of casting votes, while by some inexorable law the products and policies become more and more like each other. All this is a far cry from the Jeffersonian image of an independent man who forms his own opinion and uses his vote to protect his rights and to prevent the abuse of power.

The fading distinction between government and private enterprise is also reflected in international affairs. Outsiders do not see American society divided between individuals and authority, nor between the public interest and big business, but whole and undivided in its impact upon the world. There is much naïveté in the view of American government as the tool of "Wall Street" or the great corporations, but considerable truth in the idea that government policy and business policy are two manifestations of the same force. The world outside follows American political campaigns with intense interest, but what matters is how the President decides to use American power after his election, not the issues on which voters were asked to decide. In office the President joins the narrow world of men who direct the experts, and it is largely irrelevant that he has come to that world through political success rather than by business success or military promotion. This analysis may seem forced but it is influential enough to be taken seriously, and if it contains even a part of the truth it challenges the assumptions of a democratic society.

The concept of monolithic power has won support from informed Americans and phrases such as "the power elite" and the "power structure" have passed into common currency. According to these theories real power is concentrated in the hands of a small number of very powerful men, at the head of political, business, and military hierarchies, who gather around scientists, educators, and opinion makers. Linked by a secret and unavowed but real interest in maintaining the existing structure of society and distribution of wealth, the "establishment" uses the rhetoric of a democratic society for conservative ends. It is a part of the game to maintain a show of disagreement and debate, but the limits of argument are firmly fixed and ruin awaits the man who steps beyond them. Radical voices can be heard, but radicalism leads no man to fame or fortune. However learned or acute the critic, he will have to be content with insignificant journals of opinion, low-paid academic posts, and no television time. The "establishment" may honor a handful of distinguished dissenters, much as kings kept jesters at court, but this has little significance in a society where the road to success is marked "conformity." In the more extreme forms of radical analysis the democratic character of American life is a part of the sham; bribed by affluence the people are persuaded to resign power into safe hands and are readily persuaded to substitute ready-made slogans for independent judgment or humane impulses.

Against this radical attack many commentators and historians make a virtue of uniform trends and discover consensus as the guiding theme of American history. Democracy has operated, according to this analysis, by diminishing conflict and discovering the maximum areas of agreement. The great failure of the Civil War is the exception which proves the rule because it came about when men on both sides repudiated consensus and demanded a unilateral satisfaction of their wishes. Praise goes to men such as Stephen A. Douglas, who sought to steer around sectional divisions, but Calhoun, who demanded greater protection for minority interests as the price of union, is more admired than the Abolitionists, who attacked a moral wrong without equivocation. Antislavery men claimed that slavery and free institutions were incompatible, but consensus would have taught them to endure what could not be cured and emphasize the points of agreement among most Americans (excluding Negroes). Thus consensus is the liberal version of the radical power structure; both agree that the guiding force in American society is agreement at the center, though the one sees it as the medium of tolerance, compromise, and justice, the other as the instrument of suppression. The question is whether either understands the complex nature of society or gives adequate weight to all the pressures within it.

In broad terms both theories express some truth. In all modern societies there is a tendency for power to concentrate—and this gives a semblance of truth to the theory of the "power elite"—and no society can exist without a broad measure of agreement upon its structure and purpose which provides a hard core for the theory of consensus. But the attack upon the power elite tends to see radical criticism as the only source of conflict, while consensus deplores all conflict as harmful; a truer view might see society as an accumulation of conflicts and suggest that they contain the seed of betterment, not destruction.

There is some force in the theory of "countervailing power" elaborated by John K. Galbraith to explain the mechanism that kept economic forces in equilibrium when the old corrective of individualistic competition no longer operated. Power begat countervailing power. In all societies, and particularly in societies that respected freedom of speech and association, the use of power had generated opposing power; big business had called into existence big labor, the power of industry had been countered by the power of distributors, and irresponsible power had generated the ever-increasing power of government. In this there was a suspicion of the "unseen hand" of the classical economists: Things might seem to grow too big for comfort or justice, but somehow harmony would be restored and, in the long run, ordinary men would benefit from the battle of giants. However, the theory of countervailing force could also suggest a continuing process in which conflict would not die down and would foster not stability but constant pressure upon organized power. In this sense, too, the idea could be extended more widely in the social and political sphere. As soon as any group or individual seemed to be in a position of power, the means would be developed to counteract that power, and since power is not gladly surrendered, conflict would ensue. A further corollary might indicate that the greater the extent of authority, the more violent would be the reaction, and the more would controversy range beyond the limits of consensus to question fundamental social and political assumptions. An examination of recent trends in the history of American democracy lends support to this analysis.

It may appear that the strong Presidency initiated by the Progressive era has been confirmed, and it becomes a commonplace to describe the President of the United States as the most powerful man in the world. There is, however, a marked contrast between the potentiality of his power and his freedom to use it. In international relations the President is absolute in the sense that only he can take certain decisions, but the stakes are so high and the opposing forces so imponderable that his freedom of action is circumscribed. Enemies, allies, friends, and domestic critics not only try to bend the decision in a particular way but also confine what is politically possible to a very small area. Of course, the President has great influence upon the whole conduct of foreign relations, but this is often limited to style rather than content. He steps into a situation he did not make and can only hope to alter in a small degree and is never a man above men disposing and directing as he wishes. The most he can hope to do is to modify in detail and pray that he may not find himself in a position—like President Kennedy in the Cuban missile crisis—where only two options remain and the consequence may be nuclear war or humiliation. The balance of power limits freedom of action, and the balance exists not only between international rivals but also between sensitive allies, interests overseas, and domestic pressures.

The President is head of an enormous federal administration and Commander-in-Chief of the armed forces; in both spheres the chain of command leads to him and him only, but in both he is dealing with vast and complex organizations which have developed their own conventions and modes of action. The internal operations of government agencies and of the armed services depend upon intricate relationships between a great many experts, each with their own responsibilities. Change is possible when the focus of attention is directed upon a particular detail of administration, but for the most part the President accepts the fact that he cannot know everything and must rely upon the machine to work smoothly according to its own rules. His freedom to act becomes still more circumscribed if some agency heads and military leaders have strong and independent ideas that they are prepared to implement in the face of everything short of a Presidential prohibition. In domestic as in foreign affairs the President is more likely to impress by his style than by his specific proposals. He can inspire devotion or spread frustration, he can raise or lower morale, but a Presidential term is too short to do more than touch major problems of administration or military organization, and the success of his government may well depend upon the extent to which he learns to cooperate with the men who are nominally the principal agents of his policy.

Social needs have brought about a proliferation of executive agencies, and the separation of powers means that they come under Presidential control and only indirectly under legislative surveillance. It is true that Congress has the ultimate sanction of cutting off appropriations and does occasionally show its displeasure by reducing funds requested for government operations. In every year some agency is liable to suffer in this way, but how the dice falls depends very much upon personality, congressional fashion, and chance publicity. An agency that quietly performs the tasks for which it was created may go on for years without attracting congressional attention; yet this may be the very organization that becomes most bound by bureaucratic rules, least efficient, and most resistant to change. The golden rule for bureaucratic survival is self-effacement and mutual protection against outside interference, while the innovators and the precedent-breakers are most likely to suffer from legislative hostility. But large and active agencies, much in the public eye, also evolve their own means of resisting congressional pressure, so that activities pushed out of one door may well come in by another. The very great majority of the men staffing the government services are honest, able, and devoted to the public interest, but often they seem to win an autonomy which is hardly consistent with the principles of popular government as understood in former days. At the same time, the principle of countervailing power bids us recognize that this autonomy has succeeded in maintaining services which are welcomed by the public, but which would not be provided at all if initiative and control lay solely with Congress.

Big administration protects the framework of the welfare society against unwise economy and corrupt political pressures, and there are many examples of the way in which it helps minorities when legislative aid might be meager or nonexistent. So, in a perverse way, administration that has evaded legislative control can often protect the public interest better than one that has engaged the attention of the representatives of the people.

The picture of power concentrated in a single person or in a power elite must therefore be modified. Whether one looks at government or at giant corporations, one may well find that power is, in fact, diffused throughout a whole system that is nominally under absolute authority. Much of the world is ruled by men at desks. The lifeblood of the system is not authority and command but minutes and memoranda, precedents and rules, and the desire to avoid the stigma of being either inefficient or unpleasant. Yet with all its merits—and men at desks are usually conscientious and high principled—the system is far removed from the "wise and frugal" government so admired by Jeffersonians and Jacksonians. It has widespread ramifications, it is sophisticated rather than wise, and it is not cheap; but confronted with highly developed organization the legislature seems to blunder too often along with concepts inherited from an earlier age.

The poor reputation of Congress has been an abiding but puzzling characteristic of American society. The counterpart of the strong Presidency has been lack of confidence in Congress and an assumption that the man in the White House is better able to implement the wishes of the people than their elected representatives. The popular image of the senator, portrayed in hundreds of political cartoons, is that of a fussy, elderly man, inflated with his own importance and about to express resounding platitudes in florid oratory; while the representative is portrayed as a seedy individual more interested in poker and the pork barrel than in public policy. Congress is, in truth, neither incompetent nor corrupt: The great majority of the members are public-spirited, conscientious, and well-informed. They work harder than their predecessors, and they have more work to do. It is the sheer magnitude of the task that gives the impression of diffused and ill-directed energy, for individual members can rarely become familiar with more than one sector of the vast operations of government and general debates become less frequent and less useful. It is the man who has mastered a subject who commands influence and who, in turn, becomes the jealous guardian of his domain against attacks by the uninformed and joins with others to resist criticism of the inner ring even though they have little else in common. Congress rewards not only knowledge but also long service. The seniority system gives important committee chairmanships to the men with the longest continuous tenure of their seats, and thus confers authority upon elderly men, usually from conservative areas, who may have more experience than ability. The inevitable tendency is toward hierarchy in which the conventions that support authority may become more important than its use. The customs and procedures of Congress elevate the authority of individuals at the center while discouraging individualism at the periphery. The first lesson learnt by a freshman representative is that ambition will be best served by getting along with the party leadership. If he makes himself useful in a quiet way, begins the task of acquiring knowledge in a particular field, and does not obtrude himself by untimely criticism, he can go far; but if he speaks too much and too critically he will soon be put in his place. Favorable assignments will not come his way, local bills of interest to his constituents will die in committee, and his prospects of renomination will recede. Most legislative assemblies place radical ideas at a discount, but Congress does it more effectively than most.

In many ways, however, Congress is a sensitive reflection of public opinion. It transacts an enormous amount of business, satisfies many interests, and remedies many discontents. At the same time, Congress is often unwilling to act even when majority opinion seems clear. Its traditions engender a respect for minorities, but in practice this means minorities organized for action in Congress and the lobbies. The classic example of minority power is the resistance of Southern senators to civil rights legislation, and the best-known device is the filibuster, but there are many other minorities that can hold their own against majority wishes by an adroit use of procedure and pressure. On the other hand, ethnic minorities are always under-represented, and radical groups seldom have a voice. In the early days of the Republic the representatives of the people were seen primarily as checks upon authority, but in their modern role they do more to protect authority against the turbulence of popular democracy and to provide a cushion between opinion and power, than to act as the means by which majority will is imposed upon power.

Congress could not fulfill this role if it were not the product of a party system in which the guiding principle is to win and hold the widest possible alliance among the most influential groups. It has already been argued that there has been no party of reform with continuous traditions in American history, and though it is true that there have been occasions—most notably during the early New Deal—when one of the major parties has become committed to widespread changes, the objectives have always been limited and never embraced the idea of change as a continuing task of political life. Within the parties movements of revolt are crushed or assimilated, and all the political dice are loaded against third parties; a natural outcome of the system is a

Congress with much experience and a genuine respect for compromise, but no fire of protest.

Congress is fully aware of its traditional role as the watchdog of the executive, but it performs this by matching expertise against expertise, investigation against administrative competence, and the power of the purse against executive initiative. It is well equipped to do this because it is better staffed than any other legislature in the world. A powerful senator can employ aides, research assistants, and secretaries, and even a young representative has an efficient office; a legislative reference service draws upon the world's largest library, and committees can use the services of lawyers, economists, statisticians, research workers, and experts in every field. All this means some duplication of effort because the government departments and agencies also employ large staffs to gather and assess much the same information; but this is another example of power begetting power, and the extensive expertise of the executive demands a similar development in the legislative branch. Even so, the President normally determines the general pattern of legislative business: His proposals will occupy a large amount of congressional time, his veto, and the expectation of a veto, will influence congressional tactics, and his superior access to publicity gives him a powerful lever. It is common knowledge that a President can expect to lose half the measures he proposes and that some which become law will be greatly changed in the process; but even so, the greater part of congressional time is spent in debating, implementing, or resisting the policies initiated by the President. In other words, the President cannot always get what he wants out of Congress, but he can ensure that Congress spends a great deal of time in discussing it.

This forced partnership with the administration has been an incentive for influential congressmen to embark on investigations in which they have a much freer hand. Typically, these investigations have focused upon various forms of subversion or radical opinion, and the representatives of the people have turned with earnest purpose to investigate the people. A welcome bonus was publicity and approbation seldom given to the humdrum work of Congress. Investigations of this type may prove to have been passing phenomena, fostered by acute anxieties and dismay at the spread of communism in the world, but they presented an interesting theoretical challenge. Congress became not only a cushion to absorb popular disturbance but an instrument for the suppression of radicalism. There were ancient precedents in the Alien and Sedition Acts of 1798 but Thomas Jefferson may have shifted in his grave.

* * *

The preceding argument has suggested that the analysis of power in modern America is by no means simple. The administrative and technical instruments of power are enormous, but their use is extremely difficult. In theory there are unlimited possibilities but in practice the choices are few and the room for maneuver limited. In international affairs the President can decide policy on his own, but the gravity of the decisions required means that the President will seek to avoid doing this. In domestic affairs he is master of the Federal Administration, which is too large and too complex for one man to direct. His relationship with Congress requires a combination of tact, diplomacy, and threats, for Congress is not likely to move against the wishes of the inner ring, and even a majority can be thwarted by organized minorities. At the same time, there are occasions when the President must decide and can control events, and it becomes important to meet the charge that he is the prisoner of a "power elite." In any system there will be men of influence who are likely to be consulted and have the means of making their wishes known without consultation; but it is unrealistic to suggest that these men of influence will speak with one voice, and it is more probable that the President will be caught in a vortex of conflicting counsels and pleas. Nor is it realistic to suggest that the men of influence have more power in America than elsewhere; indeed the reverse is true, for long-standing hostility to elitist principles of authority are still strong.

It is true that modern developments make it easier for men of influence to communicate and to meet; they can speak to each other by telephone and they can travel by air to any part of the nation in a few hours. There is far greater opportunity for all the strings to be held in Washington than in previous generations; but Washington does not concentrate commercial and cultural authority in the way that London or Paris does, and other great cities across the nation put up a more vigorous claim to regional autonomy than the provincial centers of those countries. Men of influence who congregate in the national capital are out of communication with the writers, educators, and business leaders who form an integral part of the "establishment" in other countries. The purely political character of Washington gives political men the ascendancy, and they are more concerned with constituents than with a "power elite." Congressmen may sometimes seem to be confused or lacking in influence, but this continuous contact with their constituents gives them an asset not enjoyed by top administrators, generals, or heads of corporations. In this way another aspect of countervailing power emerges. Others may appear to decide great issues, but Congressmen have inside knowledge of what is politically possible. Congressional procedure tends to emphasize the insignificance of the ordinary legislator, but the constant discourse about political ends and means restores influence to men whose communications with the public are kept open.

The opinion to which a Congressman reacts is not normally that of a majority among his constituents but of politically significant minorities who are energetic and articulate enough to make their wishes known. In the last resort the overwhelming consideration is his prospect at the next election; but this may depend upon quite small numbers. He does not have to please all the people—indeed his active supporters will be disappointed if he tries to do so—but a majority of the people. The endorsement by his party will ensure automatically the support of perhaps forty percent, and in all but the largest electoral revolutions he can rely on obtaining a fair share of the uncommitted vote; his fate will therefore depend upon the remaining two or three percent, or an even smaller proportion. This fraction will be swayed partly by national, partly by local, and partly by personal considerations; yet a constant surprise in modern democracy is the uniformity of the swing across the country, and, aware that the electoral swing will largely be settled by factors beyond his control, the Congressman will pay less attention to the vital two percent than one might expect. His real concern is to maintain his place in his party, and here the goodwill of influential groups or individuals may be particularly important. At the same time the Congressman is well aware of the interaction between small influential groups and the wider circle of opinion, and he can sense the trend either on general or particular issues. Thus Congressmen are barometers of opinion, though in a more subtle way than might be suggested by their formal authority as the choice of a majority.

In the United States, as in other representative governments, the fate of candidates, governments, and vital policies depends upon decisions made by a tiny fraction of the electorate; yet a swing that gives one party or the other the barest of majorities confers the whole authority of "the people." Democracy has become "mass democracy," and minor and subtle variations in opinion are flattened out by the requirement that half the mass plus one is the sufficient and necessary authorization for the use of power.

Mass democracy is often seen as a cultural phenomenon for, as Tocqueville observed long ago, the power of the majority flows into every aspect of social life. The culture of the mass is broader than the political majority, for both parties share common cultural assumptions and tastes and what is acceptable to the greatest number of people fixes the limits and determines the central culture of a society. Mass culture in a mass society is affected by rising living standards, for as more can afford comfort and entertainment, the greater will be the efforts of commerce to satisfy their needs, to the neglect of minorities.

Advertising and salesmanship are great levelers. Yet, in a rich and varied society, there are always exceptions to mass culture: artistic coteries, minority literary movements, small magazines, and cinema and television catering to minority groups can and do flourish. The huge universities provide a home for all kinds of cultural activities that could never find enough supporters in small colleges, and the great cities, despite their gaudy downtown areas and shabby low income districts, provide the environment for all kinds of minority interests that would wither away in small towns. The very existence of standardized mass culture is an incentive for experimentation off the major networks and away from Main Street; indeed, no other modern civilization is so fruitful in cultural innovation.

What is true of culture is also true, to some degree, of politics. Mass democracy can crush individualism and minority movements, and political managers, whose main objective is to obtain a mandate for power, discourage awkward questions and cultivate harmony with as little debate and as few commitments as possible. Conversely, shrewd individuals will prefer to ally themselves with the mass party rather than risk losing their influence. The trend of politics is toward organization and away from individualism and minor movements, and it is not difficult to present a picture of mass parties whose rivalry observes an unwritten rule that neither will give countenance to attacks upon political fundamentals and both will debate within very narrow limits. The voter can choose, but only between two major parties expressing similar opinions and differing only in emphasis and style. There is nothing to stop anyone becoming a political eccentric except the abandonment of influence, prestige, and personal ambition.

If this were the complete picture the prospect would be gloomy—for variety, individualism, dissent, and the urge to reform have been the mainsprings of democratic vitality—but hopeful qualifications can be made. Mass media and political salesmanship are not all-powerful, and experience suggests that they are not effective unless there is a message the voters want to hear. If television opens wide doors to the manipulation of mass emotion, it also provides the means by which the people can study personalities and events as never before. The days when Presidential candidates could campaign from their porches and say nothing that could be of interest to anyone, are gone, and recent elections suggest that a candidate who does not grow during the campaign loses ground. Platitudes are often the stock in trade of politicians, but disaster awaits the candidate who responds with a platitude when all the world is waiting for him to discuss an issue. At the other end of the political scale the primaries provide American voters with a unique opportunity for influencing the choice of candidates for office. It is true that the majority of candidates for nomination will be either hand-picked party regulars or men with enough money to finance their own campaign, but "outsiders" can always enter the ring. It is not uncommon for them to win, and the winner of a primary is the candidate of the party however much the professionals may dislike him. Even if political dissent stands little chance in national contests, the infinite variety of the American political map may give it a footing in states, cities, or counties. Monolithic parties operating in mass democracy may seem to be terrible engines for the enforcement of conformity, but a closer examination shows that giant killers can make their mark. Modern parties are seldom blown violently off course, but they alter direction quickly enough when the wind blows strongly from a new quarter; professional politicians may like to keep parties at an organizational level without too many arguments about their purpose, but success depends upon the extent to which they can provide what the voter wants, and a sense of purpose is often more urgently demanded than material promises.

Further thought along these lines contains dangers of complacency. There are ways in which the weight of the mass can be eased, but it remains heavy, and the greatest danger lies in the existence of what may be called "invisible minorities," which may be socially significant but have neither voice nor weight in politics. If the invisible minority is small, its lack of influence may breed frustration but is unlikely to produce fundamental challenges for the political system; dangers lie ahead when sizable groups become convinced that the political system has nothing to offer them. The most striking example is that of the Negro minority: it is not completely "invisible" because there are Negro legislators and officials at every level in government, but in proportion to their numbers they are grossly under-represented in nation and states, in legislatures and executiveships. Moreover, many Negroes have come to feel that those who have achieved political success have done so only by abandoning the interests of their race. A different kind of invisible minority was formed by opponents of the Vietnam war; though numerous and articulate they seemed, for a long period, to make no impression at all upon politics. It is difficult to make more than the wildest estimate, but if anti-Vietnam opinion had been adequately represented it might have claimed about one-third of the House of Representatives. Even if this is an overestimate, it would still be true that a very large number of people, who felt deeply about a major issue, believed that they had inadequate means of making their opinions felt through the normal channels of political communication. The nearest analogy is to antislavery opinion at a time when both Democrats and Whigs were committed to avoiding the discussion of slavery.

Issues such as slavery in the past and the Vietnam war in the

1960's, about which some people feel passionately and which seem to involve the whole character of American justice and humanity, link up with other discontents and provide a focus for "invisible minorities" of every kind. A racial minority with a grievance is likely to magnify racial factors, to see every action as evidence of discrimination, and to develop more intensively the sense of ethnic identity. At the same time the stronger the protest and the more races become ethno-centered, the less willing are the dominant majorities to allow them equal participation. It is not altogether surprising that members of these minorities infer that constitutional action is of no avail and turn to unconstitutional violence. The real death of any protest movement is to be ignored, and no government can ignore violence. The truth of this diagnosis is borne out when violent protests bring rewards that have eluded years of patient and peaceful argument.

Before pursuing further this analysis of the crisis of democracy it may be well to turn aside and consider the situation of the minority whose condition worried the eighteenth-century advocates of republicanism. They were concerned at the fate of the well-born, wealthy, and well-educated under the rule of numbers, and their scheme of constitutional checks and balances was devised largely to ensure that this minority—to whom they entrusted not only the material but also the moral betterment of mankind—would not be subjected to ignorance or to the blend of selfishness and emotion which they called "passion." Since that time the minority of the highly educated have often been uneasy at the implications of democracy and attempted to counteract its influence, yet in the early part of this century they began to appeal to the principles of democratic rule and not against them. Today the former fears are seldom voiced and a belief in democracy is part of the stock in trade of every intelligent businessman, lawyer, college president, or established intellectual. This cultural minority, occupying so many positions of authority and influence have become stalwart defenders of the democratic system, and the men who might be most concerned at the implications of mass democracy seem to be little disturbed by their own minority status. Dissatisfied members of the educated middle class have provided the leadership for revolutionary movements in so many countries that their attachment to the fundamentals of the American democratic system is of great significance.

The primary factor in producing this situation is probably the economic success of America, which has ensured that there has never been a class whose economic rewards did not measure up to their education. A second factor has been the growing involvement of intellectuals and businessmen in the processes of government; neither by inclination or experience are most of them equipped to compete in popular politics, but no government can get on without seeking the aid of economists, statisticians, scientists, and skilled managers of business enterprises. Beyond the inner ring of experts government employs the services of social workers, public relations men, lawyers, technicians, and scientists. Thus the trained elite is involved with government at every level, and the local authority of political bosses becomes of little significance when the corridors of power are open. Material prosperity and the chance of exerting influence are dear to the hearts of most men, but Americans also require assurance that the nation is not at the mercy of blind and prejudiced force but subject, in all great things, to the rule of reason and of law. This assurance they receive, in large measure, from the Supreme Court.

The political role of the Supreme Court has become a striking characteristic of American history. It is a court of law and can act only when there is a case before it; but because the Constitution was, from the first, a political statement as well as a legal document, the Court has always had to depart from legal technicalities and decide upon its political meaning. The distinction between "political" and "judicial" is often a fine one; broadly one can say that a judicial decision is confined to a strict interpretation of the letter of the law and to precedent, and a political decision is more concerned with the policies that inspired or should inspire the law. Thus, as early as the days of John Marshall, the Court not only had to decide whether statutes were consonant with the letter of the Constitution but also the intention of the Constitution itself. In all the great cases before the Court, from the days of Marshall to the days of Earl Warren, the decision of the Court has been based on views of the Constitution which could be rejected by other men who were equally well versed in the law and equally intelligent in their logic. Indeed, many of the most important decisions have been taken by a majority of the judges over a vigorous dissent from the minority, and the debate between majority and minority has been as much over what the Constitution *ought* to mean as over a legal analysis of what it has meant. Thus the Court is not limited to the law as it is and becomes a law-giving body.

At the same time the Supreme Court does not operate in a void; it is not whimsical or capricious, and its reasoning grows out of the informed opinion of the day. It may sometimes appear odd that momentous questions should be settled by a majority of five to four with equally cogent arguments expressed on both sides; yet examination will usually show that both the decision and the dissents are rooted in the same soil of informed opinion. The justices differ, but their opinions on both sides exist within the same terms of reference set by the informed and thoughtful men of the day. The real authority of the Court depends upon the knowledge that its decisions are made by careful, responsible, and learned men. The Court is the least democratic of all the institutions of government, yet in a way it is also the most representative, for it distills opinion about the kind of society people want to live in and applies the principles that emerge. Through the decision of the Court these principles decide the meaning of the law and occasionally strike down laws which conflict with them. Law is made by interpreting the law, and often these judge-made laws could not have been enacted by any legislature. The famous decision of 1954, which declared racial segregation in schools unconstitutional, could not have been passed by Congress as a bill because of the blocking power of the South (and, be it added, of doubters outside the South.) Nor would legislators dependent upon over-represented rural areas have accepted a bill requiring the apportionment of representatives in proportion to population. The regulation of business and mammoth corporations might have been beyond the range of legislative competence, but over a period of eighty years the Court's interpretation of the Anti-Trust Act has built up a complex code of commercial ethics and fixed the limits for monopoly. It has also done much to help in standardizing criminal procedures and due process in state courts, whereas attempts by Congress to impose uniformity by legislation would have raised an uproar and a passionate defense of states' rights. The Court has also, with partial success, threaded a delicate path between legislative attempts to deal with subversion and the rights of individuals. Above all, the Court has sanctioned the enlargement of the "implied powers" of Congress when explicit claims by Congress itself would have run into difficulties. In these and many other ways the Court is actively evolving new laws to meet changing functions and goes beyond the judicial realm into the political sphere where men decide what policy ought to be.

For the present argument the vital fact is the representative function of the Court as it applies changing views on society. Rarely is it far ahead or far behind the consensus of educated opinion, and in this way it helps to meet one of the fundamental dilemmas of all democratic systems. There can be a "tyranny of the majority" which is vulgar, prejudiced, emotional, and unconstructive; there can also be civilizing forces which are humane, intelligent, cultivated, and decent. Given power, the minority that embodies the best instincts of a civilization can become an intolerable elite; overwhelmed by the majority it can become alienated, bitter, rebellious, and destructive. The Supreme Court provides a safety valve for intellectual resentment and guarantees that, in the last resort, all the important social activities will be required to render account to cool intelligence and rational argument.

If the Supreme Court acts as a barrier against the less attractive forces of mass democracy, it also stands guardian against abuse of administrative power. Although it has acquiesced in vast extensions of executive authority, it has also enforced the rules of fair play. Many government agencies possess powers that are executive, legislative, and judicial; under general powers conferred by Congress they can issue and execute regulations (which have the force of law) and judge when they have been infringed. It is recognized that the purposes of government cannot be effectively carried out without this merging of the separate powers, but the Supreme Court has kept a jealous eye upon these developments, insisted that administrative actions observe the principles of common-law justice, and safeguarded the right of appeal to the courts. In the light of the past the situation is ironic: the least democratic institution has proved itself, time and again, the principal defender of individual rights against authority vested in the democratic governments of state and nation.

The Supreme Court resolves some of the tensions which exist in a democratic society, but it cannot resolve them all; in particular it cannot satisfy those minorities which stand outside the consensus of educated opinion, nor those minorities which are convinced that the whole system is designed to deny them justice. The remoteness of power, and the enormous difficulty of influencing it, have fostered dissenting or rebellious groups and produced a growing crisis which the normal processes of judicial decision cannot meet. The nature of this modern crisis is widespread, but it is expressed most dramatically in black militancy, radical protest, and student revolt.

The racial crisis is the most formidable that has ever faced the United States. In politics, human relationships, economic development, welfare, and the basic principles of American democracy, it raises more problems than World War, depression, secession, or the formation of the Union itself; and there are no prophets to offer happier prospects for the future. Segregation with white supremacy offers no solution, nor does separation with black equality; integration has not advanced as fast or solved so many problems as its advocates hoped, and attempts to tackle the economic causes of racial discontent have so far failed. The solutions offered avoid the main issue, and projects for economic and educational improvement touch the periphery but not the heart of the problem. Processes that have worked with other ethnic minorities will not work with the black minority, and one is left with the intractable fact of color. The influx of Italians and Slavs in the early years of this century caused alarm, but these ethnic minorities pushed their way up the social and economic ladder to win acceptance from Americans of North European stock; material achievement and political participation bridge the gaps of nationality and religion, but not the prejudice of color. Adjustment will come only when men learn to ignore color, but this solution is nowhere in sight and some may claim that experience demonstrates its impossibility.

There is a surprising and striking parallel between black militancy and Southern secession before the Civil War. In both cases articulate leaders refuse to accept the status of a permanent minority, reject assurances by the majority, and prefer independence to compromise. Both reject the traditional democratic argument that one must trust the good intentions of other citizens; for the secessionists, Northern ascendancy could not be made acceptable by Northern promises, and for the black militant all the institutions and beliefs of a humane society are the tools of white supremacy and suppression. Here the comparison ends, for secession was born in a rural society and flourished among men who had had more than their fair share of political power; Negro militancy draws upon the discontents of the urban poor and upon lack of opportunity for Negro intelligence. And, for all their rhetoric, the secessionists had a practical strategy for independence, while an air of frustrated nonsense hung over Black Muslim talk of taking over a Southern state or establishing some shadowy black republic. Ironically, Negro separatism has grown in strength at the very time when the not so distant future may see Negro majorities taking over many of the greater cities by normal political processes. Negro mayors and predominantly Negro municipal governments may well be commonplace in the comparatively near future, though to achieve this they will have to play the political game according to ordinary American rules that militants refuse to accept. Whatever the future of militancy (and it is not inconceivable that it will wither away amid the profusion of a very rich society), it will remain significant that vocal leaders, winning the sympathy of millions, reject the principles and practice of American democracy.

Serious as is the racial crisis, revolutionary white radicalism raises questions that are equally fundamental. The scale is different, for while radical protest may disrupt a university, it is unlikely to throw a great metropolis into the confusion of civil war; the significance of white radicalism lies less in its threat to law and order that in the repudiation of American civilization by young members of the class which is its principal beneficiary. Young radicals, bred in affluent suburban America, reject the whole system of rewards and values and assert that a society claiming to be the freest and most tolerant in history is, in practice, the most oppressive. The material prosperity of America supports not only big government and great corporations but also great universities, symphony orchestras, art galleries, and sophisticated culture; but to revolutionary radicals these are all instruments used by the "power structure" to crush the human spirit. Between 1920 and 1930 many intellectuals felt alienated from the dominant culture, but for the most part they continued to believe that intelligence would reassert itself, and for many of them the New Deal vindicated their faith in American society. But radicals of 1970 claim that not only the rulers but the people as a whole are rotten. So rotten in fact that it is useless to propose policies for their reformation; destruction and a fresh start are the only answers. Though the radicals are often inspired by Marxist analyses of capitalism, they have nothing in common with Marxist planning and direction. To be fair, they also lack the Marxist ruthlessness that condemns whole groups of people to extermination in the cause of progress.

It is necessary to retain a sense of proportion. Protests against power, complacency, and materialism have been one of the driving forces in Western civilization; a society that lacks youthful idealism is a dying society, and the triumph of conservatism may mark the beginning of decline and fall. Humanitarian impulses have been responsible for achievements matched by no other civilization, and the contempt with which hard-headed men use the phrase "do-gooder" may be the symptom of a more serious disease than any campus radicalism. Men who reject the ideal of human betterment are the real traitors to a civilization that began by claiming that the pursuit of happiness was an inalienable right; radical protest ought to be the stimulant of democratic society, and when the forces of law and order combine to reject and silence the protestors, dangers lie ahead.

Yet with all these qualifications there remains something profoundly disturbing about a radicalism that aims to destroy and offers as an alternative nothing but a vague participation in everything by everyone. Modern radicalism seizes upon the theory of the power elite and goes on to repudiate all those elements in a liberal society that seem to acquiesce in its domination. For the militant radicals tolerance permits manipulation, free discussion hands over mass media to the rich, and majority rule means a mandate given to the power elite by those who have been bribed by affluence to abandon principle. The "liberal establishment" is merely a tool of the power elite, and talk about "values" or "standards" is nothing but a part of the fraud. Indeed liberals are the most frequent targets for radical protest, not only because they man the university hierarchies but also because they are temperamentally the most vulnerable.

Modern radicalism has something in common with nineteenth-century romanticism, but romantics had no great arenas in which they could present their case and tended to be solitary and individualistic or to gather in small cliques. The huge universities of modern America draw radicals together as no other institutions could. Men who are bold enough and discontented enough to be truly radical—in the sense of asking fundamental questions about the nature of society—exist in every civilization, but in most previous eras they have been scattered and unable to communicate with each other. Large cities, by drawing together masses of people, sometimes enabled the men who were radical by temperament to find each other out and establish communication, and occasional circumstances have given such radical minorities great influence. Nothing, however, equals the great modern university as a radical forum: Here, numbers mean that the radical element will be proportionately large and drawn from the most volatile age group; the environment encourages both speculation and organization; the authority is traditionally tolerant, but at the same time underlying tensions exist between students and the faculty upon whose assessment their future depends. Small incidents are easily magnified, and minds trained to generalize detect huge conspiracies where others might see only human error.

The environment of the great university gave radical minorities an advantage possessed by no other radicals in history; the war with Vietnam gave them a cause which was certain to be explosive. The war was remote, its causes were obscure, and its aims were difficult to explain. Even conservative men, who would wish the United States to take a leading role against communism, were disturbed by the way in which decision mounted upon decision, angered by a President who decided first and explained afterwards, and puzzled by the apparent inability of a great military power to control a weak Asian people even when armed force was accompanied by generous economic aid. Perhaps there has never been a war waged by a great nation in which the ordinary citizen was less able to explain why it was being fought, or what the conditions of peace should be. There were, of course, official statements to explain and reassure, but their credibility diminished with each unfulfilled promise of quick victory. Historians of the future may well justify the war and vindicate those who remained firm in the face of criticism, but the present discussion is not concerned with these judgments but with the crisis of modern democracy. An unpopular war brought millions close to the position of radicals who denied that democratic government, in its present form, could reform itself. All the channels of communication remain open, and all the democratic processes remained in working order, but the war continued and many lost confidence in the capacity of the people to control the men who exercised power in their name. Comparatively few of the critics of the war joined with the revolutionary radicals in repudiating the American democratic system, but some bridges were set up between moderate critics of excessive authority and the rebels against all authority. Indeed, a stronger alliance might have been formed—and almost was during the brief honeymoon of Eugene McCarthy's 1968 campaign for the Democratic nomination—but for the characteristic tendency of new radicals to overplay their hand. The very men who were most likely to be moved to action by dislike of war were also most likely to deplore senseless violence which disrupted the work of great academic institutions.

Wild in expression, violent in action, and flagrantly contemptuous of American civilization, the new radicals have, nevertheless, presented a case which must be answered. For the first time considerable numbers of idealistic and intelligent young people reject the basic assumptions of American democracy. Earlier radicals—loco-foco Jacksonians, Abolitionists, Populists, and even American Socialists—have appealed to American traditions and not against them. They have based their faith on the assumption that the principles of American democracy needed only to be implemented for justice to be secured and wrongs righted. The new radicals claim that the tradition has always been a sham foisted upon a gullible people by "power structures," and that reformation along traditional lines would merely give the "power elite" a stronger hold upon the country. They have a curious affinity with Thomas Jefferson in their yearning for a world of natural men uncontaminated by civilization and in their contempt for the economic leaders who offer men riches. Jefferson found his ideal in the simple cultivators of the soil, while the new radicals see their models of the natural man in dropouts from society and rebels against the moral code. Yet the Jeffersonian inspiration was wider than that of revolutionary radicalism; Jefferson's occasional outbursts against authority were made within the framework of an ordered and civilized society, and his sympathy with revolution did not prevent him from being a conservative President of the United States. Jefferson spent his life in public office, but anyone who claims any authority over anyone is an enemy of the new radicals. They seek a sense of community by cutting themselves off from the conventions of society; some go into deliberate withdrawal, while others remain in society but refuse to obey its rules. Yet the urgent question is why so many of them think in this way about a society that offers its citizens so much? There is poverty and its existence rightly stirs up protest; but most strata of the population enjoy comforts and leisure beyond the wildest dreams of earlier humanitarian reformers, and it is the pursuit of this happiness that most radicals denounce. Are they wrong to protest, or is society at fault in not wishing to understand what they say? Has American democracy reached a state of evolution at which it must reject foreign tissues, or can it assimilate and profit from these new impulses?

On the far Right there is also dissent. While the radical left condemns the "power elite" for daring to exist, the radical right blames it for not seizing the opportunities of power. For them the past half-century has been one of dangerous decadence; economic freedom was the first to go, then individualism, and finally morals. The whole tendency of modern times to break up traditional order and to substitute regulation for freedom is contained for them in the image of communism, which is not merely Marxism or Leninism or Maoism but also trade unionism, civil rights movements, and most aspects of modern administration. The great universities attacked by the new radicals are regarded by the radical right as seedbeds of communism; and the promise of the future is a dream world in which the old America will be miraculously restored by concerted action against Communists, liberals, Negro activists, and most intellectuals. The extreme right is numerically small but is amply subsidized and makes much noise in the world. As the new radicals have some links with respectable critics of government policy, so the extreme right has rather firmer links with respectable conservatism; and as the radical marriage with liberalism was temporarily consummated during the Eugene McCarthy campaign for the Democratic nomination in 1968, so the conservative alliance ran strongly during the 1964 campaign of Barry Goldwater. The magnetic center for this kind of alliance is old American tradition which the extreme right claims to respect and the true conservative reveres. Neither can explain how this tradition can be restored, and statements of policy become rhetorical and elusive. Indeed, it is not so much policy that they desire but power, though the leaders whom they would welcome have no hope of controlling a modern, city-based, mass democracy. The best for which the extreme right can hope is to win a segment of popular support by discovering new fears, and new groups who can be persuaded to be fearful. When this cannot be achieved they are apt to become contemptuous of democracy; the wildest among them dream of some kind of authoritarian regime while the more serious investigate ways in which democratic politics can be manipulated.

Two centuries of national life draw to a close with notes of anxiety sounded and with diminished confidence in the future, but the question raised is whether this is a passing reaction to temporary difficulties or a deep-seated disorder. The American experience is not unique and the same crisis of confidence is found almost everywhere in advanced countries. Change has left everyone bewildered, and political institutions have failed to adapt themselves to the greatly increased power of man to control his environment. Though little can be imagined that is beyond the reach of science, the political control of these tremendous resources remains fumbling in conception and occasionally disastrous in its consequences.

In these circumstances it is sometimes worthwhile to count blessings. The Americans did not, like the Germans, undergo a period of maniac rule ending in catastrophic defeat; they did not, like the French, experience humiliating military collapse and foreign occupation; nor did they, like the British, pass from a rapid decline from world power to a chronic economic crisis. No one has been judicially executed for political crimes, and whatever feverish imagination may make of the F. B. I. it is very unlike the secret police of totalitarian countries. American Negroes have just cause for complaint, but relatively speaking, they are better off, better educated, and have more opportunities than all but a tiny minority of African Negroes. In spite of great riches in some hands, wealth is widely diffused, the middle class enjoys a standard of life which would have been regarded as aristocratic only a century ago, and the industrial working class is affluent even by the standards of other advanced countries.

The remoteness of power, which has been so much stressed in this chapter, does not bother most Americans, and even those who are bothered can find comfort in the continued autonomy of states and great cities, which means local decision on many things affecting daily life. If mass democracy seems mindless, much American life still retains the flavor of small-town society in which everyone knows everyone else, and in spite of all the qualifications that have to be made, Americans continue to have more opportunities for political participation than any other people on earth. In spite of the new radicalism most Americans remain confident of the essential justice of their institutions, and in spite of the extreme right they have grown to be reasonably well-satisfied with their blend of private enterprise and public regulation. Set in this perspective, the anxieties of modern life can be compared to the ills of a robust hypochondriac; yet this would be too superficial a view, for in the long run society is what men think it is, and if some are dissatisfied, the whole may be weakened. Tension and criticism cannot be dismissed because they are not felt by the majority, and a more fruitful exercise is to place them in their historical perspective.

There is a tendency to regard American history as a steady progress along the middle road, interrupted only by the tragedy of the Civil War. In reality, and throughout two centuries of national existence, there has been criticism and disquiet, and the illusion of agreement has been created by the paradox that the men most convinced of the essential justice of the American system have been the most dissatisfied with its practice. There has been consensus in accepting the revolutionary and constitutional heritage, but much argument about its meaning; there has been no clash between different philosophies, but much conflict over the practical implications of a common political creed. There has always been a conservative attachment to things as they are and a radical statement of what they ought to be. Each generation has engaged in a discourse with the revolutionary traditions of American democracy, and history has been made by the outcome.

Discontent takes its place as an expected part of political evolution, and error may lie less with those who occupy extreme positions of criticism than with those who place too much emphasis upon agreement and too little on the value of controversy. Compromise has been made the major political virtue, while conflict has been identified with folly and vice; yet if one premise of democracy is respect for decisions constitutionally reached, another is the value of disagreement openly expressed. If one comes down from the higher plane of political philosophy, it is demonstrably true that schemes of social betterment have been thwarted more often by insisting upon agreement as the prerequisite of action than by conflict between the groups with interests at stake; struggles against opposition have been more effective in promoting beneficial change than exhortations to sink differences and discover a formula for compromise. Seen in this light, radical protest, however unattractive in its methods, may be less dangerous than refusal to take up its challenge.

Many of the modern discontents spring from a greater awareness of injustice and a heightened concern for suffering. The social sciences, especially sociology, originated in the hope that society could be subjected to the same kind of impersonal description and analysis as physical and biological phenomena, but this exploration revealed conditions which could not be reconciled with the promise of what American life ought to be. Historical investigation discovered an oversimplified conflict between "agrarian" and "capitalist" values, but went on to suggest that social evolution was not always moving in the direction of "a more perfect union." Fifty or sixty years ago most Americans believed that they lived in a classless society and prided themselves on the fact; today sociologists see class as an important element and discover a continuing tension between the class system and those who wish to break down its barriers. Opportunity, social mobility, and rewards for virtuous effort were prized characteristics, but social studies demonstrate the enormous advantages possessed by men born to wealth and assured status and the severe handicaps experienced by men born poor and of the "wrong" race or color. Indeed, some evidence suggests that social mobility has been slowing down and that American society is becoming more stratified than that of other advanced nations.

Widespread education and easy access to higher education have been one of the glories and assets of American civilization and remain impressive, but there are more marked variations in quality of education than in other advanced societies. The gap between the poor high school in a depressed urban area and the good high school in an exclusive residential district is enormous; the great universities are unparalleled anywhere, but in a legion of colleges the standards are low, and it is in the latter that most students of working class parents are found; college degrees are the key to remunerative employment, but the prestigious law firms, the great corporations, and high-grade faculties are most likely to be staffed by the alumni of a comparatively few rich institutions. Sociology and the new political science have investigated the mechanics of power and influence, and though their findings do not support the more extravagant notions of the "power structure," they serve to discredit simple rhetoric about government by the people.

Social science in this form has touched many springs of humanitarian concern and also sows the idea that remedies can be found. We are accustomed to regard this as an age of suffering, but this impression exists because far more people than ever before are moved by suffering, give it publicity, and demand that it should be ended. If, runs a familiar argument, resources can be mobilized for war, if millions can be spent on military research, if hugely expensive rockets can be shot off into space, then surely society has the means to solve all the problems of social life. The proliferation of administrative agencies breeds the hope that yet more can be done, and that some of the energy which goes into persuading consumers to be extravagant might be diverted into rebuilding slums, improving schools, and raising cultural standards. One of the most significant implications of power has been the demand that it should be used for more and more beneficial purposes, and when authority falls short, the discontent is proportionately greater. In earlier days reformers often met defeat through the impossibility of meeting utopian demands; but in an age when everything seems possible, the practical arguments are likely to tell in their favor.

Thus modern discontents belong to an old tradition, but appear more serious and more radical because they are voiced by people who know more, are more concerned with inequality and injustice, and believe that the means exist if the will can be found. This is the real nature of the crisis of modern democracy, but it is a sign of health, not disease, and the real danger in a developed society is not dissension but obsolescence. Idealists are unlikely to achieve their ends unless their wits are sharpened on the abrasive stone of conservative criticism, but the channels of communication must remain open. Controversy is the life of a democratic society, and democracy goes into decline when respectable people, party leaders, and men behind desks decide that controversy cannot be tolerated. The real crisis is created by the men who claim that there is nothing to discuss.

This suggests that the best remedy for the anxieties of modern society is fuller use of the democratic processes. The Progressives early in this century were reproached for trying to cure bad democracy by more democracy; yet how right they were. They modernized the nineteenth-century political system and laid the foundations for a new era of social legislation, and though, in some instances, they defeated their own purposes by making politics too complicated to be understood except by the professionals, their reforms had a tonic effect upon American democracy. Political institutions and practices must keep pace with the changes in society as a whole, and during the past quarter-century there has been enough change to fill an epoch. The United States was founded in a revolution and does not need another; but the experience of the past suggests that another installment of political evolution is overdue.

The American experiment began with the proposition that authority ought to be responsible to the governed, and all the sophistication of modern society cannot improve upon this simple principle; yet in the second century of national life the principle has been extended by the realization that politicians are not the only people who wield power. Restraints upon economic power have become as familiar as the traditional checks and balances of eighteenth-century theory, while the distinction between "public" and "private," which seemed so important to earlier generations, has become blurred. Even if government chose to abdicate many of its responsibilities, the scale of operations in the modern world would still mean that major projects could only be financed by government, while the consequences of depression would be so catastrophic that the most nostalgic defender of a self-regulating society would wish to retain public safeguards against it. As the scale grows, private economic power will inevitably be forced into even closer alliance with political power, not because there is a "power elite" conspiracy but because the two kinds of authority cannot exist without each other. A still greater concentration of power will make it ever more necessary to revive the principle that power must be responsible to the people, and history suggests several lines of development.

For over a century the pendulum has swung towards national power and away from local autonomy; the next period may see the swing reversed. This will not resurrect states' rights in the form so dear to Southern hearts, but as a means for decentralizing decision and bringing the decision makers closer to the people. National democracy has bled much of the life out of local democracy, but it might be a sign of health if some of the popular energy and emotion that goes into a Presidential campaign could be diverted into the consideration of those social problems which everyone deplores and leaves to others. The diminished distinction between "public" and "private" must lead to some new evaluation of the classic notions of authority, responsibility, checks, balances, and rights. American democracy has a magnificent opportunity for the wider application of its original revolutionary principles; it is no longer experimental but tested and mature, and its existence over two centuries provides a firm basis for its further evolution.

No political system will run itself, and if the intelligent and humane are inactive, the stupid and selfish are ready to take their place. Apathy is the greatest danger to popular government, but activity at the periphery breeds responsibility at the center. A heavy responsibility rests with the rising generation who will take the United States into its third century, but if faith seems dim in a bewildering world, no one who knows the young Americans need despair.

SUGGESTED READING

The preceding chapters have covered a wide range and even a moderately adequate bibliography would list many hundreds of books covering the history of the United States during the past two hundred years. It therefore seems best to make the following list a personal record of books which I have found significant and which have helped me, in some positive way, to understand the history of American democracy. The first section contains books that present overall interpretations, and the second books that deal with particular problems or episodes but which nevertheless present arguments influential in a wider field. I have listed a few source materials that deal with fundamental aspects of the American political system. Where possible I have given preference to works which are easily accessible and most of the titles are available in paperback editions.

I

Foreign observers have made significant analyses of American history and institutions; among them pride of place must go to Alexis de Tocqueville, *Democracy in America*. Based on observations made during a tour of the United States in 1832 the first English edition of Tocqueville's *Democracy* was published in two parts in 1835 and 1840; there have been many subsequent editions, and a new translation by George Lawrence (edited by J. P. Mayer and Max Lerner) was published in 1966. Tocqueville's observations were penetrating and his predictions were often so accurate that one is frequently moved to ask whether he did not mold subsequent opinion as well as prophesy its character. Another work of seminal importance was *The American Commonwealth* by Lord Bryce (1st edition, 1889; 2nd edition, 1893–95 was greatly revised and the last edition revised by Bryce appeared in 1914). Written at a time when the authority of the President was low and interest in external relations minimal, some of Bryce's generalizations are no longer applicable to modern conditions; but his book remains one of the most penetrating surveys of institutions and political behavior in the United States. In our own times Sir Denis Brogan has displayed an encyclopedic knowledge of American affairs and his *Introduction to*

American Politics (1954) is less an "introduction" than a mature commentary. Six years earlier Harold Laski, a British political scientist and socialist intellectual, published (1948) an ambitious work entitled *American Democracy*, which he clearly hoped to set beside Alexis de Tocqueville's classic volume; at the time of publication it was not well received by American scholars, but after twenty years it deserves reconsideration. Finally three works by British scholars do not attempt to stand in the same class as the major works already mentioned but may be interesting as foreign but friendly attempts to understand American civilization: they are *The Great Experiment* (1955) by Frank Thistlethwaite, my own *Character of American History* (1960), and *The American Presidency* by Marcus Cunliffe (1969).

Influential American interpretations of their history include Charles and Mary Beard, *The Making of American Civilization* (1937); Richard Hofstadter, *The American Political Tradition* (1948); Louis Hartz, *The Liberal Tradition in America* (1955); Daniel Boorstin, *The Americans* (two volumes to date: *The Colonial Experience* (1958), *The National Experience* (1965); and Oscar Handlin, *The Americans: A New History of the People of the United States* (1963). An ambitious and stimulating attempt to combine history, cultural studies and contemporary experience is *America as a Civilization* by Max Lerner (1957).

Most modern historical writing has been influenced in one way or another by Frederick Jackson Turner; though his emphasis upon the frontier experience as a determinant in American history has been severely criticized by many historians who look at events through urban or eastern eyes, others continue to find their major themes in the extension and application of Turner's ideas. There is a recent edition of Turner's *The Frontier in American History* with an introduction by R. A. Billington (1962), and Billington's own *Westward Expansion* (revised edition, 1967) is a distinguished general survey on Turner's principles. Some important essays have been selected and edited by Richard Hofstadter and Seymour Lipset in *Turner and the Sociology of the Frontier* (1968); among them, and of particular significance for the history of American democracy, are two essays by Stanley M. Elkins and Eric G. McKitrick originally published in the *Political Science Quarterly* in 1954. Another useful collection of readings is in *The Turner Thesis*, ed. George R. Taylor (1949) and some theoretical considerations are explored in Lee Benson, *Turner and Beard: American Historical Writing* (1960) and R. Hofstadter, *The Progressive Historians* (1968). A most interesting argument, which puts the frontier thesis into the wider context of an expansive and materially successful society, is advanced by David M. Potter in *People of Plenty: Economic Abundance and the American Character* (1954).

American political ideas, with special reference to the history of American democracy, are analyzed by Ralph H. Gabriel, *The Course of American Democratic Thought* (1940). Vernon L. Parrington, *Main Currents in American Thought* (3 Vols., 1930; single volume edition, 1958) is vigorous and readable but should be treated as an illustration of the hold of Jeffersonian ideas upon intellectuals in the first half of this century rather than as a dispassionate survey. Less subjective in its analysis of the Jeffersonian heritage is *The Jefferson Tradition in American Democracy* by C. M. Wiltse (1960), while Merrill D. Peterson makes a brillant contribution to American intellectual history in *The Jefferson Image in the American Mind* (1960). A distinguished theologian, Reinhold Niebuhr, made a brief, penetrating and critical assessment of political ideals in *The Irony of American History* (1952). Richard Hofstadter analyzes the persistent failure of politicians to understand intellectuals, and of intellectuals to influence politicians, in *Anti-Intellectualism in American Life* (1963). Hans Kohn, *American Nationalism* (1957), traces the evolution and variations of ideas about nationality, and Harold Hyman examines the implications of American ideas of loyalty in *To Try Men's Souls: Loyalty Tests in American History* (1959).

Of the several texts on constitutional history the best is probably Alfred H. Kelly and Winifred A. Harbison, *The American Constitution* (1948; 3rd Ed. 1963). Robert G. McClosky, *The Supreme Court* (1960) is a stimulating book which concentrates mainly upon the history of judicial review. W. E. Binkley, *American Political Parties: Their Natural History* (1943, and several subsequent revisions) is the best short history of the subject, though a good deal remains to be done in bringing together recent studies of party behavior (by politcial scientists) and the historical record; indications of what might be done are found in some of the interesting essays in William N. Chambers (ed.), *The American Party System* (1967). There is, curiously enough, no adequate single volume history of Congress. An outstanding good collection of documents, relating mainly to political history, is *Documents of American History*, edited by Henry Steel Commager in two volumes (first published in 1934 and frequently revised).

II

The Revolution, the Constitution, and the emergence of parties

It is highly desirable to study this period through the writings of participants and official records. S. E. Morison edited a useful collection under the title of *The American Revolution* (2nd Ed. 1929); collections which concentrate upon particular episodes or problems are *Prologue to Revolution: Sources and Documents on the Stamp Act Crisis*, edited by E. S. Morgan (1959); *The Pamphlets of the American Revolution*, edited by Bernard Bailyn (1965); *The Popular Sources of Political Authority; Documents Relating to the Massachusetts Constitution of 1780*, edited by Oscar and Mary Handlin (1966). The introduction to Bailyn's collection has been separately published as *The Ideology of the American Revolution* (1967). *The Federalist*, written by Madison, Hamilton and Jay in 1788, and many times republished, is the most impressive American contribution to political theory, but it is instructive to contrast the philosophy of republican federalism expounded therein with the persuasive rhetoric of Tom Paine's *Common Sense*, written in 1776 and still a fruitful source for radical ideas. Among the older works on revolutionary thought which retain their value are R. G. Adams, *The Political Ideas of the American Revolution* (1922); Carl Becker, *The Declaration of Independence* (1922); C. H. McIlwain, *The American Revolution* (1923); and R. L. Schuyler, *Parliament and the British Empire* (1929). A thorough re-examination of revolutionary theory and practice is *The Creation of the American Republic, 1776–1787* by Gordon S. Wood (1969), and some aspects of American law are traced back to their medieval roots in *The Origins of the Fifth Amendment* by Leonard Levy (1968).

So much writing about the Constitution has been concerned to refute or defend Charles Beard's *An Economic Interpretation of the Constitution* (1913) that one can be left with the impression that the economic interests of the Convention delegates were of greater importance than their ideas or the constitution that they made. In *Charles Beard and the Constitution* (1967) Robert E. Brown made a sharp and devastating attack upon Beard's use of evidence, and in *We the People* (1958) Forrest McDonald substantiated many of Brown's points through exhaustive research into the federal and state delegates. Much of the argument has been confused by a failure to distinguish between the relationship of political institutions to their economic foundations, and the motivation of individuals by economic interest. Good modern accounts which concentrate mainly upon political ideas and achievements are *The Great Rehearsal* by Carl Van Doren (1948) and *1787: The Grand Convention* by Clinton Rossiter (1966). There is a balanced account, seen through the eyes of the principal actor, in *Madison: Father of the Constitution* by Irving Brant (Vol. 3 of *James Madison*, 6 vols., 1941–1961).

Democracy and the Early Republic

In *Political Parties in a New Nation* (1963), William N. Chambers establishes interesting parallels between the American experience and that of new nations in the twentieth century. Leonard D. White provides an excellent account of the administrative achievements of the new government in *The Federalists* (1948). Books by C. M. Wiltse and Merrill D. Peterson on Jeffersonian ideas are cited in the preceding section and to these should be added Daniel J. Boorstin's brilliant study *The Lost World of Thomas Jefferson* (1948). Alexander Hamilton has attracted less attention than Jefferson, but the volume of literature on this controversial figure is nevertheless considerable; a good, recent and favorable appraisal is by Clinton Rossiter (1964). The best way to appreciate the force and lucidity of Hamilton's mind is to read his First Report on Public Credit and his opinion on the constitutionality of the National Bank; these can be found in H. S. Commager's collection of documents (mentioned in Section I) and in many other collections. Also in the Commager Documents are other key sources for an understanding of American political ideas: Jefferson's opinion on the Bank, the Virginia and Kentucky Resolutions, and (continuing into the nineteenth century) the opinions of Chief Justice Marshall, Daniel Webster's speech in reply to Senator Hayne, and the documents relating to the Nullification controversy.

Not much attention has been paid by historians to problems of political organization and attitudes in the first quarter of the nineteenth century, but there has been a great deal of discussion of Jacksonian politics. Arthur Schlesinger, Jr., gave an interpretation which has been much criticized but remains stimulating in *The Age of Jackson* (1948). Richard P. McCormick has some sober second thoughts (concentrating upon the mechanics of party organization) in *The Second American Party System* (1966), and there is a sensitive study of Jacksonian ideas in *The Jacksonian Persuasion* by Marvin Meyers (1957). There is an extremely interesting collection of source material edited by Edwin C. Rozwenc under the title *Ideology and Power in the Age of Jackson* (1964).

Sectional Controversy and the Civil War

This period has attracted more intensive study than any other in the world's history with the possible exception of the French Revolution; amid the huge volume of published material there is, however, surprisingly little consideration of the relationship of the political system to events. To what extent were the tensions created by political institutions and how did events react upon political ideas and democratic practice? A notable exception is the article by David Donald entitled "Excess of Democracy" (originally published separately in 1960, and republished in the second edition of *Lincoln Reconsidered,* 1965). Donald's argument is considered in Chapter V, above (p.83 ff). Another striking argument on the effect of the Constitution upon the coming of the Civil War, which can still be found only in the pages of the *American Historical Review* (Vol. LXIX, Jan. 1964), is Arthur Bestor's "The American Civil War as a Constitutional Crisis." The rival theories of government are best studied in the first messages of Jefferson Davis and Abraham Lincoln to their respective Congresses (April 29 and July 4, 1861); both are reprinted with other important writings in Edwin C. Rozwenc, ed., *The Causes of the Civil War* (1961). Surprisingly little attention has been paid to the novel problem of organizing a country for total war, but much can be gathered on this, as on a vast range of other subjects, in Allan Nevins's magisterial history of the period: *The Ordeal of the Union,* 2 Vols., 1947; *The Emergence of Lincoln,* 2 Vols., 1950; *The War for the Union,* Vol. I, *The Improvised War* (1959), Vol. II, *The War Becomes Revolution* (1960). James G. Randall (revised by David Donald), *Civil War and Reconstruction* (3rd Ed., 1969) is a good single volume history of the period with a splendid bibliography. The legislative achievement of the Civil War Congress is considered in Leonard P. Curry, *Blueprint for Modern America* (1968), and much can be gathered about changing political attitudes from George F. Frederickson's study of the impact of the war upon Northern intellectuals, entitled *The Inner Civil War* (1965). A book of first-rate importance for the study of race relations is James M. McPherson, *The Struggle for Equality: Abolitionists and the Negro in the Civil War and Reconstruction* (1964). Historians of Reconstruction have been accustomed to beginning their studies in 1865, but Herman Belz in *Reconstructing the Union* (1969) has demonstrated how much argument took place during the war over the future of the Union. George Winston Smith and Charles Judah have made a good collection of source material in *Life in the North During the Civil War* (1966). Frank L. Klement, *Copperheads in the Middle West* (1960) gives a full study of peace movements in that part of the country, but much work remains to be done on the antiwar movement in the Union (as also upon unionism and antiwar sentiment in the Confederacy). The best single volume history of the South during the war is Clement Eaton's balanced and well-written *History of the Southern Confederacy* (1954).

From Reconstruction to the Progressive Era

The later years of the nineteenth century present a field of sharp controversy; not only have historians to wrestle with the bitter controversies of the period but also with the consequences of these conflicts in the contemporary world. Modern radicalism, civil rights, black participation in politics, and white reactions in the South color the historiography of Reconstruction; while the role of politics in a society dominated by business has prompted most questions asked about the year 1875–1914. W. E. B. Dubois, *Black Reconstruction* (1935) was a pioneer work of the new school by a Negro historian which, though in some respects poorly organized, raised questions that went to the heart of the problem. Kenneth Stampp in the *Era of Reconstruction* (1965) draws together the conclusions of much recent writing and research; from a different point of view Avery Craven in *Reconstruction* (1969) demonstrates the extent to which earlier judgments have been modified. My own *American Crisis: Congress and Reconstruction 1865–67* (1963) paid particular attention to Republican policies in the context of political assumptions and constitutional limitations. The later years of Reconstruction in the South are taken up by C. Vann Woodward in *The Origins of the New South, 1877–1913* (1951) with skill and balanced judgment; the same author's *The Strange Career of Jim Crow* (2nd ed., revised, 1966) is an influential study of segregation. Harold Hyman (ed.), *Radical Republicans in Reconstruction* (1967) is an excellent collection of documents with a valuable introduction.

The economic and social background of the later nineteenth century, together with much material necessary for an understanding of political evolution, is treated in E. C. Kirkland, *Industry comes of age: Business, Labor and Public Policy, 1860–1897* (1961); Thomas C. Cochran and William Miller, *Age of Enterprise* (1944); and Fred A. Shannon, *The Farmer's Last Frontier* (1945). Samuel P. Hays, *The Response to Industrialism* (1957) is a good brief survey of late nineteenth-century society. The ideas and implications of laissez faire are treated in Richard Hofstadter, *Social Darwinism in American Thought* (1944), R. G. McCloskey, *American Conservatism in the Age of Enterprise* (1951), and Sidney Fine, *Laissez faire and the General Welfare State: a study of conflict in American thought* (1956). *Dream and Thought in the Business Community, 1860–1900* (1956), by E. C. Kirkland, is a short but successful attempt to dispel conventional generalizations about the attitudes and ethics of businessmen. Maldwyn A.

Jones, *American Immigration* (1960) is an excellent short history of its subject); Oscar Handlin, *The Uprooted* (1951) is an impressionistic but moving description of immigrants in the large eastern cities.

Reform movements since 1890 have been treated brilliantly and controversially in Richard Hofstadter, *The Age of Reform* (1955); even more iconoclastic is Christopher Lasch, *The New Radicalism in America 1889–1960* (1965). John D. Hicks, The Populist Revolt (1931) remains the best detailed study though it has been criticized for its uncritical commitment to Populism. On Progressivism there are two excellent volumes in the New American Nation Series: George E. Mowry, *The Era of Theodore Roosevelt* (1958) and Arthur S. Link, *Woodrow Wilson and the Progressive Era* (1954). There are two lively and provocative studies of the whole period in Eric Goldman, *Rendezvous with Destiny: A history of Modern American Reform* (1952) and Ray Ginger, *Age of Excess* (1965). There is a fine and sensitive study of some aspects of Progressive thought in Henry F. May, *The End of American Innocence* (1959).

Since the First World War

The impact of the First World War on American society has been strangely neglected, but William Leuchtenberg, *The Perils of Prosperity* (1958) is an admirable short study from 1914 to the depression. Arthur Schlesinger, Jr., *Crisis of the Old Order* (1957) gives a one-sided but deeply interesting study of the nineteen-twenties. Andrew Sinclair, *Prohibition: The Era of Excess* (1962) (also published as *Era of Excess: A social history of the Prohibition Movement*) is highly readable. J. K. Galbraith, *The Great Crash* (1955) is a clear exposition by an economist. As most historians express hostile verdicts upon the Hoover administration during the depression, justice demands reference to Herbert Hoover, *Memoirs: The Great Depression 1929–1941* (1952). A good single volume study of the New Deal is *Franklin D. Roosevelt and the New Deal, 1932–1940*, by William E. Leuchtenberg (1963), but the full flavor of the hectic yet constructive politics of the period can only be found in two volumes by Arthur Schlesinger, Jr.: *The Coming of the New Deal* (1959); *The Politics of Upheaval* (1960). F. L. Allen, *The Big Change* (1952) is an overall view of changes in American society in the first half of the twentieth century.

In treating modern political and social problems it is often difficult to distinguish between works of enduring significance and those which are ephemeral; especially as the latter may be important illustrations of changing moods. Two books by James K. Galbraith—*American Capitalism* (2nd ed., 1962) and *The Affluent Society* (1958)—have had wide influence. W. H. Whyte, Jr., *The Organization Man* (1956) provided much effective ammunition against conformism in the business community, and Daniel J. Boorstin, *The Image* (1962) attacked aspects of advertising and public relations in a lighthearted but highly effective manner. Michael Harrington, *The Other America: Poverty in the United States* (1963) was influential in starting the "war against poverty." Literature on the civil rights movement and the black "revolution" is voluminous and much of it is highly emotional; from the long list one might choose Anthony Lewis, *Portrait of a Decade* (1964) which considers the effect of the Supreme Court decision against educational segregation, M. L. King, *Stride Toward Freedom* (1958), L. E. Lomax, *The Negro Revolt* (1963), James Baldwin, *Nobody Knows My Name* (1961), and *Fire Next Time* (1963), Malcolm X, *Autobiography* (1966), and C. E. Silberman, *Crisis in Black and White* (1964). A somber commentary is provided by *Report of the National Advisory Commission on Civil Disorders* (1968) (also known as the *Kerner Report* for its chairman).

Several political scientists have studied the present-day operations of Congress, and from a long list the following may be selected: George B. Galloway, *The Legislative Process in Congress* (1953) (by an official of the Legislative Reference Service, Library of Congress); David B. Truman, *American Assembly: The Congress and America's Future* (1965); and Donald G. Morgan, *Congress and the Constitution: a study of responsibility* (1966). Various proposals for improvement are considered in the essays edited by Joseph S. Clark in *Congressional Reform* (1965).

The Books Yet Unwritten

The writing of American history is undergoing one of its periodic reappraisals. Will the present divisions in society produce new schools of interpretation? The historical writings of radical and black militancy have not yet produced major contributions, but past experience would suggest that intellectual turmoil and dissent cannot pass by without leaving important landmarks upon the field of historical scholarship. There are already black historians who regard white institutions and controversies as irrelevant or, at best, merely as the framework within which the emergence of the black race should be studied. There are others, white and black, who argue that racial conflict should be seen as the central theme of American history. White radicals, with their hatred of organized capitalism and their suspicion of organized government, may succeed in presenting a view of the past which challenges some of the basic premises of American democracy. On the far right the frantic cries against big government may lead in time to a measured reconsideration of the case for individualism and local self-government, while the popular demand for "law and order" may foster a historical restatement of the source of authority and its effective use. Whether the present discontents do or do not produce constructive thought about the American past, historians will face a tremendous challenge in trying to analyze and explain the discontents themselves. We live in an age in which huge new problems of organization, power, welfare and human relations are forced upon us, and each crisis is likely to demand new assessments of the past two centuries in hopes of achieving a better understanding of the processes of growth and change that have made us what we are.

INDEX